Preparing Your Business For Sale

Russell L. Brown

BUSINESS BOOK PRESS

RDS ASSOCIATES, INC.
291 Main Street
Niantic, Connecticut 06357
Tel. (860) 691-0081 / Fax: (860) 691-1145
E-mail: rds@businessbookpress.com
Internet: http://www.BusinessBookPress.com

Preparing Your Business For Sale

Copyright 1998, Russell L. Brown

The complete guide to preparing your business for a successful sale.

Published by Business Book Press, a division of RDS Associates, Inc., 291 Main Street, Niantic, Connecticut 06357.

**Publisher's Cataloging-in-Publication
(Provided by Quality Books, Inc.)**

Brown, Russell Lee.
    Preparing your business for sale: strategic moves you must make to sell your business for the most money!/ Russell L. Brown. -- 1st ed.
      p. cm.
      Includes index.
      Preassigned LCCN:98-92392
      ISBN: 0-9657400-2-1 (hardback)
      ISBN: 0-9657400-1-3 (pbk.)

      1. Sale of business enterprises.   2. Real estate business.   I. Title.

HD1393.25.B76 1998   658.1'6
                               QBI98-123

Foreword

As a financial & estate planner and an estate planning attorney, we help people understand that the time to prepare for the future is *right now!* The book you are about to read is the most comprehensive, easy-to-read guide we have ever encountered. It tells you, the business owner, how to prepare your business for sale so that you will get the most money for it, provide for your retirement, and protect your years of hard work and investment even if you plan to pass on your business to your child.

Let's face it, one way or another, you are going to sell or otherwise transfer the business you have worked for years to nurture and grow. In all the talk and discussion about financing, marketing, sales, production, quality control, and inventory management, nobody tells you what to do when the time comes that you want to "cash-out" of your business, or when someone else will need to sell your business should you be deceased or incapacitated by illness.

You owe it to yourself and your family to begin preparing for the sale of your business well in advance of these potential situations. This is the book that you *must read* to sell your business for the highest price, to protect your estate, and to provide for your spouse and other family members.

Preparing Your Business For Sale covers all the necessary topics, yet is easy to read and understand. More importantly, the hundreds of suggestions, tips and techniques inside these pages can be implemented by *every* business owner, large or small. The author, Russell L. Brown, is also straightforward about the time it will take to fully enhance the sales value of your business. We think, because you have selected this book to read and use, that you are already on a timely schedule for obtaining the best possible price for your business.

Chock full of resources vital to the execution of your plan to get the most value from your business, this book is a gold mine for all business owners, whatever the size of the company, whatever the age of the owners. Russell Brown answers the fundamental questions of why properly preparing your business for sale is so *absolutely necessary*. He shows you how to ask the "right questions," and determine what your business is really worth. And, at the book's core, there is a detailed explanation of what you can do *right now* to enhance the sales value of your business.

Also, there are chapters on the financial and tax consequences you must know if you want to receive the full value of your business and protect your estate; a chapter on the do's and don'ts of transitioning a family-owned business; and a chapter on how to select professional advisors (such as attorneys, financial planners, and business brokers) so that they work for your best interests.

Lastly, this book provides a step-by-step procedure for putting together an exit plan from your business that will provide you with the most money, and protect you and your loved ones *now and in the years to come.*

That's a lot for one book to deliver, but this book does it. This is a one-of-a-kind book that belongs in the hands of business owners everywhere.

Richard M. Kieltyka, M.B.A., R.F.P., R.I.A.
Financial & Estate Planner
North Attleborough, Massachusetts

Barry K. LaCasse, Esq.
Estate Planning Attorney
North Attleborough, Massachusetts

Introduction

Deciding to sell your business may be one of the most important decisions you will ever make, and also one of the most difficult. When your business is doing well, your income is high, your work interesting, and the future promising, you may think that there is no reason to prepare for a decision that seems a long way off. You will probably ask yourself, "Why do I have to start thinking about selling my business now?" There are some very good reasons: an unexpected decline in your health, the desire for retirement and more free time, the problem of not having an heir to pass the business to, partner/shareholder problems, or a decision to relocate to a better climate. Whatever the reason, a time will come when you *will* "sell" your business. Whether it's a sale in the conventional sense, a transition to new ownership within your family, or a disposition of the business by your estate, your business ownership will change at some point. *It's absolutely imperative that you properly prepare now for that day to ensure a smooth transfer that reflects the true value of your business.*

Simply stated, the only time a business can be sold for a favorable price, which will enable you to realize the highest return on your investment of time, money and sweat equity, is when conditions surrounding the business are strong and the future looks good. Many business owners wait too long and never properly prepare their business for sale. Consequently, they will only receive a fraction of what they once could have sold the business for. The process of preparing your business for sale and completing the transaction can take a great deal of time, even years. *Now* is the time for you to begin planning your business sale.

When you sell a successful company, you are in a position to realize at least three important benefits. First, the sale will allow you to make a profit on your substantial investment in the business. Second, the sale converts the equity you presently hold in your company to cash. Third, the cash itself allows you to pursue new and alternative opportunities in both your business and personal life.

You will sell your business only once; therefore you must plan for the sale very carefully. Preparing your company for sale is almost as important as the sale itself. But getting the best price for your business is not simply a matter of driving a hard bargain. There are numerous factors to be considered in addition to your readiness to sell, including the cost of money in the financial market, the interest level of prospective buyers, the current business outlook in your trade or industry, the way your company is presented for sale, and the manner in which the purchase is structured. All of these factors are covered in this book.

Ideally, most small-business owners should begin preparing to sell their business about one or two years prior to putting it on the market. I realize, however, that many business owners wait until the last minute and will not have the time to make an optimal preparation. I address both situations in this book. I discuss the ideal approach, and also offer recommendations and suggestions for taking action to sell your business for the most money in a much shorter period of time.

There are many reasons for preparing your successful business for sale now. For example:

- Every day in business is a risk. Just because the business is successful today does not mean that it will continue that way. As in the stock market, you should sell at the top when all the news is good and everyone else is buying. Take the opportunity to beat the odds and take your money off the table. If you do not, the law of averages may eventually catch up with you.

- Estate taxes can ruin even the most successful small business. Leaving a business to heirs who are financially unprepared will put an enormous burden on them and could threaten a successful transition by creating a forced sale. Proper estate and financial planning can eliminate this risk.

- Small-business owners tend to look at their business as if it was their child. They have conceived, nourished, and guided the business into a mature, successful enterprise. Giving it up can be emotionally traumatic and they tend not to plan for the inevitable. Lack of planning for an orderly transition of the business is a gross disservice to the work and capital they have invested in growing the business.

- Statistics show that only 10 to 15% of family-owned businesses are passed on to members of the same family past the second generation. Many problems develop in family-owned businesses that hinder a smooth transition. Sometimes the business owner's heirs lack the competence, knowledge, or capital to successfully run a business. A well-conceived succession plan can overcome many of these problems for the owner who wants to keep the business in the family.

- Many business owners work so hard in the early years of developing their business that they experience burn-out in their later years. Things are finally good, the profits are rolling in, and they do not have to drive themselves nearly as hard as they did in the beginning. This is when many business owners start to let things slip. Their successful business begins to decline before they realize that the value is slipping away.

One of my favorite sayings is: "Any fool can start a business. It takes a smart or lucky person to make it profitable. But it takes a genius to exit a business successfully." My objective in this book is to give you the information you need to make a successful exit from your business without having to be a genius.

If you have an established, profitable, operating business with a track record of at least three years, you *will* be able to sell your business at an excellent price, if you are prepared. There is no question about it. There are far more potential buyers than there are good quality businesses for sale. I estimate that at any given time in the United States there are 850,000 businesses of all types and sizes for sale with at least five prospective buyers (on average) for each one. That's over 4 million potential business buyers! The key to selling your business will not be finding a buyer, it will be finding a *qualified* buyer who can and will purchase your business under the right conditions, and at a price and terms that are acceptable to you.

To attract a qualified buyer who is ready, willing, and able to buy your business on your terms, you must prepare your business for sale in order to present it in its best light. You have taken the first step in this crucial process by reading this book. If you develop an exit plan for your business along the guidelines that I lay out, you will be able to sell your business on your timetable and on terms that are the most favorable to you, your family, and your employees. This will also work in the best long-term interests of the business itself.

I wish you success in preparing and selling your very special business! Thank you for allowing me to help.

Other books by
Russell L. Brown

Strategies for Successfully Buying or Selling a Business

ISBN: 0-9657400-0-5
© 1998

Table of Contents

This book is dedicated
to my wife, Susan, and my son, David.
They have contributed much to the writing of this book
through their understanding and faith in me.

*"Selling your business is perhaps
the only financial endeavor for which
no preparation is thought necessary."*

Paraphrase of a quote by
Robert Louis Stevenson

1

Why You Need to Prepare Your Business for Sale

- *Introduction*
- *The Partial Liquidation Option*
- *The Types of Business Buyers*
- *The Buyer Most Likely to Buy Your Business*
- *Methods of Sale for Your Business*
- *Preparing Yourself for Selling Your Business*

Introduction

Many business owners operate their companies to minimize their exposure to federal, state, and local tax obligations as well as to maximize value for themselves. Business owners also continuously invest in new product and/or service development, major facility improvement/expansion programs, or engage in ongoing philanthropic activities. These actions may make good sense during normal business operating periods but they generally do not help to create value in a potential buyer's view during the business sale process.

In order to create a strong sense of value from a buyer's perspective, you must begin to operate your business in a substantially different way during the one- or two-year period leading up to offering your company for sale. You will need to demonstrate the maximum net profit-generating capability of your business, while maintaining reasonable operating expenses. This will help to ensure that you receive the highest value for your company. You will need to take as much care and pay as much attention to detail in preparing your business for sale as you took in starting it and growing it to the success that it is today.

Other factors also can work against you in receiving the best value from your business when it comes time to sell. They must be addressed and corrected as early as possible in the sale process. For example, many businesses have:

- Out-of-date or incorrectly documented business legal structures.

- Sloppy management resulting from a long-time owner's late-stage complacency.

- Owners with a greatly inflated sense of what their business is worth.

- A deteriorated physical plant and operating equipment resulting from a long period of neglect.

Out-of-date or incorrectly documented business legal structures are very common in many small businesses that have been owned by the same person(s) for many years. There are a substantial number of partnerships that have no Partnership Agreements or Buy/Sell Agreements in place, only long-standing verbal agreements. There are also many closely-held private corporations that have not properly documented the officers' loans, sales and/or gifts of corporate stock, or annual Board of Director's meetings (as is usually required by state statute). Many times a buyer has to struggle to figure out who owns what and just what exactly is for sale. This lack of structure will frequently work against the seller in trying to accomplish a smooth and orderly sale of the business.

Some owners get sloppy in their management style in the later years of their business ownership. Many simply get tired of the continuous grind and competitive pressures over the years. They become complacent about the business which they used to operate with a close eye to detail. Revenues slip, operating expenses rise, and employees lose their motivation. By the time the owner decides it's time to sell, the company is a shadow of what it once was. While this is an understandable consequence of human nature, it clearly erodes the value of the business and is not easily or quickly reversible.

Some owners have a greatly inflated sense of what their business is worth to a potential buyer. They forget to take into consideration the needs of most buyers: earning a fair wage (which is usually higher than the present owner realizes), earning a return on the buyer's cash investment, and most importantly, servicing the debt that they take on in buying the business. The buyer must do all this while covering the operating expenses of the company. Consequently, some business sellers put their business on the market for an unrealistically high asking price that tends to scare off otherwise good, prospective buyers who may move on to another opportunity. And all too often the business does not sell, and the owner becomes increasingly frustrated and anxious. In this situation, the owner sometimes pays less and less attention to overall day-to-day management, resulting in an increasingly poor operating performance. This, of course, lessens the business's value even further and a downward spiral begins. It is this situation that causes some owners to end up liquidating what was once a very valuable business.

Some owners let the physical plant and/or facilities of their company deteriorate over the last years of their ownership. This is primarily because of inattention to details, but it can also be a result of a desire to maximize the income from the business and defer these kinds of normal expenses to the eventual buyer. While deferring some of these expenses into later years is possible, many business owners underestimate the amount of time it will take to actually sell the business. Months turn into years, and inattention to maintenance and repair issues takes its toll. Consequently, the business's physical assets may not only look like they are in poor condition, but also present a potential buyer with a relatively large initial bill to bring things back up to proper quality standards. It is almost impossible for a seller to receive anywhere near top value for a business under these conditions.

For these and many other reasons, you will need to carefully plan your exit from the business so that you can maximize the value you will receive when you sell. This book contains many strategies, recommendations, ideas, hints, and resources to help you avoid or overcome many of the pitfalls that can befall a business seller.

This is a good time to clarify some terminology and concepts that I will be using throughout this book. I use the terms "business" and "company" interchangeably in the text. I do this for the sole purpose of relieving the tedium of sticking to one term or another.

In some places in the book, I may introduce business terms and concepts that you are not familiar with. If the terminology is not defined in the text, you will find it in the Glossary. The Glossary also contains many other business terms associated with the purchase, sale, and valuation of a business even if they are not specifically addressed elsewhere within the book. The Glossary is intended to assist you not only in preparing your business for sale, but also in providing you with information concerning terms relating to the actual purchase and sale of your business.

Definition of a Small Business

When I refer to a "small" business, I am doing so within the broad definition established by the U.S. Small Business Administration (SBA). The SBA says that most businesses are considered small and they have an elaborate set of categorization criteria that is substantially different by industry and subcategorizations within an industry. For example, the SBA considers small businesses to be:

Retail and Service Businesses	Up to $13.5 million in sales
Construction Businesses	Up to $17 million in sales
Agriculture Businesses	Up to $3.5 million in sales
Wholesale Businesses	100 or less employees
Manufacturing Businesses	500 or less employees

Of the approximately 6.2 million full-time operating businesses in the United States today, approximately 5.6 million are considered to be small businesses by the SBA. So it's a good bet that your business falls into the category of a "small" business.

Incorporated Versus Non-Incorporated Businesses

A more important distinction concerning your business is whether it's an incorporated or non-incorporated business. Some of the methods of sale such as MBO, LBO, ESOP, and IPO (which I will cover later) will not normally be available to a non-incorporated business because there is no corporate stock to use in the transaction. But there is no reason a non-incorporated business cannot be sold. Actually, hundreds are sold every day. The sale will take the form of an asset sale rather than as a corporate stock sale. In fact, even in the purchase of an incorporated business, many buyers prefer to buy only the assets of a business rather than its corporate stock in order to minimize their future exposure to hidden (unknown) liabilities resulting from past corporate actions.

Of course, if your business is not a corporation and you want to pursue one of the methods of sale that will require corporate stock, then incorporate. The process is relatively easy and inexpensive and also fairly fast to accomplish. Contact your Secretary of State's office for the details about incorporating your business.

Business Size Considerations

Please keep in mind that most of the concepts, ideas, recommendations, and strategies contained throughout this book are applicable to every business regardless of its size. The need to prepare a major oil refinery that produces petroleum products for sale is also true for a modest two-pump gasoline station that sells those products. However, some of the information provided may not be directly applicable to your particular type or size of business. The local card and gift shop owner may not be very interested in considering an Initial Public Offering for the sale of their business. The company owner with several million dollars in sales but only a handful of employees will most likely not be interested in an Employee Stock Ownership Program. Also, no matter the size or sophistication of your business, if you are not planning to transfer the ownership within your family, then the discussion regarding Family-Owned Succession Planning may not be of interest to you. You may choose to skip these topics as you read this book but I recommend that you at least scan the information provided. It's better if you have the "big picture" view of the process of preparing a business for sale for every situation. The information may spark an idea or approach specific to your business that you might not have otherwise considered.

A Word About the Strategic Moves

Sprinkled throughout the book are various highlighted strategic moves that you should consider in preparing your business for sale. Each strategic move is fully explained in the text and is marked for emphasis through the use of a chess piece icon. Not all strategic moves may be of equal importance, depending on the specific circumstances of your particular business sale. I recommend that you consider each one relative to your own business sale objectives and decide on its relevance and level of importance to your situation.

The Partial Liquidation Option

When making the decision to detach yourself from your business and extract as much money from it as possible, you have two basic courses of action to choose from:

- Close the business as a going concern and sell (liquidate) all of the assets for the maximum amount possible. Or,

- continue to operate the business and sell or otherwise transfer it as a going concern.

The premise of this book is that you have a business with at least some profitability and reasonable prospects for the future. In almost every case, you should choose to sell your business as a going concern. This will maximize the ultimate benefit which you can gain from the sale. Accordingly, you will need to prepare your business for sale in order to properly showcase its current and future potential value.

In preparing your business for sale, it's assumed that you have already considered and decided against another alternative for extracting the value from your business. That alternative is to:

- Maximize the cash flow of the business to yourself over a relatively short period of time using extraordinary sales and cost-cutting measures to the possible overall detriment of the business as an ongoing concern;

- Then sell the remaining shell of the business for the fair market value of its physical assets.

I refer to this as a partial liquidation. Sometimes business owners see this as a good way to extract as much cash as possible from their business before they offer it for sale. They begin to cut back as much as possible on all expenses in order to maximize the cash flow to themselves. They:

- Eliminate all research and development expenses.

- Eliminate all employee training expenses, and minimize employee benefit programs.

- Cut back on marketing and advertising expenses to a dangerous level that may not maintain the normal revenues.

- Cut equipment maintenance and repair expenses to a bare minimum.

- Replace high quality suppliers with less expensive but inferior quality suppliers.

- Cut back on employee incentives and bonuses.

- Eliminate employees not required for immediate business activity, but needed for long-term business development.

Additionally, some business owners will dramatically reduce product costs across the board to move their inventory off the shelves and out of the warehouse. This can have the effect of reducing product value in the customer's eyes and creating expectations of lower product pricing in the future that cannot be maintained in the long run for sustained business profitability.

Although this is one way of extracting some of the value from your company, it's not a very good way because you could very easily ruin the overall business for ultimate sale. You could lose your competitive advantage, drive away long-time major customers, alienate high-value employees, and generally run your business into the ground. It also presents a potential taxation problem: the increased corporate profits are taxed and then taxed again as dividends as they are passed on to shareholders. However, there may be ways to overcome this depending on your business's legal structure. For example, a sub-chapter S corporation has all its profits flow directly to its shareholders for personal taxation without a corporation or dividend tax. But, changes to a company's legal structure are cumbersome and can be expensive. Many times the IRS rules will not allow a change depending on how the company has been operated in the past. In almost all cases, an outright sale of the company as an ongoing profitable concern is the best way to minimize your tax liability as well as to maximize the value you receive for your business.

The partial liquidation approach could ultimately leave you with a company that is not salable as a going concern, but only as a tangible asset sale. Used company assets are then typically sold far below their replacement value, as well as significantly below their value to an ongoing business. In almost all cases, you will realize the most money as a result of selling your business as a healthy, growing, operating enterprise. The true value in your business will be its ability to generate net operating profit based on your product and/or service name recognition, your proven customer base, proprietary or patented products, good business reputation, and experienced employees, as well as on your tangible asset base (such as real estate, equipment, tooling, inventory, etc.).

You should almost always choose to sell your business as an ongoing, profitable, operating company to maximize the value you will receive at the time of sale. There are many factors which will affect your ability to sell your business and for what amount. By understanding the characteristics of the different types of buyers and the various methods of sale available, you will better appreciate why you need to prepare your business for sale. The following discussion covers these and other important issues for your consideration.

The Types of Business Buyers

Early in the sale process, you should very carefully consider the types of buyers who may buy your business. Just as you would thoughtfully target a business marketing campaign to a specific customer base, you should also target the potential buyers of your business. This will enable you to tailor your preparations for selling the business in the best possible manner. This leads us to the first of the 60 strategic moves I have identified for you to consider in preparing your business for sale.

Strategic Move #1:

"Understand the key characteristics of the potential buyers for your business to help target your sales approach."

Buyers come in all shapes and sizes: public and private companies, wealthy individuals and cash-poor wannabes, strangers and family members, friends and partners/shareholders, competitors and suppliers. But they all can be categorized into basically five classes:

- Financial Buyers.

- Strategic Buyers.

- Family Buyers.

- Partner, Shareholder, and Employee Buyers.

- Industry Buyers.

Financial Buyers

Financial buyers are motivated by many things, but are primarily interested in the immediate income producing capability of their investment in the business. They tend to look for companies that offer financial opportunity within a business field with which they are familiar, have a track record of profitability, and have sales of less than $10 million. The vast majority of financial buyers purchase businesses with less than $1 million in annual sales.

Financial buyers tend to have the following characteristics:

- They are individuals rather than companies.

- They are primarily motivated by profits and a return on their investment, rather than by strategic issues.

- They want to minimize their cash investment in the business and, consequently, their risk.

- They want the seller to substantially finance the purchase price of the business.

- They are willing to pay for goodwill, if the investment justifies it.

- They are by far the most common buyer for a business with sales under $10 million and/or a selling price less than $1 million.

- They are usually undercapitalized and overly ambitious regarding the type of business they want to purchase.

- They are very susceptible to their sometimes conflicting emotions of optimism and pessimism as well as the problems of "cold feet."

- They want a business that fits or enhances their self-image.

- They seek businesses in fields they are familiar with and feel that they have the know-how to run.

Whether you want to or not, you will most likely find yourself dealing with a financial buyer for your business. They are the most plentiful and usually the most motivated, but also the least sophisticated buyers. Accordingly, if a financial buyer is the most likely type of buyer for your business, you must do everything you can to maximize the provable profits in your company and eliminate any negative aspects that could inhibit the sale. It's most important to fully prepare your business for sale if it will be sold to a financial buyer.

Strategic Buyers

Strategic buyers are generally large, publicly-owned corporations or very large, privately-owned companies that have a strategic reason for buying a company. Some of these reasons include:

- Access to new technology without the customary lead time and development costs.

- Penetration into established markets without the need for the time or cost of new customer development.

- Quick boosts to earnings (and consequently their stock prices) in rising stock market periods.

- Suppliers looking for better control over channels of product distribution.

- Customers looking for better control over sources of supply.

- Companies in a related industry looking for new products/services to add to their existing base.

Some of the other benefits that strategic buyers may seek to obtain are:

- Reduced administrative overhead costs by combining similar functions.

- Reduced material costs because of larger purchase volume and related discounts.

- Increased revenues and profits as the acquiring company cross-sells related products and/or services.

- Improved pricing flexibility by removing a competitor.

- Stronger market presence leading to increased sales and profitability.

Strategic buyers tend to be:

- Competitors (local, regional, and national) with a strategy of expansion through acquisition.

- Suppliers (including subcontractors) with a desire to protect an important account.

- Distributors wanting to add products to existing channels of distribution.

- Customers wishing to protect their sources of supply.

- Regional or national chains of similar businesses.

Strategic buyers typically consider only companies that have a solid market position, an expanding track record, added earning opportunities, and sales of $10 million and up. Of course, there are exceptions to every rule, but strategic buyers generally only pursue opportunities that will have enough ultimate positive future financial impact on their operations to make the purchase cost-effective.

I have deliberately used the words "tend to" in describing both strategic and financial buyers, because there are so many exceptions that it is hard to establish a rule. In the past several years, many deals have been made by strategic buyers for very small companies in what is an extremely interesting, and so far, profitable phenomenon. For example, small funeral homes are being swallowed up by much larger, publicly-traded companies that operate funeral homes on a national basis. So, too, are trash haulers, regional truckers, home heating-oil companies, pharmacies, restaurants, auto-parts manufacturers, and radio stations. The reason for this is really very simple. With the stock market at continuing record highs for several years, many publicly-traded companies are enjoying very high share prices on record-high earning multiples. Consider the fact that most smaller companies normally sell in the range of four to six times earnings (net profit). The larger, publicly-traded companies are selling at anywhere from 15 to 30 (or more) times earnings. If a strategic buyer acquires a small company at a price that is eight times its earnings, and then folds that company into its operations, the stock market will most likely reflect the new earnings in the acquiring company's stock price at the higher earnings multiple. For example: Company A is a large waste recycling firm which is trading on the NASDAQ market at $16 per share with earnings of $1 per share. This company currently has a price to earnings ratio (p/e) of 16:1. The company finds a regional, privately-held waste recycling company that it is able to purchase for eight times earnings. Company A adds this company to its corporate structure for cash and stock options and boosts its share price at the next earnings reporting period by a factor of two to one for what they paid for the acquired company (16:1 p/e ratio vs. 8:1 p/e ratio). This is a great deal for everyone involved as long as the stock market remains at high levels, and the average price to earning ratios stay at their relatively high multiples. Of course, this bubble may eventually burst, but as long as this financial phenomenon continues, the medium-sized company seller, whose business fits the criteria discussed here, is well advised to seek a strategic buyer.

A note of caution is in order relative to strategic buyers. As the business seller, you may be offered stock and/or stock options by the strategic corporate acquirer as a substantial part of the purchase price for your company. Frequently, the stock and/or options will be tied to a "no-sell" period of time that could be as long as one to several years. Remember that "cash is king" and try to take as much in cash that you can and settle for as little corporate stock as you can get away with in these heady times. We all know that someday the financial markets will come back down to their historic averages, including price to earnings ratios. Watch out for selling your business for, say, $5 million, which includes $1 million cash and $4 million in stock in the purchasing company that cannot be sold until at least two years later. You may well find at that time that you actually sold your company for millions less than you thought because of a significant drop in the share price. On the other hand, you could realize a windfall gain if the share price has moved up. The point to keep in mind here is that if you accept any portion of the sale proceeds in stock, you have become a stock market investor with all of the attendant risk and uncertainty.

Not very many businesses can be sold to a strategic buyer, but this may be your best course of action if at all possible. In the final analysis, both strategic buyers and financial buyers are ultimately concerned about the same thing: making money. It's just that strategic buyers sometimes see methods to make money from acquisitions in different ways and take a longer-term view than financial buyers, and they tend to pay more for the same business. Sometimes, much more. Accordingly, I recommend that you do not establish an asking price for your business if you attempt to sell it to a strategic buyer. It will be to your advantage to seek bids for your company and evaluate the bids relative to your private valuation of what the business may be worth to a financial buyer. This will leave the door open to possibly receiving a price for your business in excess of any value a traditional valuation method will provide. I will cover this and other issues of valuation in detail in the next chapter.

Family Buyers

I have devoted Chapter 5, "Succession Planning for the Family-Owned Business," to "selling" your business to close family members. More than half of the small businesses in the United States are now family-owned; that's over 12 million family-owned businesses! Consequently, it's likely that you will at least consider this form of business transition. Although it presents you with different issues, you still need to prepare your business for sale. Many sales within a family are not possible due to a multitude of factors including a lack of necessary capital, inability of offspring to effectively manage the business, and poor timing relative to availability of the particular parties. Proper preparation of your business may allow you to overcome these impediments to transition.

If you are seriously considering selling your business within your family, you should read Chapter 5 before reading Chapter 3, "Enhancing the Sales Value of Your Business," and adjust the recommendations accordingly to fit your specific needs. For example, if you have little or no need for more money and you are primarily interested in transferring ownership of your business to your children in the least tax-intensive way, then you most likely will not want to maximize the reported net income of your business.

Partner, Shareholder, and Employee Buyers

If you plan to sell your share of the business to your partner or close private shareholders, you absolutely need a Buy/Sell Agreement in place as soon as possible. This agreement can be written in such a way as to cover a buyout by either party under specific conditions. In a Buy/Sell Agreement, the parties all agree ahead of time to a formula or procedure for valuing the business and for passing ownership to the succeeding partners or shareholders. The timing, terms, and conditions of the agreement have to be carefully worked out ahead of time to ensure a smooth transition of ownership. In the event of the death of one of the partners/shareholders, a life insurance policy paid for by the business is typically used to pay the survivors of the deceased owner for their share. If you already have a partner or major shareholder that you want to sell to and you do not have a Buy/Sell Agreement already in place, you may find that you will have a difficult time agreeing to the valuation of the business and the terms and conditions of sale. Just as in a divorce, one of you will want the price as high as possible and the other as low as possible, depending on whether you are the buyer or the seller. One approach under this adverse situation is to hire an outside appraiser/arbiter and agree to be bound by their judgment. Another way is to hold an auction of the business. This is actually fairly easy to accomplish. It can be done quickly and very inexpensively. Most importantly, it will avoid litigation between the partners. In brief, this is the way it's accomplished:

- The partners agree to the auction concept and establish a date, time, and place (usually the corporate attorney's office).

- Ground rules are established, such as method and time frame of payment for the winning bidder.

- The bidding process is decided upon with the use of one-time sealed bids, or by open bidding with multiple rounds.

- The bidding process is accomplished according to the rules, whereupon the winning partner takes title to the business and pays the losing partner the agreed-upon amount.

Some business owners find it advantageous to sell to one or more of their employees. Sometimes the senior managers will want to buy out the departing owner and in other situations, all of the company's employees will share in the purchase of the business. If the business is strong and has good prospects for the future, the company's employees may know this better than anyone else. Many business owners at least explore the possibility of selling their business to someone within the company. Usually, the sale process is greatly simplified and the selling costs are substantially reduced.

A sale to a partner, shareholder, or employee is essentially a sale to a financial buyer and all of the considerations previously discussed will apply. Accordingly, you should prepare your business for sale for any one of these types of buyers in the same way as you would if they were an "arms-length" financial buyer.

Industry Buyers

An industry buyer is a company most likely similar to yours and usually within the same industry. They are sometimes referred to as the buyer of last resort. This is because they have no strategic reason to buy your company and have no reason to pay for any goodwill value. They already have a going business and the know-how to do what your business does. What they may be interested in is your assets (if you were to liquidate your business) such as inventory, equipment, and vehicles. They may even be interested in your location for their own expansion purposes. Typically, they will pay very little for your company's assets and are primarily looking for a bargain price. Generally, you should only consider selling to an industry buyer if you need to liquidate your business because it cannot be sold as a going concern.

The Buyer Most Likely to Buy Your Business

Strategic Move #2:

"Identify the most likely type of buyer for your business early in the sale process."

Now that I have described the various types of buyers, you should make a preliminary decision as to which one is most likely to buy your particular business.

Targeting a particular type of buyer early in your preparation process will help you to focus on the kinds of preparations you should make, aid you in selecting the type of sales representative you need, guide you in setting an asking price, and lead you to an effective marketing approach for your business.

The vast majority of business sellers will find that their company is most attractive to a *financial buyer*. The characteristics most common to businesses attractive to financial buyers include:

- Annual sales less than $1,000,000 (but may range much higher).

- A retail, restaurant, or service business.

- Less than 10 employees.

The next largest group of buyers likely to buy your business are *family buyers,* typically your own children. Many small businesses are family-owned and their owners hope to keep the business within the family, although this does not usually happen. Characteristics of businesses likely to be transitioned within a family include:

- Businesses with owners having offspring of a suitable age, capability, and desire.

- High enough company profitability to allow the business profits to buy out the owner.

- Annual sales greater than $1,000,000.

- Any type of business.

Strategic buyers are much less apt to buy your company than either financial or family buyers. Many business owners would like to sell to a strategic buyer because they tend to pay the most money for a business. However, as their description implies, they must have a strategic reason to buy your company that they perceive will enhance their own business operations. Typical business characteristics include:

- Annual sales greater than $10,000,000.

- A proprietary product or business process.

- A unique marketing strategy or share.

- A strong management team.

- Any type of business.

Although business sales to *partners, shareholders, and employees* certainly occur, they represent a very small percentage of the total. The most prevalent form within this category is the sale of the business from one partner to another. There are no typical characteristics for this type of business, because all kinds and sizes are included.

Industry buyers with no strategic motive are basically bottom feeders, looking for a bargain in buying the assets of a liquidating business. These types of buyers will most likely pay the least amount for your business. Characteristics of businesses most likely to be sold to an industry buyer are:

- Sales less than $10,000,000.

- An unprofitable company operating history.

- A business in a "forced sale" situation due to an owner's death, divorce, or some other serious problem.

- A business that cannot be sold as an operating entity.

Whichever buyer is the right one for your company, you most likely will want to prepare your business for sale. Of course, the right buyer can mean different things for different sellers. In one case, the right buyer might be the "all-cash" buyer, independent of the type. In another case, the right buyer might be one that you develop a strong rapport with and who you are convinced will maintain the business focus and ideals of your company better than anyone else. If you plan early enough and take the time to properly prepare your business for sale, you will have the luxury of carefully selecting the buyer for your business who will best satisfy your personal as well as financial criteria.

This book primarily addresses the issue of preparing your business for sale by positioning it in its best light in the eyes of a strategic or financial buyer (although Chapter 5 is devoted to transitioning your business to a successor family member). This means presenting it as an ongoing profitable operating business. In selling your business to either a strategic or financial buyer, you will want to take the steps necessary to maximize your business value to them. Although it's true that something (including a business) is only worth whatever someone is willing to pay for it at a particular point in time, experience has shown that buyers of businesses tend to buy based on the immediate past net operating profit and the outlook for its continuation. In general, by increasing the bottom line, you will increase the sales price of your business! In Chapter 3, I will discuss many of the things you can do to increase your net profit in preparation for sale without hurting the overall operation of your business.

It's possible for you to "reconstruct" or "recast" your profit and loss statement without actually realizing the financial improvements on your books, and try to sell these potential earnings to a buyer. However, with the exception of excess depreciation and amortization expenses, you will find it difficult to convince a buyer that certain expenses are not needed. In the case of additional sales, you will find it nearly impossible to convince a buyer that you could have had more sales revenues and expect them to factor the increased phantom sales (and therefore, increased profits) into their determination of a purchase price. So it's absolutely essential that you take the steps recommended in this book to prepare your business for sale if you expect to realize your business's maximum value.

Before you consider the specific things you can do to enhance your business value, you should understand the various methods of selling a business which are available to you.

Methods of Sale for Your Business

One of the next things that you will need to do is to decide (at least as a starting point) on the method that you will use to sell your company. There are several different ways to accomplish the sale of your business, and many of the recommendations for preparing your business for sale presented in this book apply equally well to each situation. Keep in mind a very important point. No matter what your preferences are, you will eventually sell your business. Either you will use one of the methods I have described, or your estate will do it on your behalf! No matter which way it's done, you owe it to yourself and your family to have a well-thought-out exit plan for your business. This will maximize the value you and/or your heirs receive as a result of your many years of hard work.

Strategic Move #3:

"Make an early decision as to the planned method of sale of your business in order to properly position it for sale."

By deciding early the method you plan to use to sell your business, you will be able to tailor your preparations to maximize the sale price. As someone once said, "You will never get there if you do not know where you are going." So carefully review the following discussion of the possible methods of sale of your business and choose the one that seems to be most approriate for you.

The principal methods you may want to consider to accomplish the sale of your business, are:

- The sale of your business to a private party.

- The sale/transition of your business to a family member.

- A management buyout by your in-house company managers (MBO).

- A sale to your employees through an employee stock ownership program (ESOP).

- A merger with, or acquisition by another company (M&A).

- An initial public stock offering (IPO).

- A leveraged buyout (LBO).

The vast majority of small businesses in the United States and Canada are sold by their owners to a private party, so I'll concentrate my recommendations with that premise in mind. However, a significant number of businesses are sold or transferred to a close family member. Even in this case, the current principal owner will need to extract the value in the business in order to realize enough cash to pursue their next phase of life, whether it's retirement or engagement in another business endeavor. Chapter 5 is devoted entirely to the issue of succession planning for the family-owned business. The other methods of sale (MBO, ESOP, M&A, IPO, LBO) are used much less frequently by small-business owners but should be considered as part of the thought process and planning that you will be putting into your business exit plan.

I will address the pros and cons of each of these methods for selling your business with the understanding that no matter which approach you take, you will need to make careful plans which must be enacted in order to properly prepare your business for sale.

Sale to a Private Party

The sale of your business to a private party is the most likely transaction process for companies with annual sales of less than $10 million. Larger businesses are also sold to private individuals, but as sales volume and selling price begin to go into the millions of dollars, the most frequent buyers are companies acquiring or merging with other companies. This issue was covered in an earlier discussion about mergers and acquisitions.

Some of the key differences you will encounter in dealing with an individual private party typically involve the following:

- The potential buyer is much less sophisticated about business operations.

- The potential buyer will almost certainly require some sort of seller financing with the primary security being the business itself.

- A business broker or other intermediary will be very valuable to facilitate the sale of the business by "hand-holding" the buyer and resolving the many questions and issues that will arise requiring a third party to assist in mediating.

- Although your involvement in the sale of your business will most likely be extensive under any situation, it will probably be the most significant when you are dealing with a private individual.

There are many advantages and disadvantages in dealing with a private party in the sale of your business. Here are some of the most important ones to consider:

Some advantages of a sale to a private party are:

- There are many potential buyers of small businesses in the market (I estimate there is an average of 20 for every business for sale), so you should be able to find a qualified and motivated buyer.

- The transaction costs will be the least of any of the other methods of sale, with the possible exception of a sale to a family member or employee.

- The actual transaction will generally be the least complicated in terms of legal issues, and therefore faster to accomplish.

- There are many experienced professionals available to advise you in this most common form of business ownership transfer.

Some disadvantages of a sale to a private party are:

- Because there are many potential buyers of small businesses, you may find it difficult to find the truly motivated buyer with the financial wherewithal to complete the transaction. Unfortunately, many potential buyers are just "lookers" and, if not properly screened and qualified, will waste your time and delay the sale of the business.

- Although the transaction costs are lower relative to most of the other methods of selling your business, they will still be significant. A good business broker may take up to 10% of the total selling price of the business, plus you will also pay attorney and accountant fees.

- You will have to deal with a large number of conflicting emotional issues when dealing with private individuals. Many buyers may get "cold feet" during the sale process for no rational business reason. Many transactions never close because of this.

- You will most likely need to finance a significant portion of the business sale. This will delay for several years your receiving the full selling price of the company, and will keep the funds owed to you at significant risk for that period of time.

- The process of finding a private party buyer will often result in a lack of confidentiality that the business is for sale. The more that your business is discussed with potential buyers, the greater the chance that it will become general knowledge that your business is on the market. This could result in customer and supplier confidence problems.

Sale/Transition to a Family Member

There are significant numbers of family-owned businesses in the United States. In fact, it has been estimated that more than 50% of all small businesses are family-owned. If your company is a closely-held private business and you have offspring of an age and capability to take over the business, then this is a sale option that you should consider. But beware. Less than a third of all family-owned businesses survive the transition from the founders to the second generation. Almost nine out of 10 fail to survive into a third generation. There are many significant reasons for this poor track record which has raised government and private concerns about the long-term health of small-business. This has led to a dramatic increase in the number of SBA and university-backed programs that are available to help business owners deal with the special problems of family-owned business management and succession.

Although there is no hard data on how many privately-held, family-owned businesses are candidates for succession transfer to the next generation, a recent insurance company study sheds some light on this issue. The Massachusetts Mutual Insurance Company recently sponsored a survey of over 600 family-owned businesses with revenues of $2 million or more. The findings indicate that 65% plan to pass the business on to family members, 24% specifically do not, and 11% are undecided. A huge 75% of the respondents who plan to transfer the business within their family have no succession plan and are not really sure how they will address the details when the time arrives. This information tends to point towards at least a partial reason for the inability of family-owned businesses to successfully make the transition: poor preparation and planning.

Because this is such an extensive and complicated issue affecting so many small businesses, I have included a separate Chapter 5 devoted to this subject. You should still read this entire book even if you decide to transfer your business ownership to a son, daughter, or other family member, because you still need to prepare your company for transition, establish the "true" value of the business, and devise a plan to exit the business gracefully. Of course, you will most likely also need to determine a way to "cash-out" your ownership position so that you can live comfortably in your retirement. You need an exit plan no matter what method you choose to sell your business.

Some advantages of a sale to a family member are:

- You will avoid the problems of dealing with a stranger who will want to investigate every nook and cranny of your company, potentially disrupting your normal course of business.

- You will have a reasonable assurance that the business will continue on as you prefer, maintaining your ideals and vision for the future.

- You will typically be better able to control the timing and condition of transfer to suit your needs than with an open market transaction.

Some disadvantages of a sale to a family member are:

- Your family members may not be prepared to assume ownership of the business when you are ready to exit.

- There may not be enough financial resources available from the business for your successor family members to adequately buy you out.

- Family conflicts may result in cases where there are multiple family members desiring a "piece of the action."

An In-House Management Buyout (MBO)

An in-house management buyout (MBO) is just what the term implies. If your company is large enough, its management forms a team to buy the business from you. There are many advantages to this method since your managers probably know almost as much about running the company as you do. You will have a better than reasonable assurance that the company's success will continue and that you will eventually receive your full payment for the sale of your company. In all likelihood, the management team will not have the funds to buy you out in cash, but will require you or another party to loan them the money for a buyout. This is very similar to what's called a *leveraged buyout* accomplished by a third party and is discussed later in this chapter. There are some strong advantages and disadvantages with an MBO.

Some advantages of an MBO are:

- The management team as a collective group already knows and understands your business.

- You intimately know the capabilities and shortcomings of your management team and you will be better able to make a good decision about personally financing the sale of the business to them.

- The impact of the sale on your business will be lessened because the key managers will stay on and most likely continue business as usual, at least for a while. In a sale of the business to a third party, some of your management team may become apprehensive about their future and leave, or they may be replaced by a new owner.

- You will be better able to maintain confidentiality that your business is for sale by keeping that information within the company. Knowing that a company is for sale usually creates uneasiness among customers and vendors. The members of the management buyout team, however, will have an incentive to keep the pending transaction confidential until it is completed.

Some disadvantages of an MBO are:

- Unless you personally finance the sale to your management team at a reasonable rate, the cost of funds from commercial lenders, venture capitalists, and other sources of buyout money may greatly weaken the company's ability to sustain operations over time. In many cases, the only way a company can remain intact and prosper through an MBO is if the seller holds a significant portion of the financing for the buyout at less-than-normal commercial rates and terms.

- Although the managers attempting the MBO may have extensive experience and knowledge about their specific functional area of the company, do any one of them have an overall picture of running the business? Generally, a collection of individually capable people may not have the entrepreneurial spark or leadership capability necessary to successfully run a company.

- If you are financing a significant portion of the MBO, there may not be enough financial incentive on the part of the new owners to be prudent in their actions. A danger could be that they take extraordinary risks which backfire and drive the company to ruin. Of course, this is a risk that you will have to take with any buyer for whom you provide a significant portion of the financing.

Sale to Your Employees Through an ESOP

A sale of your company to your employees is a very real option for closely-held, incorporated small businesses. The formal terminology for this type of sale is: employee stock ownership plan (ESOP). Although the most widely used purpose of an ESOP is to provide a benefit or retirement plan for a company's employees, it can also be used very effectively as a method of selling the business to them. In fact, according to the National Center for Employee Ownership (NCEO), over 10 thousand companies now have ESOPs covering over 10 million employees. Here's a snapshot of how it works. The company establishes an ESOP and guarantees any debt incurred by the ESOP in the purchase of the company's corporate stock. The ESOP then borrows money from a lender for the purpose of buying the owner's stock, in whole or in part. The corporate stock shares are placed and held in a trust, and the company makes annual tax-deductible payments to the trust to retire the loan. As the loan is paid down, the corporate shares are released and distributed to the employees. Of course, there are some legal restrictions on the use of ESOPs. For example, ESOPs cannot be used with partnerships or professional corporations. Additionally, sub-chapter S corporations have been restricted from using ESOPs in the past. Effective January 1, 1998, federal legislation will extend this opportunity to all sub-chapter S companies but restrict some of the tax incentives enjoyed by C corporations. As with any other method, there are advantages and disadvantages with selling your business to your employees using an ESOP:

Some advantages of an ESOP are:

- The ESOP provides a ready market for the shares of the business owner.

- There are very attractive tax advantages to the seller, the company, and the employees involved in an ESOP.

- Many companies that are purchased through ESOPs do very well because each and every employee feels a real sense of ownership in the company. This helps many of them to personally excel and further benefit the company. Each employee becomes a true stakeholder in the financial success of the business. This has the tendency to improve productivity and reduce operating costs.

Some disadvantages of an ESOP are:

- Entering into an ESOP requires an extensive amount of otherwise private corporate information to be given to the employees. Information such as profits, management salary, corporate perks, etc., may not be something some owners wish to divulge to their employees.

- Information provided to employees may also be inadvertently transferred to the business's competitors. It's hard enough to keep sensitive company information private between yourself and a few key managers, and it may be impossible when the information is spread out across many employees.

- The ESOP will not only be the ownership vehicle for the employee, but will also be their company retirement plan as well. Some employees may be unwilling to accept this potential double-jeopardy risk. If the company fails, they lose their job and their source of retirement income.

For those of you interested in pursuing this option further, Chapter 8, "Resources for Preparing Your Business for Sale," lists some information sources about setting up an ESOP in your company.

Mergers and Acquisitions (M&A)

The phrase "mergers and acquisitions" (M&A) is a commonly accepted term in the business community. Merger is generally defined as the process of joining your company with another in the sense that a new corporate entity emerges and the assets and liabilities of the joined firms are comingled. In an acquisition, another company purchases your company and operates it as a subsidiary or as another entity under a larger corporate umbrella. This process is distinctly different from selling your closely-held business to another private party.

The trend for mergers and acquisitions of companies peaked in the 1980s. There was a steady decline in popularity in the early 1990s, but they have experienced a resurgence in the mid- to late-1990s and continue as a very viable method for selling your closely-held business. The market for mergers and acquisitions has been as robust in recent years for some types of companies as it was in the 1980s, and is once again a good way to sell a business. The primary reason for the decline in M&As for some types of businesses has been due to the reduced access to financing; the easy credit market for acquisitions is not as broadly available today as it has been in past years for all types of companies. Accordingly, it may be difficult to pursue an M&A transaction for your company when you are ready to sell. A notable exception to this is the high technology/communications/Internet field as well as otherwise strategically attractive companies, both of which have seen an explosion of M&As in recent years. Here are some of the advantages and disadvantages of pursuing an M&A for the sale of your business:

Some advantages to an M&A are:

- There may be excellent tax reasons to take this approach. Secured payment for your business can be spread out over several years which will minimize your tax exposure.

- If you are selling your business for reasons other than cashing-out entirely and leaving for other pursuits, this approach may provide expansion capital for your business while still allowing you to retain a significant ownership position.

- If you take part of your selling price in shares of the acquiring company, you may minimize your financial risk by diversifying your overall investment.

- If you are looking for an all-cash buyout, this is probably the best approach to take. There are companies within certain industries (primarily high technology) that have a significant amount of cash available for acquisitions as a result of their own successful IPOs.

Some disadvantages to an M&A are:

- Selling a company through an M&A process is very difficult and time-consuming. The goals and objectives of each company can be very different and may result in an inability to reach a meeting of the minds even after extensive negotiations.

- The M&A process tends to be very complicated, including stock swaps, cash, stock options, contingencies, etc., that are very expensive and time-consuming to negotiate, and frequently may not result in the desired sale. The wasted energy and lost enthusiasm on the part of everyone involved in your company may be detrimental to the overall business.

- The negotiation process itself requires disclosure of sensitive corporate information and the likelihood is high that the company most interested in a M&A is one of your current competitors. Just how much information are you willing to provide about your company to a competitor? If the deal doesn't proceed, you may have done irreparable harm to your competitive position.

- Because many M&As involve some kind of stock swap, you may be trading in a known risky asset (your company) for an even riskier asset (the acquiring or merging company). Sometimes the devil you know is better than the devil you do not know.

Chapter 8 provides some information and assistance resources for you to pursue if you are interested in further exploring this method of selling your business.

Public and Private Corporate Stock Sales

Selling your business through an initial public stock offering (IPO) is the Holy Grail for many entrepreneurial business owners. Some have called it "super money" because it offers the possibility of making a business owner extremely wealthy in a very short period of time. The truth is that most businesses will never qualify for the process of bringing their company to the public market-place. The vast majority of businesses are too small, in the wrong market sector relative to public interest, or undercapitalized to be able to afford the extensive cost of an IPO process. For those of you interested in how the process works, here is an overview of what you will need to do.

Once a business owner decides to try the IPO route, they must:

- Select and hire an investment banking firm to serve as an underwriter for the IPO. The underwriter, in turn, brings together a group of investment firms who will ultimately attempt to sell the corporate stock to the public.

- Dedicate one or more senior corporate managers to work full time for six to 24 months with the underwriter, attorneys, CPAs, auditors, Security and Exchange Commission (SEC), etc., to prepare the required prospectus in accordance with very specific legal requirements.

- Begin, once the SEC is satisfied and the prospectus is prepared, an extensive marketing campaign using the investment firm brokers who will be selling the stock of the IPO to the public.

- Decide with the investment banker/underwriter what price to put on the shares of the IPO. This is always a contentious event with the business seller wanting as high a price as possible and the underwriter concerned with keeping the initial price low enough to sell out the complete inventory of initial shares.

- Offer the shares to the public.

There are less complicated approaches to selling corporate stock other than through a full-blown IPO. These take the form of Private Placements and Direct Public Offerings. These approaches are usually used by a company attempting to raise expansion capital and are generally not used by a business owner to cash-out of the company, although it's certainly possible.

A *Private Placement* sale of corporate stock involves the sale of company shares to an investment institution or other private party. There is generally no Security and Exchange Commission involvement in this type of stock sale. A private placement of stock falls under Regulation D of the federal securities laws and generally lets a company raise capital relatively quickly and with much lower costs than a public offering (except perhaps under a Small Corporate Offering

Registration (SCOR) method; see below). Private placements are available to all companies, large and small, private or public, but are usually used by private companies. Private placements are easier and less expensive to do than public offerings in that they do not need to be registered with federal and state securities regulators, but they still carry a great deal of restrictions. For example:

- Depending on the size of the offering, they are limited to a maximum number of potential investors.

- A certain number of "accredited" investors will be required. An accredited investor will have net worth ($1 million or more) and income ($200,000 for two years) requirements.

- The stock must be held for a specified time period (usually two years).

- Investors must be provided with full, fair, and complete disclosure of all material facts.

- A company may not use press releases, advertisements, or general advertisements to offer the stock for sale.

A *Direct Public Offering (DPO)* is also usually used by a company to raise expansion capital, but could be used by a business owner as a way of raising capital for the company to use for a partial buyout. The most popular DPO approach for small businesses is the Small Corporate Offering Registration (SCOR). The SCOR method of initial equity financing allows a company to raise up to $1 million by selling common stock directly to the public for a price set at no less than $5 per share. Stock can be sold directly by the company without any limitation on the number of investors or their financial expertise. In fact, many owners have been using the Internet and their product catalogs to promote the sale of stock in their companies! SCOR also allows your company to establish a trading market for its common shares on the NASDAQ electronic bulletin board. The great attraction to this is that the shares are able to be freely traded. This greatly enhances the outlook for investors who initially invest in your company. This can all be done without the expensive and complicated disclosures required by the SEC for other IPOs. As of this writing, all states except Alabama, Delaware, Florida, and Hawaii accept the SCOR method of financing.

There are other DPOs and all are individually regulated within the state in which the company is incorporated. Chapter 8 lists sources of information to explore for a better understanding of the IPO/DPO process.

As I stated previously, the vast majority of small- to medium-sized businesses will find the IPO route to selling the business tantalizing and seductive, but far beyond their reach. The up-front costs in time and fees paid to all the professional experts involved is usually considered exorbitant. In addition, the uncertainty of the outcome generally weighs against taking this course of action for most small companies. In summary, some of the advantages and disadvantages to public and private corporate stock sales are:

Some advantages to an IPO are:

- It has the potential for generating the most amount of money of any of the methods of sales for your business.

- You will most likely be able to retain a significant ownership position and management control after the sale if you so desire.

Some disadvantages of an IPO are:

- It is very expensive and extremely complicated to accomplish.

- It will take a relatively long period of time to complete.

- Very few businesses will qualify for this method of sale. Only a fraction of all businesses become publicly traded companies.

Leveraged Buyout (LBO)

A leveraged buyout (LBO) is very similar to the MBO discussed earlier in this chapter. The principal difference between the concepts of an MBO and an LBO is that in an LBO the sale of the business is made to an outsider, while with an MBO the sale is made to inside management. In the case of privately-held companies, whether they are incorporated or not, an LBO is almost always initiated by the seller, although occasionally a business owner is approached by an investment firm looking for LBO candidates. An LBO is a mechanism of sale that is commonly used by very large companies (both publicly- and privately-owned) but it's possible to accomplish an LBO with a relatively small company.

Some advantages of an LBO are:

- The seller is usually able to realize an all-cash sale thereby eliminating any risk in holding financing

- The transaction is usually accomplished very quickly by strategic buyers who have already decided they want your company and have pre-arranged the financing.

Some disadvantages of an LBO are:

- The professional fees associated with the extensive requirement for legal, accounting, and investment banker expertise may make an LBO financially impractical for most small businesses.

- An LBO could be a "hostile takeover" resulting in a sale of your business under conditions unacceptable to you.

In addition to thinking about who you will sell your business to, the method of sale you will use, and preparing your business for sale, you also need to consider preparing yourself for the eventual sale of the company. In the next section, I address some of the considerations you should have about preparing yourself for the sale of your business.

Preparing Yourself for Selling Your Business

Equally as important to preparing your business for sale is to prepare yourself and your family for this major transition in your life. You may have spent many years building the business, seeing it through good times and bad, making tough decisions that kept you up all night. Eventually, you were able to enjoy the fruits of success. To actually sell your business to others and forever give up the control, power, and exhilaration of running a successful business can be very traumatic to many entrepreneurs. What do you do with yourself next? And what about your family? How will they react to you selling your business? They need to be prepared to understand and accept this momentous decision because it will affect them as well as you. This leads to the next strategic move you should make to prepare your business for sale:

Strategic Move #4:

"Prepare yourself for selling your business as carefully as you prepare the business for sale. Be absolutely sure you want to sell!"

Some sellers regret selling their business after they have completed the sale. They find that managing the money from the sale of their company is not nearly as rewarding as managing the business that they have taken so long to nurture and grow. Sometimes it's as important to prepare yourself for selling your business as it is to prepare the business for sale. In this section, I will explore some of the personal considerations you need to ponder as you begin to make the decision to sell your business.

- Do you really want to sell your business now?

- Would you rather keep the business in the family than sell it to strangers?

- What will you do next with your life?

- What are your objectives in selling the business?

Identify Your Reasons for Selling the Business

The first thing you need to do is to honestly assess your motivations for selling your business. Be absolutely sure you want or need to sell your business! Changing your mind during the sale process will cost you money, will waste the time of many people, will hurt your reputation, and could possibly lead to litigation by a jilted suitor. Before you can deal with the emotional issues that arise with your decision to sell, you must fully understand why you are planning to sell. Some of the most common reasons are:

- *Failing health* or other personal difficulties such as the death of a loved one that precludes you from continuing the intensive level of involvement in the company necessary for its continued success.

- *Retirement* to a quieter, more relaxed lifestyle in order to enjoy the financial rewards of your hard work while you still have your health. There are many business owners who cannot conceive of sitting on the beach, playing golf, or traveling, day after day for the rest of their lives. Their enjoyment of life is their business and they would likely be disappointed by a retirement lifestyle.

- *Burn-out* from all of the stress, anxiety, problem solving, and responsibility of keeping a business running. There is no doubt that, as a business owner, you are on the job 24 hours a day, seven days a week. Even when you are not in the office, you are constantly thinking of the business and the issues that you need to resolve. Some of the best entrepreneurs can be overwhelmed by this and feel that the only escape is to sell their business.

- *Divorce* can certainly cause serious problems even in the best-run businesses. About 50% of the marriages in the United States end in divorce, and business owners are certainly not immune from this sad statistic. In many cases, a spouse plays an integral role (whether actively or passively) in a business's operations and when a divorce enters the picture, the business inevitably suffers. Frequently, the details of a divorce settlement center upon financial issues that can only be resolved by selling the business to raise the necessary cash for compensation to the parties involved.

- *Business problems* that can only be solved through a sale, merger, or acquisition of the business. Sometimes businesses are unable to raise the capital necessary to deal with a sudden downturn in sales, or conversely, to efficiently handle a dramatic increase in product orders. In addition to new capital, new management may be needed, or new sales' outlets opened. For a myriad of reasons, both good and bad, business problems can sometimes force the sale of a business.

- *Partnership or shareholder problems* can also be a significant factor in deciding to sell a business. Many times, partners in privately-held businesses find that they have developed substantial differences which cannot be resolved and that threaten to significantly hurt the company. Also, in privately-held corporations with a number of shareholders, serious disagreements may evolve over the future direction of the company, a proposed expansion, the addition of a new product line or service, or the taking on of new debt. Sometimes the only resolution to a shareholder or partner impasse is the sale of the business to an outside party.

Prepare Yourself Emotionally for Your Business Sale

Once you have satisfied yourself that you understand why you want to sell your business, the next important step is to prepare yourself emotionally for this major life transition. The reason you need to prepare yourself emotionally is because it can be one of the most tiring, frustrating, and unpleasant events of your business life. It can also be the most financially rewarding! Potential buyers will poke and prod into the most private financial matters of your business and almost certainly disrupt and distract you from the daily running of the company as they conduct their due diligence. You must be absolutely certain that you want to sell your business.

You may not think about it in this regard, but you most likely love your business in much the same way you love your child. Chances are that you created your business, nurtured it through the early years when it could not stand on its own, and then guarded it through great challenges as it came to maturity. As you progress through the process of turning control of your business over to another person, whether a stranger or even a family member, you will most likely experience strong emotional conflicts that could interfere with your business judgment. Prepare yourself for this by addressing your feelings early in the sale process. I recommend that sellers write down the reasons that they have decided to sell their business as part of their exit plan. Then, when those emotions start to creep in as the business moves toward a sale, you can refer back to those written reasons that you arrived at in a more logical and unemotional manner. Usually this will help you to keep moving towards your goal.

Plan to Stay With the Business for a Time After the Sale

You should also plan on staying with the business for some period of time after the sale. Almost all business sales will benefit from the continuity provided by the seller remaining with the company for some period of time. Frequently, business sellers take either employment contracts or consulting agreements as a term or condition in the sale of the business. Although this is done primarily for economic reasons for both the buyer and the seller, it can also be an important emotional bridge you can use to separate yourself from your business over a gradual period of time.

Many small businesses are extensions of the founder/owner. The business may have difficulty maintaining successful operations without that person's continued involvement for some period of time for many reasons:

- Some long-time customers may remain as customers only out of a sense of loyalty to the present business owner, and time will be needed for new relationships to be established.

- The sales charisma of the business owner may be so strong that a buyer is unable to match it right away and will require the seller's involvement for a period of time.

- The unique know-how of the business owner may not be able to be easily and quickly transferred.

Business sellers sometimes remain with the company for extended periods of time after the sale beyond the initial transfer period. It may be in a new owner's best interest to retain you to stay with the company for six to twelve months or even longer. You may want to make it a condition of the sale that you remain with the company for a period of time to ease your transition to retirement. I know of cases with larger companies where the seller has been provided with an office, secretarial services, and the use of a company car for up to a year after the sale. In some cases this is for the benefit of the company, and in others it's strictly for the benefit of the outgoing business owner.

Generally, the size and complexity of your business will determine the length of the transition time needed. Small retail businesses can be transitioned in as little as one to four weeks and small personal services companies range between two and eight weeks. Much larger companies, especially manufacturing businesses average three to six months. No matter what type or size of business you have, I recommend that you plan to stay with the business at least one to three months after the sale. The buyer will most likely want and need you to stay on for that length of time to answer the one-thousand-and-one questions that are bound to arise but cannot be anticipated before the sale. Also, because you are most likely going to be holding financing for the sale of your business, you will want to ensure that the new owner starts off on the right foot to keep the business moving ahead properly to protect your investment. Do not forget that if you finance the sale of your business in any way, you are in fact an investor in that business until the money owed to you is fully repaid. Finally, it may be best for you emotionally to ease out of the business rather than leave it "cold turkey." It can be very traumatic to suddenly stop going to work at your business as you have done for so many years.

In Summary

I have now discussed some of the reasons why you need to prepare yourself and your business for sale. I have also covered the different types of buyers and the methods of sale that you will need to consider and for which you need to make a preliminary decision. The next necessary step is to determine a "ball-park" estimate of valuation for your business as of the present time. This can serve as a benchmark for you to use as you begin actually preparing your business for sale in order to enhance its value in the eyes of a potential buyer. In the next chapter, I will cover the different ways of valuing a business. I will demonstrate how to "reconstruct" an income and expense statement, and I will recommend a valuation method for you to use with your business.

2

What Is Your Business Really Worth?

- *Introduction*
- *Business Valuation Methods*
- *Reconstructing the Income and Expense Statement*
- *Applying the CAP Valuation*
- *Timing Is Everything*
- *Finding Value in a Business Without Net Income*

Introduction

It's very important in the early stages of preparing your business for sale to have a good idea of what it might be worth. By personally going through the exercise of determining a "ballpark" valuation for your business, you will be better able to understand what must be done to enhance its selling value. The bottom line in most business sales is just that—the bottom line. Most businesses are sold to financially motivated buyers and are valued and sold based on the net operating profit of the business. Although there are many other ways of valuing a business, including various rules of thumb for specific types of companies, the most important aspect of almost any business is its ability to generate profits for its owners. Accordingly, most of the discussions in this chapter are based on the business being a relatively mature and profitable business. However, I have added a section at the end of this chapter titled "Finding Value in a Business Without Net Income" for those businesses that are not producing a net operating profit.

This chapter will not be a definitive treatise on the extensive subject of valuing an operating business. Many books cover this subject in great detail. I have included some references to these publications in Chapter 8, "Resources for Preparing Your Business for Sale," if you are interested in exploring this topic further. Unless you are concerned with establishing a business value for minimizing estate taxes, gift-giving purposes, bankruptcy, or divorce, the approaches outlined in the following pages are sufficient in providing you with a close approximation of what your business may be worth to someone in an arms-length purchase and sale transaction. My approach will provide you with all of the analysis you need to establish a baseline value for your business as you prepare it for sale. Later, you can use this figure to establish an asking price for your company.

No number of expensive business appraisal reports will convince a buyer to pay more than what they perceive as the worth of your business. The real value of your business will evolve through the natural give-and-take of the negotiation process, and will be based on compromise and expectations. Furthermore, your business may well be worth more to a strategic buyer who has a far different perspective of value than a financial buyer. Either way, when you offer your business for sale on the "open" market, the best you can hope for relative to a business valuation is a reasonable ballpark estimate of an asking price that will not scare away potential buyers nor cause you to "give away" the business for significantly less than you could otherwise receive.

Rules of Thumb for Valuing a Business

Before we begin talking about the more traditional professional business valuation methods, I want to mention the subject of "rules of thumb" regarding the valuing of a business. Rules of thumb have been developed by various business brokers, mergers and acquisitions specialists, and investment bankers to provide a quick, broad-brush assessment of a private company's value on the open market. These estimates are based on a variety of factors specific to a particular type of company and are unique to the individual or activity using them. Rules of thumb will not only vary by experience and opinion, but by areas or regions of the country. The result is that they are notoriously unreliable in establishing a reasonable asking price for your particular business. One way to think of business valuations is that a traditional valuation approach will at least get you into the right ballpark and a rule of thumb will, at best, only get you into the right city. To give you an idea of the broad range of rules of thumb that are kicking around in the business buying and selling world, I have included a few in Table 2-A for your consideration.

Table 2-A

Rule of Thumb Business Valuation Examples

Automotive Dealerships (new cars)	50% of annual net profit plus inventory and equipment
Automotive Parts (retail)	4-5 times monthly sales plus inventory
Beauty Salons	15–25% of annual net profit plus $2,500 per station
Book Stores	40–50% of annual net sales plus inventory
Campgrounds (with real estate)	8 times annual net profit
Dental Practices	1.5 to 2.0 times annual net profit plus current market value of all equipment and inventory
Distributors	25–50% of annual gross sales
Fast-Food Restaurants	40–50% of annual gross sales
Hotels	2 to 3 times annual gross sales
Insurance Agencies	1 to 1.5 times gross annual commissions
Manufacturing Companies	40--50% of annual gross sales
Marinas (with real estate)	8–10 times annual net profit
Motels	$20,000 per room
Pharmacies	Total daily sales times 80-120, plus inventory
Publishers (books)	2–3 times gross annual sales
Retail Businesses	25–50% of annual gross sales, plus inventory
Trucking Companies	$2,500-$5,000 per driver

Please note that I specifically do *not* recommend using rules of thumb to determine even a ballpark value for your business. If you notice in the examples in Table 2-A, the actual return on investment is completely ignored, and in many cases so is any concern with profitability! For example, in the case of Hotels, the rule of thumb for a business valuation is two to three times the annual gross sales. What if the yearly sales for a particular hotel are $500,000 but the business is losing $100,000 per year because the occupancy rate is only 50%? Will someone be willing to pay $1 to 1.5 million for the opportunity to lose $100,000 per year? I think not. Remember that the value of a business as a "going concern" is directly linked to its ability to generate profits for its owner(s). When you discuss the specifics of your business with a serious potential buyer, whether strategic or financial, you must be able to show them why your business is a good investment on their part. General rules of thumb will never do that.

Establish a Benchmark Valuation

Because it's so important to establish a valuation for your business as it's currently operating, I have made this the fifth strategic move to take in preparing your business for sale.

Strategic Move #5:

"Establish a benchmark valuation of your business before you change anything or offer it for sale."

The key operative word in the strategic move wording is "benchmark." You will want to establish a benchmark valuation for many reasons:

- To have a baseline valuation against which you can measure results of changes you will make to your business to increase its value.

- To have an estimate of the value in your business so you can select the best method of sale and the right members for your business sale team.

- To have an idea of what your business may be worth in order to compare it against a "professional" valuation prepared by a business broker, investment banker, business consultant, or CPA.

- To demonstrate to yourself the many opportunities you have to enhance sales and increase profitability, and thereby potentially increase the selling price of your business.

Many attempts have been made by appraisers, brokers, accountants, lawyers, and business writers to standardize the methods of valuing a business, but a significant diversity in approach still prevails. Many specialists, and various learned authorities, will try to sell you a cornucopia of workbooks, computer software, and lately, interactive CD-ROMs. Almost every one is different except in its approach to valuing your business in terms of either net assets or some form of return on investment. I believe that the process of valuing a business will always remain more of an art (beauty is in the eye of the beholder) than a science (plug in standardized formulas). That is why there are different reasons to value a business other than to estimate what the selling price will be on the open market. These reasons include:

- Selling or acquiring a partial interest in a business.

- Forming a joint venture arrangement with another company.

- Selling or acquiring a product or service line.

- Putting together a buy/sell agreement for a partner or minority shareholder.

- Dissolving a partnership or corporation.

- Reorganizing a company under the bankruptcy rules.

- Establishing an estate plan and determining value for estate and gift taxes.

- Divorce settlements.

In all of these cases, it's difficult to choose a valuation method since the forces of a free and open market are generally not in effect when arriving at a fair-market price. For example, arriving at a value for a buy/sell agreement between business partners can be fraught with difficulty as the two parties decide what is a "fair" approach. What may seem reasonable to one may be totally unacceptable to the other. In the situation of estate planning where trusts are established and the transition of the business to succeeding family members is desired, you will want the business valuation to be as low as possible (as viewed by the IRS) to minimize potential estate and gift taxes. If you are going through a divorce, then there is an obvious problem in that one party will want to value the business highly while the other will seek to minimize its value. Although this valuation process also occurs in the sale of a business to a stranger, no actual free-market sale takes place in the above situations. Only estimates, perceptions, and someone's arbitrary valuation will ultimately prevail. So for these cases, the method used for valuation will be different than that used for valuing a business for sale as an arms-length transaction.

In the situation where you are planning a sale of your business on the open market, you only need to establish a ballpark estimate of value for your business to begin a sales and negotiation process that will ultimately lead to the true value of your business (at least at that point in time). Even if you are planning to sell your business to the next generation of family members, the valuation process need not be as rigorous as it might otherwise be for some of the other cases cited. After all, your goal presumably will be to transition a company that cannot only provide financial rewards to you, but will also provide a prosperous future for your children, and not squeeze the last dime out of the business.

All businesses that follow even the most rudimentary accounting practices will already have a written value for the business. This is the book value or shareholder's equity that appears on the balance sheet. This value is almost always an unreliable indicator of the company's true-market value. This is because the value is based on the historical cost of a business's assets, rather than their current market value and also does not reflect the value of a company as a "going concern." That is, it does not take into consideration the ability of the company to use its tangible and intangible assets to generate future income for its owners. Additionally, the book value of a company can be significantly impacted up or down by the type of accounting methods that are used. Accordingly, book value and shareholder's equity are usually not used in the determination of an ongoing business value.

Therefore, in this book the discussion of valuation will center upon the concept of establishing an estimate of a "going concern" value as a result of free-market forces based on perceived financial or strategic value in your business. The premise is that you will be able to influence this "going concern" value by the actions you take in preparing your business for sale. ***By following the guidance I provide for you, not only will you most likely be able to increase the value that you ultimately receive for your business, but you will also make the business much easier and faster to sell.***

Do not forget that the true or "actual" value of your business will ultimately be determined by the marketplace for a particular instant in time. Whatever someone is willing to actually pay you for your company when you are ready or need to sell is what your company is actually worth. And why should this surprise any of us? Just take a look at the companies that you can relatively easily put a value on at any given point in time. Today's price for Apple Computer, Inc. is $2.98 billion ($24.00 per share times 124 million shares issued). So if you have about $3 billion handy and you want to own a computer and software manufacturing company, you have some idea of how the investing public values Apple Computer. But is this really the value of Apple Computer? It most likely is not because as soon as you approach the tens of thousands of individual shareholders with an offer to buy their shares at that price, the price of the stock and therefore the overall valuation of the company will likely rise. Why?

Because of expectations. The shareholders are likely to suspect that you know something good relative to the future profitability of the company (why else would you be willing to buy the company?) and they immediately want more money to relinquish their shares, because their expectations rise. As a result, company valuation on the public market is constantly changing and reflects not only expectations, but also history, general economic climate, investor mood, and a host of other variables. So why should valuation be any easier or straight-forward for a private company? It is not. In fact, it's much more difficult because there is no public market to even provide a hint of what the company might be worth. But you still need to estimate the value of your business to establish a benchmark and ultimately an asking price as you proceed to prepare the business for sale. Consequently, the following methods of valuing a business are available for your use.

Business Valuation Methods

Although there are many different ways of valuing a privately-owned and closely-held business, there are only two basic approaches that are the basis for all traditional valuation procedures; the valuation of assets and the return on investment. These further break down into four fundamental methods:

- Asset based valuation (liquidation value).

- Market comparison valuation.

- Present value of the business's future earnings valuation.

- Capitalization of current net earnings valuation.

Each of these four methods is important in estimating the valuation of your business, depending on the type of sale that you plan to use. In the following discussion, I will provide an overview of each of the valuation methods and then recommend the best one for you to use in establishing a valuation for your business.

Asset Based Valuation

The asset based value is also known as the liquidation value and is relatively easy to determine. The assumption in this valuation method is that you will not sell your business as a going operation but rather, you will sell all of the assets separately, pay all of the outstanding bills, and keep whatever is left over.

This is usually an unreliable method for arriving at a good estimate of a business's value if the company has net operating income. This is true because it does not take into consideration the value of the business as a "going concern." Although many of the tangible assets can be appraised as to their current market value, it's very difficult to assign a meaningful value to the intangible assets such as goodwill, trademark, or trade name. In fact, the intangible assets usually have little or no value outside of the company. However, as the business owner, you should do an asset based valuation to have as a reference to measure against the other valuations. In some cases, you may discover that there is more value in your business if you separate out the tangible assets for sale than if you sell the business as a whole.

The first step you should take in valuing your business based on its asset value is to make a comprehensive list of all of the assets owned by the business. I recommend that you separate the assets into two categories: tangible and intangible. Tangible assets are generally things that you can see, touch, feel, count, or measure and for which you can provide an accepted fair-market value. Intangible assets are usually things that exist more in perception than in physical space, and consequently are much more difficult to value. Each business is different and will necessarily have a unique list of assets. The following Table 2-B presents some possible examples of assets in your business in order to spur your thinking.

Table 2-B

Typical Business Assets

ASSETS	
Tangible	**Intangible ***
Cash	Trade Name
Accounts Receivable	Trademarks
Inventory	Patents
Furniture and Furnishings	Licenses
Equipment (incl. commercial software)	Covenant Not To Compete
Real Estate (land, buildings, leases)	Customer Lists
Customer Contracts	Customized Tooling and Dies
Open Customer Orders	Copyrights (incl. print, software, music)
Automobiles	Proprietary Information
Leasehold Improvements	Proprietary Computer Software
Prepaid Expenses	Trained and Assembled Work Force
Franchise Agreement	Brand Names

* *Note:* I have specifically not listed the term "goodwill" as a separate intangible asset. In most business valuations goodwill can be characterized as the sum of all of the intangible assets of the company. One exception to this is if you are valuing a business that has already been sold at least once. In this case there may be an actual balance sheet item valued as goodwill. In this situation you should use goodwill as a separate intangible asset for valuation consideration purposes.

After you have carefully listed all of your business assets, you need to assign a value to each one. There are several accepted ways of valuing the assets of your business:

- Book value.

- Net book value.

- Replacement value.

- Value in place.

- Fair-market value/liquidation value.

The *book value* is the non-depreciated value of the asset as of the day the asset was purchased and as it is currently carried on the balance sheet.

The *net book value* is the depreciated value of the asset. This value could be less than the liquidation value.

The *replacement value* is simply the current purchase price of the same or a similar asset.

The *value in place* is the value of the asset as it's used in the business including installation costs, upgrades, etc.

The *fair-market value* is the value of the asset in a liquidation sale on the open market.

The fair-market value is the only realistic value you can use to determine the value of the asset since it represents the price the asset would receive in a free and open market. By the way, this should not be an exercise in wishful thinking. You owe it to yourself to assign very realistic values to your assets based on what they would sell for in the open market. Usually, an in-use asset's resale value is much less than its purchase price or replacement cost, if sold outside of the operating business. Some possible exceptions to this are real estate, heavy machinery, and machine tool equipment. I have listed some resources in Chapter 8 that you may want to consult for assistance in placing current fair-market value on your tangible assets.

Also, it's very difficult to objectively put a value on a trade name or trademark or any of the other intangible assets. For the purposes of an asset based valuation using liquidation values, it's best that you use only a value for your intangible assets that you are confident you will receive in an outright sale of the asset. For example, a patent may in fact have some value on the market outside of your business if there is a reasonable length of time remaining in its protected life of 17 years. On the other hand, customized tooling and dies for the manufacture of your product may have no value as assets in themselves outside of your operating company.

As to valuing your other intangible assets, the best way is to assign a value to them as a whole. Estimate the cost to start the business as a new venture and assign this value to your intangible assets. In many businesses, this tends to be an impractical undertaking because the cost of startup is extremely difficult to estimate.

After you have listed and assigned a fair-market value for all of the business's assets, you will need to subtract out all of the company's liabilities to arrive at a *net* asset based value. The following Table 2-C lists some of the typical liabilities found in an operating business.

Table 2-C

Typical Business Liabilities

Liabilities	
"Real" Liabilities	**"Phantom" Liabilities**
Accounts Payable Accrued Expenses Accrued Taxes Notes Payable—Bank Mortgages Deferred Income Taxes Legal Judgments or Liens	Notes Payable—Officer (Note 1) Notes Payable—Personal Items (Note 2)

Note 1: Any Promissory Notes payable to an officer are not considered liabilities in an asset based valuation. If paid, both sides of the ledger would be reduced and the net asset value would remain unchanged.

Note 2: Any items such as an automobile that are used primarily for personal use and which would be retained upon sale should not be counted as either an asset or the outstanding Note as a liability.

Therefore, to arrive at the business's net asset value:

Assets (at fair-market value) less Liabilities = Net Asset Value

This will most likely turn out to be the least value of any of the business valuation methods unless there is extraordinary value in any of the business's assets, such as the real estate. If this is the case for your business, and the business is not tied to that particular location, then it may be prudent to move the company to another location and sell the real estate separately. More about the real estate issue later.

Market Comparison Valuation

Market comparison valuations are very difficult to accomplish unless you can identify a similar publicly-traded company for which you can obtain key operating data. Presumably, the outstanding share valuation will help to determine the marketplace's view of the value of the company. To determine the business's total valuation, simply multiply the number of issued shares for the company times the per share price. For example, if a company that you determine is very much like yours has a share price of $5 per share and their issued (or outstanding) numbers of shares (also known as the "float") are 500,000, then the total market valuation of that company is $2.5 million. A ballpark price for your similar company might then be in the $2.5-million range. Of course relying on the value of publicly-traded stock to accurately reflect the true value of a company is chancy at best. Is the stock market in general in a bull (up) or bear (down) phase? Is the industry out of or in favor at this point in time for some unknown reason? Is the stock price reflecting investors' optimistic anticipation of future earnings or reflecting a pessimism based on past disappointing earnings? Because you most likely do not know the answers to these questions, a valuation comparison of a publicly-traded company to yours is not realistically feasible.

Another way of doing a market comparison valuation is to find a similar privately-owned company which has recently been sold and for which there is enough information to make a reasonable comparison to your company. Some resources for information about recent business sales are contained in Chapter 8. The problem will still remain for you to obtain enough data to be able to do a reasonable apples-to-apples comparison. Frequently, you will not be able to find enough information about the selling business's sales and profitability as well as its purchase price and structure of the sale, to allow you to make any kind of meaningful comparison. For these reasons, I recommend against trying to do a market comparison valuation for even a ballpark estimate of the value for your business. However, a good business broker/investment banker or professional business appraiser with specific recent experience with companies like yours in your industry may be able to shed some light on the potential value of your business as compared to recent sales.

Income Based Valuations

For most potential buyers of your business, especially financial buyers, the value will be based on the bottom line. Most buyers usually want to buy a business based on its ability to generate income for them. The higher the income, the higher the price for the business (all other things being equal). To get at the price for a business based on income there are basically two ways to approach the valuation:

- Present Value (PV) of Future Earnings and,

- Capitalization (CAP) of Current Net Earnings.

I contend that these two approaches will generate a valuation, based on the assumptions you make, that are very close to each other. The PV approach is more complicated and requires you to use financial compounding which only accountants and MBAs love to do. The CAP approach is more straightforward, and easier to use and understand. Accordingly, I recommend that you use the Capitalization of Current Net Earnings approach to obtain a ballpark estimate of your company's value. However, never forget two important points:

1) The true value of your business will be what a financially qualified buyer is willing to pay for it at a particular point in time.

2) A financially qualified buyer will most likely base a buying decision on your company's proven ability to generate income and the likelihood that it will continue to do so.

With that said, let's go over the two income based approaches to valuing a business (although lightly on the PV approach) and then cover an extremely important concept related to both approaches; reconstructing the income and expense statement.

Present Value (PV) of Future Earnings Valuation

This method of valuation will provide a much better indication of the true value of a privately-held profitable business (and what someone may be willing to pay for it) than the asset valuation and the market comparison valuation.

The present value method attempts to put a current value on a stream of future earnings. There will be many variables to consider, such as the time value of money, whether the future earnings are expected to increase, decrease, or remain flat, the projected inflation rate, and how far into the future one wants to project earnings. After all of these variables have been taken into consideration, you apply the compound interest formulas, using a business calculator or computer, to determine today's value of a future stream of earnings from the business.

The biggest problem I have with this approach, besides its complicated nature, is that when you try to use this with an arm's-length buyer (as opposed to a family member or partner), you will receive a great deal of resistance. Most buyers do not want to make a valuation decision for a business based on nebulous projected *future* earnings stretching out over several years, which many owners want to show as robustly increasing. Who can predict the future? Even if it is possible to make some learned predictions as to future income from the business, is it reasonable to expect a buyer to pay for those earnings? Let's face it, running a business of any kind is risky and to continue to maintain a given earnings stream, the manager/owner of the company will have to be continually adjusting and fine-tuning the company's business approach. A wrong move could send those attractive, historically consistent earnings right into the toilet. On the other hand, a fresh, bold approach to the business could take the company to higher levels of sales and profitability. Most buyers, whether strategic or financial, will want to personally benefit from the opportunity for increased sales and profitability as a compensation for the risk they are taking by acquiring your business. This is not to say that you do not sell your business for as much as you can get, but being realistic about establishing a value for your business will make the selling process much smoother and faster.

For those of you who want to understand and, perhaps use this valuation approach as a comparison with the other methods, the following synopsis is provided. The basic premise for determining the present value of a future stream of earnings is that money in hand today is worth more than future income. There is more risk attached to the possibility of receiving a dollar several years from now then there is in receiving that dollar right away. Many things can happen to the business to negatively affect its ability to continue to generate a projected income stream. For example: inflation, economic downturns, loss of key employees, natural disasters, technological obsolescence, and so on.

A business buyer can attempt to take into consideration these future unknowns in valuing the business by applying a discount rate to the projected future earnings of the company. The discount rate is a percentage applied to the expected earnings over a number of years. It attempts to "normalize" the projected income to account for the inherent risk.

The main difficulty with this approach (besides getting both you and the buyer to agree on the level of future earnings) is for you and the buyer to agree on a discount rate and the period of time over which to project the earnings. One way to approach the issue of the discount rate is to consider a floor or absolute minimum rate as a baseline and work from there. Probably the safest investment someone can make at this point in time is the purchase of 30-year U.S. Treasury Bonds. At the time of this writing, the 30-year T-Bond rate is 6.5%. This means an investor can invest risk free (other than the risk of inflation or a default by the U.S. Government) a sum of money that will return 6.5% annually for 30 years. This rate establishes the floor rate for comparison purposes relative to any other investment. Unfortunately, that is all it does, and the issue of establishing a discount rate for the projected cash flow from your business still has to be determined by taking into account the other future uncertainties listed earlier.

The problem is that there is no generally accepted formula or method for determining a discount rate. All we know is that it certainly must be more than the safest investment rate (6.5% today). One way to try to get at the rate is to compare the discounted cash flow rates of businesses in your industry that have recently sold. This information is very difficult to come by and comparisons are therefore very difficult to make. In general, accountants using the present value approach will use a discount rate of 8% to 12% for a projected 10-year earning period for a well-established company in a stable industry.

An example of a net present value calculation looks like the following using a 8% discount rate, $100,000 of earnings, a $5,000-per-year increase in earnings based on past performance, and a 10-year period:

Year	Earnings	
1	$ 100,000	
2	105,000	
3	110,000	Discount Rate: 8%
4	115,000	
5	120,000	Net Present Value: $800,892
6	125,000	
7	130,000	
8	135,000	
9	140,000	
10	145,000	
	$1,225,000	Total Cash Flow to the Business Owner

Note: The calculated net present value of $800,892 is arrived at by using compound interest formulas as performed by Microsoft Excel for a series of 10 annual unequal, end-of-year payments.

This means that a business buyer might pay $800,892 for the right to own your business if the reasonable expectation exists that the business will return $1,225,000 in earnings over the next 10 years. Some of the problems with this approach are:

• The buyer must agree that it is reasonably likely that the earnings stream will continue to improve at historical rates for the next 10 years, or whatever period is selected.

- The buyer and you must agree that the risk factor return (discount rate) of 8% is a reasonable premium over the guaranteed 6.5% from a 30-year T-Bond. If the percentage rate is lower, the estimated value of the business will go up and vice versa.

- You both will have to agree on the projected annual earnings which is a problem with any valuation method. I will discuss this issue further in the section on reconstructing the income and expense statement later in this chapter.

- It does not address the issue of debt and financing relative to the business purchase and subsequent operation by a new owner.

Forecasting the company earnings can be an extremely complicated undertaking that most businesses will find almost impossible to do with any acceptable degree of accuracy. Some of the factors that must be considered in an earnings forecast over any length of time beyond the next operating year include the effects of:

- Inflation and interest rates on borrowed capital.

- Competition and customer preference changes.

- Government actions (such as NAFTA, EPA regulations, etc.).

- Labor costs and availability.

- Product/service mix and pricing.

- Cost of raw materials, inventory, etc.

- Inventory turnover rates.

- Accounts receivable rates of collection.

- Increases in federal, state, and local taxes.

- Insurance rates.

- Pension plan costs.

- Overhead operating costs.

This will certainly help an accountant (or two) keep busy for quite some time and when everything is done, all you will have is a collection of educated guesses based on arbitrary assumptions. Not, in my opinion, a good basis for establishing a baseline value for most small businesses that are to be sold as an arms-length transaction.

Capitalization of Current Net Earnings Valuation (CAP)

The next valuation approach which I recommend as your primary method for valuing your business is based on what the company has proven it can earn. Of course, there is a "future" factor here as well. The expectation will be that the current rate of actual earnings of the company will continue for some time. The payoff for the buyer will be if they can increase those earnings to greater and greater levels through their efforts after they take over the business. This is the future opportunity factor which will be part of the purchase attraction for any buyer.

Capitalization of Current Net Earnings (CAP) is a powerful way of valuing a business which allows a business to be fairly evaluated as an investment opportunity without many of the uncertainties that other valuation methods introduce. This method assumes that business owners are entitled to a fair return on the value of the business (their investment) over and above their fair wage if the owners work in the business. This approach is also known as the Excess Earnings Method. The Small Business Administration (SBA) recommends a form of this approach for establishing a business valuation. In fact, the Excess Earnings Method is the approach taken by the IRS in determining the value of business estates or gifts. Specifically, you may refer to IRS Revenue Ruling 59-60 for more information regarding the IRS approach to valuing a closely-held corporation. The actual approach in this book is the author's own based on sound business practices as well as real life experiences in buying and selling businesses. This approach works equally well whether the business to be purchased is operating as a sole proprietorship or as a corporation!

One of the variables that you have to concern yourself with when using this method is the "fair return" percentage. Because the ownership of a small-business is a somewhat risky investment and future profits are not guaranteed, a return on investment or ROI, (also known as a capitalization rate) of 20% to 25% is not an unreasonable range of return to be expected. However, this range may even be too low in many service-related businesses that have a low startup cost, little or no inventory, and "soft" accounts; in other words, riskier businesses. In these types of businesses, a 30% to 35% ROI (or even higher) is a good range to use. Conversely, a long established business with a solid reputation and stable or growing revenues may be more fairly valued using a 10–15% return on investment.

The best approach I have seen written relative to the selection of capitalization rates is by Shannon P. Pratt ("Valuing a Business," 2nd edition, Business One Irwin, 1989). Pratt grouped businesses into five types with a range of risk premiums that are to be added to whatever the current risk-free rate of return is.

As I mentioned previously, at this writing the rate is 6.5%, so for each of the following rates, you would add 6.5% to the risk premium range specified.

Type 1: Very well-established businesses with good trade positions, good management, stable or increasing past earnings, and a reasonably predictable future: 6% to 10%.

Type 2: The same kind of business as *Type 1* except the company is in a more competitive industry: 11% to 15%.

Type 3: Businesses in highly-competitive industries, with low capital investment and mediocre management, but having a good historical earnings record: 16% to 20%.

Type 4: Relatively small businesses that depend on the skill and expertise of one or two people, or large companies in very cyclical industries with poor predictability relative to sales and earnings: 21% to 25%.

Type 5: Small, personal-service businesses with a single owner/manager upon which the business is dependent: 26% to 30% (or even higher in some high risk cases).

It has been my experience, and that of many business brokers, that the above rates (when combined with the current risk-free rate of investment return) tend to be reliable capitalization rates to use in establishing a baseline business value suitable for conducting negotiations with a financially-motivated buyer. The resultant rates not only take into consideration the degree of risk in purchasing a company, but the cost of capital as well. However, as the seller, you may want to select the next best rate for which you honestly believe your company fits to establish an acceptable negotiation range that allows for some downward movement in the negotiated selling price from the asking price.

In order to illustrate this approach, the following simplified example of how to apply the CAP valuation method is presented. Note that a more definitive example that includes other factors such as reconstructed earnings, income taxes, and cost of capital is covered in the later section of this chapter titled "Applying the CAP Valuation."

Making the same business assumptions as I did for the example in the PV discussion, I will select a capitalization rate of 12.5%. This rate is chosen by determining that the business is a *Type 1* as defined by Pratt (well established with good trade positions, good management, stable or increasing present earnings, and a reasonably predictable future). Using the low end of the Pratt range of 6% plus the current risk-free investment rate of 6.5% determines a CAP rate of 12.5%. The business valuation calculation looks like this:

Capitalized Value = Current Year Earnings divided by CAP Rate (as a decimal)

= $100,000 / .125

= $800,000

The resultant CAP valuation estimate looks very much like the PV valuation estimate ($800,000 vs. $800,892) because similar assumptions about risk have been made. The biggest difference between the two approaches is the amount of work and detail involved. For your purposes of establishing a benchmark valuation as a measure to begin preparing your business for sale and then as a ballpark value to begin sale negotiations, the capitalization of current net earnings approach is a good choice.

Once a gross valuation is arrived at using the capitalization method, all of the assets will be physically listed with an approximate liquidation value apportioned to them (except for the inventory, if any, which will be separately valued). This, less any contingent debt, constitutes the overall valuation of your business. You should understand that the difference in price between the valuation using the capitalization of net profits method, and the fair-market value of the tangible assets of the business, is assigned to the intangible assets of the business, collectively referred to as the goodwill. This procedure automatically accounts for the value of all tangible and intangible assets without actually considering them individually. It assumes that the business assets are just the tools of the trade that enable the earnings stream to be realized. I contend that without an earnings stream, a business essentially has no value as a going concern. You should note that in using this method, a business may actually be worth less than its asset value, or in some cases worth substantially more. You will be able to get the most you can for your business by showing a buyer the investment value in your business. In most cases, buyers will pay the capitalization of net profit valuation of a business rather than its asset value (even if the asset value is substantially lower). It's much harder to get buyers to pay the asset value of a business if a reasonable return on investment is not available.

Let's look at a simple example to clarify this concept of valuation. Consider the previous example where a company is currently earning $100,000 and has been tentatively valued at $800,000 using the capitalization of net earnings approach. If the fair-market valuation of the tangible assets (except for cash, accounts receivable, and inventory) is estimated at $400,000, the inventory value is approximately $100,000, the cash and accounts receivable valued at $100,000, and the business debt is $100,000, the intangible assets, also known collectively as the goodwill, will be valued at $100,000. Mathematically this looks like this:

	$ 800,000	overall business gross valuation
(less)	100,000	business debt
	$ 700,000	net business valuation
(less)	400,000	fair-market value of business's tangible assets (except cash, accounts receivable, inventory)
(less)	100,000	all inventory (work-in-process and finished)
(less)	100,000	cash and accounts receivable
	$ 100,000	goodwill value

The reason the inventory is valued and accounted for separately is because you and the buyer will want to adjust this number up or down to reflect the actual dollar value at the time of closing. Also, the tangible assets to be conveyed should be exclusive of cash and accounts receivable. You will want to take the cash out of the business prior to closing (or be compensated separately dollar for dollar). In addition, accounts receivable are often collected separately by the seller, thereby avoiding any argument relative to "collectability" of the receivables. Other methods for receivables can also be worked out where the buyer acquires them at a discounted rate consistent with the bad debt experience of your company. However you approach this issue, the tangible assets which have variable values should be separately priced to allow for adjustment at the time of sale of the business.

If the company you are valuing also owns the real estate necessary for the conduct of the business and you are including it in the sale, the real estate should be valued separately as to its current use. The real estate value should then be added to the CAP value of the business to determine an overall valuation. There are two issues that are key to this consideration:

• The business expenses must include a fair-market value payment for the use of the premises (a mortgage or lease cost).

• The value of the real estate must be determined as to its use in the conduct of the business and not necessarily as to its "highest and best use."

In the previous example, if the real estate is to be sold as part of the business and $100,000 of company earnings are counted as fair-market rent for the premises, the real estate value should be added to the CAP valuation in order to arrive at an overall valuation of the business:

	700,000	net business valuation
plus	$ 300,000	real estate value (separately appraised)
	$1,000,000	overall business valuation (with real estate)

The following concept in the valuation of an operating business is extremely important in any income based valuation. But you will need to reconstruct your company's past and current financial statements so as to eliminate the effect of accounting practices on your company's earnings. This is done to demonstrate the true cash flow available from your business. I have made this the next strategic move you should consider in preparing your business for sale.

Strategic Move #6:

"Reconstruct the income and expense statements to show the maximum cash flow available from your business."

Reconstructing the Income and Expense Statement

No income based valuation of an operating business can be done properly without reconstructing the company's income and expenses to reflect the *potentially* available cash flow to the owner. This process is also known by several other terms:

- Recasting the earnings statement.

- Determining actual "free cash flow" in a business.

- Reconstituting the net operating income.

- Normalizing the earnings.

No matter what term is used, the concept remains the same: reconstruction determines the actual cash flow available to a business purchaser if the company was not operated to minimize exposure to income taxes. While some of the adjustments to the income and expenses may be straightforward, many are not, and a potential buyer may look at these items quite differently than you do. This is one of the key points of this entire book. Most buyers, whether financial or strategic, will be buying your business based on the amount of return on their investment that it can provide. Accordingly, you must do everything you can to demonstrate as much actual proven profit to maximize the perceived value and therefore the selling price of your business.

Looking at how a business broker, investment banker, or other professional would reconstruct your income and expenses will do two things for you:

- It will allow you to calculate an estimated value for your business as of a point in time if you are able to convince the buyer that the reconstruction is accurate, and

- it will highlight those income and expenses that you should begin working on to prepare your business for sale.

With that background in mind, let's go through the process of reconstructing an income and expense statement for the fictional Precision Products Company in order to illustrate this concept.

Precision Products Company Example

Mr. John Smith is 55 years old and is the founder and president of the Precision Products Company which manufactures intermediate market products ultimately used in consumer appliances sold in the retail marketplace. Mr. Smith is in good health, has a happy family life and a son, David, who is in his third year at the Rhode Island School of Design pursuing a degree in Fine Arts. (He is doing quite well and shows promise of being an excellent creative artist.)

The Precision Products Company is also doing well ($1,500,000 of gross sales last year) and is enjoying an average increasing sales volume of about 5–8% per year for the last several years. Profits have been increasing proportionately (currently $75,000 of pretax net income) and it appears that the economy in general is, and is likely to continue, doing well.

John has recently been thinking about the future for himself and his company. He sees new opportunities for even faster growth of the business but the costs to pursue them are high and would have to be financed. In fact, John has been able to retire almost all of the business debt with only a $50,000 balance remaining on a business loan he took out five years ago. John is also a little bored with what he has been doing for the last 25 years and he's wondering if now is the time to start thinking about cashing in on the business that he has built. He's thinking about doing something new and totally different with his life.

His son has not shown any interest or aptitude towards manufacturing or business issues in general, so John knows that he will eventually have to sell the business. What better time than within the next few years? There's sure to be another economic downturn and things will definitely not look so great then. In fact, the company has already been through three such times over the last 25 years and John has little stomach for another period of austerity and crisis management. So John has begun thinking about preparing his business for sale and he would like to come away with enough money that he can take up sailing for the rest of his life if he chooses.

John has managed to realize a nice financial life from the company after the early years when he often did not bring home a paycheck. The first economic slide in his fifth year in business almost bankrupted the company but with family loans he was able to pull through. Now, since many of the mistakes have already been made and hard lessons learned, John has been able to stay current and even a little ahead of the inevitably changing market. He works six days a week and drives an expensive Mercedes convertible for the short commute to the office from his nearby home. He owns the real estate the company occupies although it's in his wife's name. The property is leased to the company for a relatively high rent compared to other space available. John's older brother, Bob, works in the company as a production supervisor. His wife does all the bookkeeping and office administration, and even his son, David, works there in the summers when school is out.

Finding the right buyer for his business will take time, and John knows that whomever the buyer is, they will want to know how much money the business can generate. So he decides to take a look at how much real cash flow could be generated by the company if he wanted to maximize the reported net profit. He has read several books on the subject and decides to do this himself rather than get anyone else involved at this early point. There will be plenty of time later for all of those other folks (with their fee meters running) when the business is actually put up for sale.

John takes the last full fiscal year's income and expense sheets to begin a reconstruction of the expenses to get an idea of just how much cash the company could generate for a new owner if all the perks, philanthropies, and tax shelter schemes were eliminated. Table 2-D shows what John came up with in a reconstruction and the accompanying notes explain his thinking.

Table 2-D

**Precision Products Company Expense Reconstruction
for Fiscal Year ending December 31, 1997**

Expense Item	Statement Expense	Reconstructed Expense	Explanatory Note
Cost of Sales	$1,050,000	$1,050,000	
Operating Expenses			
Salaries & Wages	70,000	60,000	Note 1
Workers Comp. & Taxes	6,000	5,500	Note 2
Employee Health Insurance	9,000	8,500	Note 2
Equipment Depreciation	10,000	6,000	Note 3
Equipment Maint. & Repair	16,000	14,000	Note 4
Equipment Insurance & Taxes	5,000	7,000	Note 5
Real Estate Rent	24,000	18,000	Note 6
Utilities	5,000	5,000	
Miscellaneous	5,000	3,000	Note 7
Total Operating Expenses	$ 150,000	$ 127,000	
Gen. & Admin. and Selling Expenses			
Officers Salaries	75,000	60,000	Note 8
Administrative Wages	50,000	35,000	Note 9
Workers Comp. & Related Taxes	10,000	8,000	Note 10
Employee Health Insurance	15,000	12,000	Note 10
Officers Key Man Life Insurance	4,000	0	Note 11
Sales Promotion & Advertising	10,000	10,000	
Sales Vehicles	40,000	25,000	Note 12
Office Expenses	6,000	6,000	
Professional Services	4,000	3,000	Note 13
Dues & Subscriptions	5,000	3,000	Note 14
Contributions	1,000	0	Note 15
Depreciation, Office Equipment	2,000	2,000	
Bad Debt Expense	2,000	2,000	
Miscellaneous	1,000	1,000	
Total G&A and Selling Expenses	$ 225,000	$ 167,000	
Total Expenses	$1,425,000	$1,344,000	

Note 1: John employs two full-time people in the company's production operation; his brother, Bob, who earns $40,000 annually and an unrelated employee who earns $30,000. Bob has agreed to retire at the time of the business sale and John has agreed to provide him with 10% of the net proceeds of the business sale as retirement compensation. Bob can be replaced with an employee at a wage of $30,000, yielding a net expense reduction of $10,000 for this item.

Note 2: The reduction in wages discussed in Note 1 will result in expense reductions in worker's compensation insurance, payroll taxes, and health insurance costs.

Note 3: The actual (versus tax-code allowable) depreciation cost for the company's equipment replacement has been running at about $6,000 per year, rather than the $10,000 allowable expense.

Note 4: John's Mercedes is a perk and will be taken out of service as a company expense since it is not actually needed in the actual conduct of business. The annual maintenance expense reduction (oil, gasoline, repair) will be about $2,000.

Note 5 The company has just received its property tax assessment for the next year. John discovers that the business property taxes are expected to rise by $2,000. Accordingly, this expense item is adjusted *upward.* This is an important point to keep in mind. To arrive at a fair and reasonable reconstruction of income and expenses, both positive and negative adjustments should be made.

Note 6: The business real estate is owned by John's wife and is leased back to the company at higher than going market rates. This has helped to get some of the income out of the business without the double taxation problem of a C corporation. John has decided that he will either sell the real estate separately to the buyer of this business or lease it to them at a triple-net rate of $18,000 per year which is more in line with comparable market rates.

Note 7: The miscellaneous expenses include about $2,000 paid to John's son, David, for summer work that could realistically be absorbed in the maintenance and repair expense item.

Note 8: John has been paying himself $75,000 per year, but he figures a salary of $60,000 would be more appropriate relative to the other wages paid in the company. He believes that a buyer should "pay their dues" as he has done before expecting a salary at the higher level.

Note 9: John's wife does all the bookkeeping and administrative chores and receives a $50,000 company salary for this. John believes that he can find a capable replacement for her for a $35,000-per-year salary.

Note 10: The reduction in salary in Notes 8 and 9 will result in expense reductions in worker's compensation insurance, payroll taxes, and health insurance costs.

Note 11: Key Man Life Insurance is not a requirement for running the business and John considers this a perk that can be eliminated.

Note 12: By taking John's leased top-of-the-line Mercedes out of service, the annual expense savings in this item will be $15,000. Also, see Note 4. John plans to lease a Dodge Neon at his own expense for the time his business is for sale.

Note 13: John has been using the same CPA for 25 years and knows that he can get comparable competent services for a lesser fee of approximately $3,000.

Note 14: This expense item includes various costs for participation in trade organizations that are important to continue for the benefit of the company. However, about $2,000 of this expense item is for John and his wife to attend the annual convention in Las Vegas every year. This is an optional expense and not necessary to the company.

Note 15: John contributes to the local charities every year but considers this a purely discretionary expense as local community goodwill is not crucial to his type of business.

If John can convince a buyer that these are the "real" expenses that they can expect if they purchase the business, the net pretax income goes from $75,000 to $156,000 and the business valuation and eventual selling price will go up substantially! There is good news and bad news here. The good news is that most, if not all, of these expense reconstruction items can actually be realized by John's business. The bad news is that a potential buyer is not likely to believe many of them and will not accept most of the reconstructed expenses in establishing a purchase price for the business. John will be well advised to establish a one- or two-year plan for preparing his business for sale so that he can begin implementing the expense item reductions, as well as many of the other business value enhancements recommended in the next chapter of this book. Once the expense reductions are reflected as the increased profitability of the business in its financial statements, John will have no trouble convincing a potential buyer of the true value in the business.

Before we leave this subject of income and expense statement reconstruction, I want to address the subject of income (revenue) item reconstruction. Although a buyer is reluctant to accept a reconstruction of revenues which includes income not reported as received by the company, there is at least one situation where this is possible. In the case of a company that is basing its valuation on the prior fiscal year and has a cash (versus accrual) accounting method, it may happen that a major receivable is paid late by a customer shortly after the close of the fiscal year. For income tax purposes, this revenue is properly accounted for in the current fiscal year. For business valuation purposes, you may be able to convince a buyer that the revenue is more properly attributable to the prior fiscal year (the year in which the business valuation is based) if you can show the following:

- The account is a long-standing customer.

- The customer historically pays before the end of the fiscal year and the revenues have been consistently reported accordingly in past years.

- The slippage of payment into the current fiscal year is an anomaly that will not likely be repeated in future years.

In the next section, I will put together a capitalization of net earnings valuation for John's business and compare the valuation using the expenses before and after reconstruction.

Applying the CAP Valuation

As an example of how to use the capitalization of net earnings valuation and assign a tentative value to a business, let's continue to consider John's business from the previous section. A recap of the vital statistics of his business shows that:

Annual Sales	=	$1,500,000
Annual Expenses	=	$1,425,000
Annual Pretax Profits	=	$ 75,000
Long-Term Debt	=	$ 50,000 (to be assumed by the buyer)

Because the business is very well established with a 25-year track record with a recent history of increasing earnings and what looks like a promising future, John initially wants to classify his business as a Type 1 in order to establish a capitalization rate in the 12 to 16% range. However, after discussions with his accountant and an experienced business broker, John is convinced that the fact he is the sole owner and manager of the company and intends to retire and not stay with the business after the sale will increase the risk to a buyer. He agrees to a compromise capitalization rate of 20% as being more realistic to attract a qualified potential buyer.

John wants to establish a benchmark valuation that considers both the unreconstructed and reconstructed expenses in the calculations. By considering the valuation both ways, John discovers that he can increase his business value by about $243,000 to $418,000, using a capitalization rate of 20%. Let's look at the mathematics of this:

Before Expense Reconstruction:

Latest Year Company Sales	$1,500,000
Less Total Expenses	1,425,000
Total Pretax Earnings	$ 75,000
Estimated Earnings After-Tax Rate	x 60%
After-Tax Net Earnings	$ 45,000

Business Valuation = (After-Tax Net Earnings / Capitalization Rate) – Debt
= ($45,000 / .20) – $50,000
= $225,000 – $50,000
= $175,000

After Expense Reconstruction:

Latest Year Company Sales	$1,500,000
Less Total Expenses	1,344,000
Total Pretax Earnings	$ 156,000
Estimated Earnings After-Tax Rate	x 60%
After-Tax Net Earnings	$ 93,600

Business Valuation = (After-Tax Net Earnings / Capitalization Rate) – Debt
= ($93,600 / .20) – $50,000
= $468,000 – $50,000
= $418,000

Assuming that the capitalization rate of 20% is acceptable to a buyer, John will still have a great deal of difficulty in selling his business for this larger amount of money. He will find that it will be very hard to convince someone that all of these reconstructed expenses can actually be realized. Accordingly, he plans to start right away to cut the expenses over the next operating year so the benefits will show up in his next full year's business income and expense statements. He also plans to implement many of the other recommendations discussed in Chapter 3, "Enhancing the Sales Value of Your Business," not only to cut expenses, but to increase the revenues and minimize the perceived risk for his company.

Note that this business valuation of $418,000 does not include the value of the business real estate which should be separately appraised and then added to the calculated business value. The key to properly determining the value of the real estate will be to have it appraised as to its current use rather than its highest and best use. The latter appraisal may be different and drive the price unrealistically higher. One way to arrive at a good estimate of real estate value is to use a present value calculation process based on the income-producing capability of the property. The net rental payments are $18,000 annually in our example, a reasonable payoff period for a commercial real estate loan is 25 years, and a current market level interest rate is 10%. Accordingly, the real estate value and the overall business value is calculated as follows:

PV = 25-year period, 10% interest rate, $1,500 monthly payments ($18,000 annually)
   = $165,584

Therefore, the overall estimated value of the business is:

CAP Business Valuation   = $418,000 (using reconstructed expenses)
Real Estate Value   = $165,584 (based on current use
                             income based valuation)
Overall Business Valuation = $583,584 (with the real estate)

I want to point out that my use of after-tax earnings to calculate a business value is not embraced by all professionals in the field of business valuation. This is primarily because tax rates are very specific to the person buying the business, how they set up their accounting procedures, and how they handle and account for the business purchase expenses. While this is true, you still have to deal with some basic facts:

- In most business sales, the dollars used either to pay off the purchase debt incurred and/or reimburse the buyer for their cash investment will come out of the profits from the business, *after paying taxes* on them.

- Almost all business purchases must be paid for out of the available cash flow from the business. This is taxable income.

Accordingly, I recommend using a representative tax rate and calculating your business value using after-tax dollars. Perhaps the best way to select a reasonable tax rate is to use your own rate since the buyer of a small-business under $1 million in value will most likely have a tax rate similar to your own. For larger businesses, a tax rate of 40% is a good estimate. Do not forget that you must consider state and local taxes as well as federal taxes. I have used a tax rate of 40% in the example shown above for mathematical illustration only.

Another concept which I will address further in Chapter 7, "Putting It All Together: Preparing an Exit Plan," involves what to actually ask for as the selling price for your business. By following the guidance I have provided in this chapter and the recommendations I will discuss in the next several chapters, you will arrive at several preliminary valuations for your business. For example, by just looking at your business income before doing any expense reconstruction or implementing any improvements, you will establish a "benchmark valuation." After "reconstructing" your income and expenses, you will have another, probably much higher valuation for you to use before you undertake any of the suggestions contained in Chapter 3. After realizing as much of the reconstructed expense item reductions as possible and also implementing the improvement recommendations appropriate to your business, you will hopefully come up with a valuation that is even higher, based on your new profitability. That is the valuation for which you will offer your business for sale, but it's best to develop a negotiation range for the price of your business.

Following the maxim that something is worth only what someone else is willing to pay for it at any given point in time, it becomes obvious that there's no magic or concrete way to absolutely value a business. Consequently, you should carefully place a tentative valuation on your business using the methods I prescribe in this chapter and then establish a private negotiation range that you can work within. I recommend setting a negotiation range that is plus or minus 10 percent of the estimated value of your business. You should set the asking price for your business at the high end of the range, but privately be willing to take the low end of your range for the absolutely right buyer.

Selecting a Valuation Method

I have recommended that you use the CAP method for valuing a business that is profitable and has an operating history of at least three years. This is the best approach to valuing a business if you expect to sell to a financial buyer. But what if you plan to sell your business to another of the five types of buyers? The following table and discussion will help you to select the best valuation method for your business.

Table 2-E

Valuation Methods Versus Most Likely Buyer Type

	Types of Buyers				
Valuation Method	**Financial**	**Strategic**	**Family**	**Partner/ Employee**	**Industry**
Capitalization (CAP)	X	X	X	X	
Asset Based			X		X
Present Value (PV)	X	X			
Market Comparison		X			

The *CAP valuation* method is by far the best method to use to estimate the value that a financial buyer will pay for your business. It is income based, and relates the value of the business directly to the financial return that a buyer can expect to receive. The vast majority of small businesses have selling prices less than $1 million. They are sold to financially-motivated buyers who look at the business in terms of an investment (at least for valuation purposes). This method is also frequently used for the sale of the business to family members, partners, employees, and shareholders who all tend to have the same perspective on value as arms-length financial buyers. Strategic buyers also sometimes use this valuation method, but are typically more liberal in their use of capitalization rates and reconstructed income which results in higher business valuations.

The *asset based valuation* uses the fair-market value of the business's assets outside of the company as an operating entity. This is the valuation method most likely to appeal to industry buyers. It typically results in the least value for your business, and is usually used only in a liquidation of your company. Sometimes, the asset based valuation is used in valuing the business for transition to a family member. Usually the objective is to keep the business value as low as possible in a family succession in order to minimize the taxes involved. The IRS generally requires a form of the CAP valuation method, but businesses with low or well-hidden profitability may be able to use an asset based valuation for succession planning purposes.

The *present value of future earnings* method can be used with financial buyers, but due to its relative complexity and emphasis on a long-term future of earnings, it is usually not the best choice for this type of buyer. Strategic buyers are more likely to use this valuation method to financially justify their acquisition of a company, but it will most likely not be the basis for an acquisition decision. As discussed previously, strategic buyers are primarily interested in business attributes other than your company's bottom line. They may desire your customer base, your distribution network, a proprietary product or process, or they may even want to eliminate some of their competition.

The *market comparison* valuation method is generally unreliable for small privately-held company transitions, because it's difficult to obtain similar data for comparison purposes. Consequently, the greatest application for this approach is with larger companies. They can be compared to the transfer of publicly-traded companies where financial details are more readily available. Accordingly, strategic buyers who acquire companies in the range of $20 million and higher in annual revenues tend to use the market comparison valuation method more often than other types of buyers.

A Final Point: If you plan to sell your business to a strategic buyer, I recommend that you do not establish a formal asking price for your business. You should determine the asset based valuation for your company to establish its minimum value and also use the CAP valuation to determine what a financial buyer might pay, but do not use these estimates to establish an asking price with a strategic buyer. Rather, you should hold these valuations for your own personal reference and ask a strategic buyer to provide a bid for your business. The exact reasons why strategic buyers purchase a business are extremely diverse and, therefore, generally unpredictable. This makes it almost impossible to estimate what they will pay for your company. Coupling this fact with the knowledge that strategic buyers tend to pay more for a company, you want to make sure that you do not underprice your business. Accordingly, it is better to prepare a detailed prospectus for your company, emphasizing the areas you think will appeal to a strategic buyer, and solicit bids from potential buyers without establishing an asking price that you might set too low. With your privately prepared asset and CAP valuations, you will be able to judge the true merits of a strategic buyer's offer and negotiate accordingly. This approach will ensure that you do not leave any money on the table by valuing your business lower than a strategic buyer might be willing to pay.

Timing Is Everything

What's hot, exciting, and valuable today could have much less value tomorrow. You have to watch your industry trends to see where your company fits into the scheme of things. At this writing, high technology companies with anything to do with telecommunications and/or the Internet are hot. Privately-held companies in these areas have many opportunities for selling not only to a private buyer, but through the merger/acquisition process or a public stock offering. Not too long ago, real estate development companies were on the top of the heap. Then the Savings & Loan (S&L) crisis came and companies once worth billions of dollars barely survived. Many even filed for bankruptcy.

The only time you will be able to sell your business for a favorable price that will enable you to realize the highest return on your investment of time, money, and hard work is when your business is strong, industry conditions are on the upswing, and the general business climate is promising. If it's at all possible, do not attempt to sell your business when you "have to." The worst time to sell your company is when you are experiencing either business or personal problems. For example, avoid trying to sell your business under these conditions.

You have personal problems such as:

- You are discouraged, tired, depressed, or feeling burned out.

- You or a close family member are ill or you are facing a divorce.

- You have just lost a partner or key employee.

You have business problems such as:

- The sales and/or profits of the company are declining.

- The company is involved in or facing major litigation.

- The company is experiencing cash flow difficulties or loan foreclosure.

- New technology developments are forcing you into major changes.

- The company has lost its lease for the business premises and must relocate.

Do not confuse the above points with your overall ability to sell the business. Sometimes, businesses sell much easier and quicker if they have the "right things wrong." For example, buyers may see opportunity in a business with a "burned-out" owner, an older owner unable to comprehend and keep up with new technology, or a business with declining sales that a buyer believes they can turn around. The problem for you is that the buyer will most likely drive a hard bargain to purchase a business with problems for much less money than it could otherwise be sold. To maximize the opportunity to realize the best price for your business, you must resolve these significant difficulties before offering the business for sale.

Strategic Move #7:

"The best time to sell your business is probably the exact time you do not want to sell it."

You must pick the time to offer your business for sale very carefully. Paradoxically, the best time to sell your business will be exactly the time you do not want to sell it. If you have prepared an exit plan for yourself as I advocate throughout this book, you should follow it even if things seem great and you begin thinking about staying with it for "a few more years." Eventually business cycles turn down, people become ill and pass on, technology moves relentlessly on, always changing the way business is conducted. One of these (or something else that you cannot even guess at now) will catch up with you eventually. Only you can decide when the time is right to take your chips off the table, but never forget that every day in business is a risk. It may be far better to sell "too soon" than too late. A favorite quote of mine I have heard repeated over the years goes something like this: "A very successful and wealthy stock market investor upon being asked to share his investment wisdom replied, 'I always sold too soon!' " In other words, he took his profits earlier than the peak was reached—but always avoided the inevitable downturn.

Finding Value in a Business Without Net Income

As you learned from the previous discussion, the recommended way of valuing a business is based on the company having some sort of profitable track record. How, then, to sell a business that is in its startup phase (usually in the first three years of operation) or one which has fallen on hard times? In either case, you can try basing a valuation on the assets of the business. Also, in either case, there is certainly value in the fact that the business has a legal entity, has established a location and product/or service, done some advertising, and developed some level of clientele and sales. In general, a business should be worth, at a minimum, whatever the cost is of starting the business from nothing, if there is a market for its product or service. Of course, the business must have viable prospects for the future. The following is a further discussion of each of these two types of businesses.

Selling a New Business

The biggest problem with selling a new business is that there is usually no track record upon which to base a valuation. A new business can be defined as one that has been in existence for less than three years. To sell a business without a substantial track record, all you really have to sell is hope. This does not mean that the business cannot be sold. You will need to develop a realistic but attractive pro forma. It will also be useful to list (and value) all of the expenses you have incurred to get the business started, the expenses that someone beginning a similar business would have to pay for. For example:

- Legal and accounting expenses for corporate entity set-up.

- Logo design, stationery, brochures, catalogs, flyers, etc.

- Salable inventory and other material costs.

- Some portion of advertising costs which have promoted the company name and existence.

- Special tooling, fixtures, and other capital expenses to outfit the business.

If you are fortunate enough to have a profitable business which has not been in existence for long, you may still be able to sell it based on a traditional valuation. But, most buyers will want to use a capitalization rate of 30% to 40% or even higher. This will, of course, drive the business valuation down, but that will be the price you pay for someone assuming a very risky and basically unproven business enterprise. The real key to selling this type of business will be to have a very plausible story to tell about why you want to sell. If the business is relatively new and making money, then "Why in the world does the seller want to sell?" will be an obvious question. Some of the better reasons I have run across include:

- Divorce proceedings initiated after the start of the business where the business must be dissolved to satisfy the settlement.

- Geographic relocation of a spouse's lucrative job outside of a reasonable commuting area.

- Not enough capital to realize the full business potential and unable or unwilling to attract lenders or investors.

- Early stage burn-out caused by the long business hours and daily pressure of meeting the business obligations. (Some people find they are not suited for the life of an entrepreneur, while others thrive on it.)

- Unexpected serious illness or some other catastrophic event such as a seriously debilitating accident.

- Absolute inability of partners to get along with each other, and neither having the resources to buy out the other.

Selling a Turnaround Situation

The biggest problem with selling a turnaround situation *is* that there is a track record. Usually a very poor track record. It is definitely possible to sell a business that is having a poor or nonprofitable period but it's generally very difficult, especially to a financial buyer. Some of the steps that you should take are:

- Develop a three-year financial snapshot of the business when times were good, including a reconstruction of the expenses.

- List the problem(s) that you believe to be the reasons for the business's current woes (e.g. poor health or death of the owner, increased competition, rising material or employee costs, etc.).

- Develop a plan of action to overcome these problems that you would pursue if you were to stay on as the owner.

- Develop a realistic pro forma, including new capital costs, that it will take to accomplish the plan of action.

- Come up with a convincing reason why you cannot stay on as the owner and see the company through the implementation of the "get-well" plan.

- Price the company in accordance with the pro forma out-year projections, taking into consideration the additional capital costs.

The best approach for trying to sell a turnaround situation for more than its liquidation value is to find a strategic buyer. Strategic buyers of businesses often have motivations other than the financial profitability of your particular enterprise. For example, the cost of acquiring new proven customers that your business is able to provide for your type of product or service may well exceed the sales price of your business. Let's say you have a proven customer base of 10,000 who have purchased a product from your company within the last year. Your company has not been able to sustain profitability from this relatively small customer base and you do not have the resources to pursue improvement, so you are trying to sell out. A similar, but larger and more profitable acquiring company may want to tap into your customer base. That company may have determined that it costs them an average of $20 for every new active customer developed through their normal sales and marketing efforts. Buying your business for $150,000 may see like a bargain to them and may well exceed the fair-market value of the assets in your company. They will most likely not care about asset value or capitalized valuations as long as they can obtain access to your customer database. Refer back to Chapter 1, "Why You Need to Prepare Your Business for Sale," for a list of some of the other purchase motivations for a strategic buyer.

Sometimes the key to selling a turnaround situation to a financial buyer is to use an earn-out to reduce the risk for a buyer. An earn-out is a method of sale whereby you receive all or part of the sales price of the business in the form of future payments based on some negotiated performance factor. You may be able to structure a deal whereby a financially-motivated buyer takes over your business for an up-front payment consisting of the fair-market value of the assets plus payments tied to increases in future revenues higher than the last fiscal year as a baseline. You both may come out winners in a transaction of this nature if you carefully select a buyer that will bring to your company whatever it's now lacking for success:

- New capital infusion.

- Greater market penetration.

- New, innovative products and/or services.

- Fresh energy and ideas.

- Stronger management expertise.

As the business prospers with a new owner, you will receive payments above what you would have received in a liquidation sale. Depending on the terms of the earn-out, the increased funds to you could be significantly higher. Even if the business fails under the new ownership, you have still received the fair-market value of the assets up-front.

Selling a new or turnaround business presents unique problems that require unique solutions. I have presented some thoughts for you to consider if your business falls into one of these categories. Hopefully, you will not have to face these specialized problems, but are rather grappling with the issue of selling your profitable business which you have been running successfully for many years.

In Summary

In this chapter I have covered several different ways to value a profitable operating business. I have suggested that you first perform an asset based valuation to determine a liquidation value for your business as a "floor price." I have covered the use of rules of thumb and the traditional business valuation methods and have recommended that you base your valuation on the CAP method using both the current earnings and the reconstructed earnings for comparison purposes. The valuation based on current earnings represents a "benchmark" valuation, a snapshot of the business's current value. The valuation based on reconstructed earnings represents a potential value if you are able to prove these earnings to a prospective buyer. These valuations are all considered to be "ballpark" valuations because they are only estimates of what a buyer may be willing to pay for your business on the open market. Your business will ultimately be worth only what someone is willing to pay for it at a given point in time. In the next chapter, I will present you with many ideas, recommendations, suggestions, and strategies to enhance the overall value of your business in the view of a typical buyer as you prepare it for sale.

Enhancing the Sales Value of Your Business

- *Introduction*
- *Maximize Your Operating Profits*
- *Streamline Your Financial Operating Ratios*
- *Improve Business Income and Minimize Expenses*
- *Other Enhancements You Can Make*
- *Anticipate Buyer Concerns*
- *Give a Buyer a Good Reason to Buy*
- *Properly Organize Your Company*

Introduction

As you have seen from the previous chapter on valuation, the principal value determinant for most business transfers will be the financial bottom line. In the vast majority of business sales, the business must be able to generate enough available cash flow to handle the debt structure entered into by the buyer for the purchase of the business, provide a reasonable return on their cash investment, and provide opportunity for growth. Even in those cases where the buyer provides an all-cash deal, the business profits must still justify the buyer's use of their investment money. For these reasons, it's absolutely imperative that you maximize the profitability of your company to its fullest potential before offering it for sale to ensure that you receive the best value for your business.

It's widely understood that most privately-held businesses operate in such a way as to minimize their tax exposure to the IRS as well as state and municipal taxing authorities. Frequently when businesses are offered for sale, the most recent income and expense statement will be "reconstructed" as part of the business selling process to find the hidden value in the operating business as demonstrated in Chapter 2, "What Is Your Business Really Worth?" There are three main problems in doing this:

- First, you should be cautious about creating a written reconstruction of profits that may be significantly different than that reported to the IRS. If the reconstruction falls into the wrong hands, business owners may find themselves in difficulty with the IRS regarding back taxes due, penalties, interest, and perhaps even more serious issues of a criminal nature. While many reconstruction elements are perfectly legitimate, such as excess depreciation and amortization, the recasting of entertainment expenses, travel expenses, and other personal benefit items along with the inclusion of unreported cash sales on the income side could very well cause problems for you with the IRS.

- Second, it may be difficult to convince the potential buyer that many of the reconstructed financial statements truly represent the actual income and expenses that a new owner may expect to experience. Do not forget, it's most likely that you are both relative strangers to each other and that you are in an adversarial position. A buyer wants to pay as little as possible for the business, while you will want to maximize the sales price and net proceeds to yourself. It will be extremely hard to "sell" your full reconstruction, even if it's totally viable.

- Third, it's generally difficult to convince a third-party lender such as a bank or other institution to base a loan amount on a reconstructed earnings statement. If you do not want to hold a significant amount of financing and you expect a potential buyer to provide a full cash buy-out to you, then you will need to do more than provide a reconstructed earnings statement to justify the selling price of the business.

This whole issue can be summed up in the words of some unknown, but often quoted wag: "Show me the money!"

To overcome these three major difficulties and enhance the overall sales value of your business, you should begin "cleaning up" your income and expense statement at least one year, and preferably two years before you offer your business for sale. Yes, you're going to increase your tax exposure to Uncle Sam (and to the state and local governments), but you will more than make up for it in the sales price of your business. In the next section I will show you mathematically how this works out.

To emphasize the importance of this concept, I've made it the eighth strategic move you should make to prepare your business for sale.

Strategic Move #8:

"Maximize your business's net operating profit in the one or two years prior to a sale, even at the expense of higher income taxes!"

I realize that many of you will not have, or want to take, the time necessary to make the changes which will result in an increase in your provable bottom line. You will still need to identify those expense items where you believe costs can be cut and reconstruct your income and expense statement accordingly. Providing documentation as to why and how these expense reductions can be made will be important in "selling" these items to a prospective buyer. Convincing a buyer that certain expenses such as some depreciation charges, luxury items, and provable personal benefits can be eliminated or reduced will be easier than items such as employee payroll costs, vendor charges, and professional services. In Chapter 7, "Putting It All Together: Preparing an Exit Plan," I provide a section with recommendations about how to prepare your business for sale in a short time.

Maximize Your Operating Profits

Assume that your business is showing a net unreconstructed operating profit of $100,000 per year after taxes. If you operate your business for the next year at a level that minimizes your discretionary expenses, reduces the operating expenses, and maximizes your sales, it's possible that you can show a new operating profit of $150,000 (before taxes are applied to the increase). Looking at the impact this could have on net cash in your pocket if you sell your business one year later, the math looks like this:

$150,000	new operating profit
−100,000	status quo net operating profit
$ 50,000	gain subject to additional taxes
x 40%	representative tax rate (federal, state, and local)
$ 20,000	increase in total taxes
$ 50,000	additional operating profit
− 20,000	additional income taxes
$ 30,000	increased after-tax net income

So at this point you are out $20,000 to the tax collector and you have had to forego some of the benefits that the $20,000 may have brought you: a nicer company car, a luxurious vacation as part of a business meeting, a subsidy to George (your brother-in-law), etc. Although some of the increase in your bottom-line profits will be due to a reduction in your discretionary personal benefit expenses, the most significant increase in profitability will most likely come from other cost-cutting techniques discussed later in this chapter. These will result in actual expense reductions and increased profitability well beyond a recapture of personal benefit expenditures.

But consider this: Working with a multiple of five times net after-tax earnings (which equates to a capitalization rate of 20%), a buyer will pay $150,000 more for your business than they otherwise might have. Even if you consider the increased capital gains taxes of approximately $30,000 that you will have to pay on the business sale, you are still significantly ahead. Again, look at the math:

$ 30,000	increased after-tax net income
x 5	earnings multiplier (20% capitalization rate)
$150,000	increased business value
x 20%	representative tax rate (federal capital gains)
$ 30,000	increase in capital gains tax due for sale of business
$150,000	increased business value
– 30,000	increased capital gains income taxes
$120,000	net gain
– 20,000	additional operating income tax
$100,000	additional net business value after taxes

So, an increased tax bill for one year of $20,000 could net you an additional $100,000 value for your business at the time of sale. This is a large gain on a one-year investment of $20,000! Even if you maximized the business's net operating income for two years, and therefore increased your yearly income taxes even higher, you will still be way ahead of the game.

Keep in mind that the above example uses a capitalization rate of 20%. In some small businesses that have an associated high risk (refer back to Chapter 2 for a discussion of this topic), the capitalization rate may be much higher resulting in a lower benefit from reducing expenses. This will, consequently, mean a lower business valuation. However, it's clear that to maximize your business selling price and minimize any disagreements with a prospective buyer, you should enhance your reported operating income as much as possible. But there are other financial aspects of your business a savvy prospective buyer will want to examine to ensure that you are not cutting expenses too deeply or otherwise operating the business unwisely to maximize short-term profitability for the sake of the sale. These are usually examined in the form of business operating ratios.

This leads to the ninth strategic move you should make as you prepare your business for sale.

Strategic Move #9:

"Ensure that your business's operating ratios are as good or better than others in your industry!"

Streamline Your Financial Operating Ratios

You should examine your business operating ratios and compare them with similar ratios within your industry. The "Almanac of Business and Industrial Financial Ratios," published annually by Prentice-Hall, is a good source of financial ratio data that is representative of most businesses in the U.S. If your business ratios do not compare favorably with your industry averages, you should take the action necessary to improve them. Knowledgeable prospective buyers (or their accountants) will examine your company's operating ratios very carefully to help them determine your overall business performance. For example, a buyer will be able to tell if your current accounts receivable are too low, your inventory turnover sluggish, or your cost of sales too high relative to other companies in your industry. To help ensure that you maximize your sale price, you may need to streamline your particular operating ratios to correspond with or exceed the industry averages.

Improving your business's operating ratios will usually take a much longer period of time than any of the other recommendations I provide. You cannot improve your past year's operating performance figures, and these types of numbers generally take one or more years to change, once they are identified. If you are allowing a one- to two-year period to prepare your business for sale, you will have the opportunity to impact these important financial operating ratios. If you do not have the time or ability to improve weak ratios, you should at least identify them and prepare an explanation to satisfy a buyer, if they show concern during the due diligence process.

Not all types of financial ratios are as significant or as relevant to all businesses. Some of the most important financial ratios for all types of businesses are:

Is the business solvent?

$$\frac{\text{Current assets}}{\text{Current liabilities}}$$

This is called the Current Ratio and is a test for solvency. It provides a clue to the magnitude of the financial margin of safety for the business. The standard guideline is for a ratio of 2:1 or higher.

Is the business liquid?

$$\frac{\text{Cash \& accts receivable}}{\text{Current liabilities}}$$

This is called the Quick Ratio, and is also known as the Acid Test Ratio. It's used to determine the company's general liquidity (its ability to pay its current debts). A general standard for this ratio is 1:1 or higher.

Has the business borrowed wisely?

$$\frac{\text{Total debt}}{\text{Net worth}}$$

This operating ratio reveals the extent to which the business has borrowed money. Too much debt may indicate insufficient capital and could weaken the business's competitive position.

How is the business performing?

$$\frac{\text{Working capital}}{\text{Sales}}$$

This ratio shows the relationship of working capital to business transactions. Compare this ratio with averages in your industry and related businesses to determine business performance.

Are the products selling?

$$\frac{\text{Cost of sales}}{\text{Inventory}}$$

This ratio shows the number of times the inventory turns over. A comparison with industry and related business averages can be revealing. Slow inventory, relative to similar businesses within the industry, could indicate problems that will show up in future profitability.

How's management doing?

$$\frac{\text{Net profit}}{\text{Net worth}}$$

This ratio shows the return on invested capital. Compare it with industry and related business averages. Also compare this ratio with the rate of return you could expect to receive in the equity or financial markets. The risk of running a small-business is not worth mediocre returns on investment capital.

Is the business earning a profit?

$$\frac{\text{Net profit}}{\text{Sales}}$$

This ratio measures the profit margin of the business. Compare it with industry and related business averages to see how well your business is doing. This ratio could be used as a strong selling point if your business exceeds industry averages.

Are profits adequate?

$$\frac{\text{Cost of sales}}{\text{Sales}}$$

If this margin appears thin compared to the industry average, it could mean future trouble. This indicates how much money is available to pay expenses. Even a small decline in sales for a company with a weak ratio may have serious consequences.

Now let's turn to specific things you may be able to do right away to enhance the net operating performance of your business as you prepare it for sale.

Improve Business Income and Minimize Expenses

Even better than reconstructing the income and expense statement is to actually improve the bottom-line profitability of your business before you begin the sale process. This way, there is no question as to the business's ability to generate the claimed cash flow. Of course, some reconstruction will always be required with such items as depreciation and amortization, which are generally not actual expenses. But there are many other income and expense items that you may be able to adjust to improve the selling value of your business. Before we get into a discussion of the possible things you can do, you should be sure that you understand the impact of what an increase in the bottom line means to the potential sales value of your business. For example, let's assume that:

- Your business is well-established and profitable, and

- has moderately increasing profit and sales, and

- is in a stable or expanding industry.

In this case, a reasonable ROI of about 20% can be assigned to your business for valuation purposes (refer back to Chapter 2 for a detailed discussion of this issue). A ROI of 20% (which will also be the capitalization rate used in a CAP valuation) will mean that for every $1 of net after-tax profit that you add, the potential value of your business could increase by approximately $5. Assuming that you are in a 40% income tax bracket, that means you will have to pay 40¢ for each extra dollar of increased profit per year. If you operate your business at the increased profitability level for a period of three years, this means that you will pay an extra $1.20 in income taxes over that time (3 x 40¢) which will reduce your net gain at sale time to approximately $3.80 on the dollar ($5.00 – $1.20 = $3.80). But this is still a very powerful reason to improve the bottom line of your business. A $3.80 return for a $1 sustainable decrease in expenses (and a commensurate increase in profits) is well worth the effort! In fact, you may not have to demonstrate the increased profitability for three years to convince a buyer that it is sustainable. Frequently, two years (or even one) are enough. However, knowledgeable buyers may want to use a higher CAP rate to account for the increased risk inherent in valuing the business using shorter-term profitability increases.

As I discussed in the previous chapter, some business appraisers will value a business using pretax earnings. On the face of it, this would seem to increase the overall valuation of your business. However, it usually does not because the same appraisers will then use a higher capitalization rate to bring the total calculated valuation back down. I recommend considering the tax impact on business earnings for valuation purposes because, in reality, the buyer will have to pay for the business in after-tax dollars. Either way, if you can increase the actual provable bottom-line profits of your business, you will almost certainly increase the value of your company by a multiple of the improved earnings.

As a further example of this multiplier effect consider the fictional Wonderful Widget Company. In 1995, its net profits were $100,000. Using the capitalization of net profit valuation approach, the gross selling value of this business will be approximately $500,000. If the owner of the Wonderful Widget Company is able to raise the net profit to $120,000 over the next three years, the estimated selling price of the business will jump to $600,000. The increase of $100,000 will be offset by the new taxes paid on the additional profit by about $24,000 ($20,000 x 3 years x 40% tax rate), but the seller will realize an additional $76,000 of value at sale time! In actuality, the gain will be even greater because the increase in profits may be realized gradually over the three-year period rather than all at once as this simple example assumes. Therefore, the income tax payments will be less. For this reason and to keep the math simple in the following recommended actions, I will round the earlier estimate of a $3.80 increase in business selling price for every dollar up to $4 for every dollar.

Keep in mind that this example of an approximate $4 increase in the selling price of a business for every $1 increase in net operating profit is based on several variables and meant to be illustrative only. In other words, this example translates to a selling price for a business of four times the after-tax earnings. The actual amount could be more or less for your particular business depending on the variables finally agreed to by you and the buyer. However, it should be clear that increasing the provable bottom-line profits in your business can translate into a much higher selling price for your business at the time of sale. You should do everything that you can in the time leading up to the sale to increase the business income, decrease the actual expenses, and consequently increase the net operating profit.

The following sections contain more detailed discussion of what you may be able to do to increase your bottom line. As a lead-in to this discussion, the next strategic move is offered.

Strategic Move #10:

"Evaluate all leased and financed assets for possible conversion to owned assets to increase your business profitability."

Evaluate All Leased and Financed Assets for Conversion to Owned Assets

Think about converting leases and financed business assets into outright owned assets, if you have the cash available. This may seem a little strange as you first read this advice, but consider the implications. I have already shown that a well-established, profitable business in a stable or expanding industry can increase its gross selling price by $4 for every $1 added to its net operating profit. Depending on the costs to realize the increased profits and the time frame required by a buyer to prove that the decreased expenses and increased profitability are not an anomaly (usually one to two years), you may be able to obtain a 30–50% return on your investment!

Consider this example for the fictional Lithograph Printing Company. The owner is planning to sell the business after many years of successful operation. After careful evaluation, the seller believes that a multiplier of five times the net operating profit may be used to reasonably determine the business value. Because business has been good, the company has $100,000 of "free" cash in its accounts (cash not needed for day-to-day operating expenses). At first, the seller is tempted to take the cash as a personal disbursement, but then considers the newly leased printing press that the company has acquired. The lease payments are $40,000 per year for three years and the current payoff on the lease is $100,000. If the owner pays off the $100,000 to purchase the machine outright, the company will realize $40,000 more net profit per year (after the year in which the payoff occurs). At a sales price of five times net profit, the $100,000 payoff becomes a short-term investment with a return of $200,000 ($40,000 x 5 = $200,000) before taxes. This is a 100% return on investment for the business owner if the company is sold within one year, or 50% for two years, or 33% if it takes three years to sell the business. Where else can the business owner get this kind of return on a cash investment? Even when the tax consequences are considered and the loss of interest income from $100,000 invested in certificates of deposit (CDs) is factored in, it's still a smart business move.

The business owner contemplating a sale of the business should carefully consider all of the business's leased and financed assets for possible conversion to owned assets. These assets can be placed in three categories:

- Automotive.

- Equipment.

- Real estate.

Automotive Assets:

Consider all of your automotive assets, including delivery and service vehicles, salespersons' cars, and your personal auto if it's leased or financed through the business. Most automotive leases are not cost-effective to pay off before the lease period expires due to the high cancellation fees usually incurred. I will discuss more about the owner's auto in a later section of this chapter.

Equipment Assets

Determine if any of your production or office equipment is leased or financed. Then perform an analysis to decide if it makes sense in your particular circumstance to convert them to owned assets for the purposes of selling your business. In many equipment lease programs direct from the vendor, you will find that the effective interest rate is quite high relative to conventional financing (frequently in the 18% range). This may be a good area for you to decrease your expenses and increase your bottom line proportionately.

Real Estate Assets

In many small businesses, the real estate rent or mortgage payments are a significant expense sheet item. For example, rent payments as a percentage of total operating costs for restaurants averages about 6%. For general merchandise stores and business services, the rent payments average about 3%. For medical practitioners rent costs can be all the way up to 8%. If you can find some way to lower these costs, it will have a significant positive impact on the selling price of your business. If you own the real estate, you may be able to decrease the monthly payments by refinancing the mortgage. Even if you do not reduce the principal balance or get a better interest rate, you may still be able to significantly reduce your monthly expenses by extending the mortgage term. For example, consider a 25-year term mortgage at 12% where there is still an original principal balance of $500,000 with 10 years remaining on the mortgage note. The current monthly payment is $5,266. The remaining principal balance after 15 years is $367,047. If the mortgage is refinanced for a new 25-year term with no payment towards the principal balance of $367,047 and the interest rate remains at 12%, the payments are reduced to $3,866 monthly. This will improve the business's bottom line, dollar-for-dollar, and could boost the value of the business by over $60,000. This is calculated as follows:

$5,266 – $3,866 = $1,400 monthly expense savings
$1,400 x 12 months = $16,800 annual expense savings
$16,800 goes direct to the bottom line as an increase in net profit
$16,800 x $4 (business value multiplication factor) = $67,200

Note: I want to point out, in the above example, that the portion of the mortgage payment that goes towards the loan principal cannot be expensed. However, in the first few years of a refinanced mortgage, approximately 95% of the payment amount will be interest and may therefore be expensed. Accordingly, the above calculation is approximate only and the exact amount in your case will depend on the actual interest portion of your mortgage payments.

You will most likely have to pay some fees to refinance the mortgage, but the amount of the increase relative to the selling price for your business will be minimal. You will also have to be willing to lease the space to the new owner of the business at the reduced mortgage amount. Reasonable escalations for inflation and related property maintenance costs can be included in the lease without hurting the overall selling price of the business. You may also sell the real estate as part of the sale of the business. In this case, it will greatly help if the property mortgage is assumable by the new owner. Have a clause to this effect added to your mortgage when you refinance the property.

If you do not own but are leasing the property, you may want to consider offering to purchase it. This is a major step and usually only makes good sense for the business owner over the long run. If you have not done this so far and are considering selling your business within the near future, it probably is not a viable alternative at this time. Many business sellers want a complete separation after the sale of their business and holding the real estate as a lease-back to the new owner for many years is not desirable. However, for those business owners who lease their business space and who are not planning to purchase the real estate, you should make every effort to renegotiate the lease to obtain lower monthly rental payments. This is not an easy task and may be impossible in some situations. The principal bargaining position that you may have is to offer to extend the lease term for a reduction in monthly rent payments. Some property owners may be willing to take less in monthly payments now for the stability of a longer lease term. Keep in mind that a longer lease term will probably also work in your favor with a potential buyer who will want some assurances that the business location is solid (if location is important to the business). I have run across many business owners who are contemplating the sale of their company, but are not taking any action to "lock in" their leased premises for the future. I believe they want to leave their options open as to the potential relocation of the business or possible liquidation, if the business cannot be sold. In most cases, this is a poor strategy because many businesses are very dependent on their physical location for continued operation. For example, retail, service, and food and beverage businesses are a few of the business types that tend to be dependent on their location for success. If your business needs to stay where it is and you do not own the real estate, you should seriously consider locking in a long-term lease (if possible) as part of your preparation of the business for sale.

Of course, you need to have free cash available to make the conversion of leased or financed assets to owned assets, and not all leases are cost-effective to convert. For example, many automotive leases have a relatively high buyout clause that makes it prohibitive to purchase the automobile during the lease term. Additionally, the real estate owned by another party may not be available for sale or the price may be extremely high. This could negate any increase in the value of the business. You should carefully consider all of these types of assets and determine what the benefit might be to buying out the lease or paying off the financing.

I will also caution you about going into personal debt to make these or any other enhancements to the bottom line. At first, it may appear that borrowing $100,000 on your home equity at 10% is a prudent move to pay off a business debt if it results in a 50% (or higher) average annual return when you sell your business. But, consider what happens if you have a sudden business downturn, or the general economy goes into a tailspin, and the potential business buyers disappear. It's never good to put all of your financial eggs into one basket, and borrowing against personal assets to potentially increase the purchase value of your business is extremely risky. Proceed with caution!

The next strategic move will produce a significant amount of improvement to the bottom line for many small businesses.

Strategic Move #11:

"Carefully evaluate all ongoing service and material contracts with the objective of reducing their cost by at least 10%"

Evaluate All Ongoing Service and Material Contracts and Agreements

You should make a list of all of your major service and material contracts, including the date you entered into them, their duration, cost, and benefit provided. Your objective here is to renegotiate and/or re-compete some or all of these contracts and agreements to ensure that you are receiving the lowest possible price at an acceptable level of quality and reliability. It may surprise you to learn that some of your long-time suppliers may not be as competitive in price as they once were. Many business owners become comfortable with suppliers who have proven to be cost-competitive and reliable over the years. Now is the time to take the action to make sure that you are spending as little as necessary. Now is not the time to concern yourself with loyalty to your provider even if you have developed a personal friendship! When you sell your business, the new owner most likely will renegotiate all of the business's contracts and agreements anyway, so you should take action at this time to accrue the financial benefits to yourself.

A listing of your service and material contracts and agreements will look something like this:

Table 3-A

Service and Material Contracts and Agreements

Vendor	Date Start/End	Service/Material	Cost
AT&T	Jan 1992/open	long distance telephone service	$25/monthly plus $0.19/minute
Web "R" Us	Nov/ 1996	Internet access	$29.95/monthly
Realty Inc.	Jan 1990/Dec 2005	business real estate lease	$5,000/monthly increasing at 5% per year
Computer Kare	Jun 1995/open	computer and office equipment maint. and repair	$200/monthly plus $45/hr repair labor
We Care Insurance	1986/open	fire and liability insurance	$500/monthly
Automotive Leasing	Mar 1996/Feb 1999	truck and car leases	$3,000/monthly
Abacus Accounting	1985/open	bookkeeping	$12,000/year
Joe's Lawn Care	Apr 1993/open	lawn maint., snow plowing, etc.	$6,000/year
Sam's Office Supply	1985/open	office supplies	$10,000/year
Visual Image, Inc.	1988/open	printing services	$8,000/year
Product Distributor	1985/open	inventory	$100,000/year

You get the idea. Just record every ongoing expense item in a format similar to the above example and evaluate whether you might be able to obtain these or similar services for a lesser cost. One important indicator is the length of time a vendor has been with you. Frequently you will be able to obtain a better price by renegotiating or re-competing for a particular service that is being provided by a long-time supplier to you. You may even find that you end up keeping your original vendor but at a lower overall cost. For example, has your printer kept up with technology and switched to electronic pre-press capability with the resultant lowered costs? Or, are you still being charged for manual paste-up of your advertising copy at very expensive labor rates? Another key indicator of a potential cost reduction is the magnitude of the cost itself. The larger the cost, the greater the opportunity to find an equally good supplier at a lower price and the greater the size of the potential savings.

A note of caution is in order here. When you re-compete your supplier contracts, be sure to factor in quality and responsiveness as well as price. It will not do you any good to get a lower price from a new company for your printing work if the quality is poor or they miss your marketing deadline requirements. It may also be a disaster to get a lower priced inventory supplier who cannot keep your shelves stocked with merchandise when you need it. Only you can weigh the cost savings against these other potentially damaging factors that may arise with the selection of a new supplier.

Evaluate the Business's Physical Plant

Whether you own or lease the physical facilities occupied by your business, you should undertake a careful evaluation of the usage of the space. Keep in mind that every square foot is costing your company money and you need to determine if all of the space you have is really needed for your business operations. In general, less space will cost less to rent, maintain, provide with utilities, and insure.

Strategic Move #12:

"Evaluate the business's physical plant for innovative ways to decrease expenses and increase income."

If you own the space occupied by your company and determine that a significant portion of the real estate is not really needed, and that business location is not crucial to your success, you may want to consider selling your present facility and moving to smaller, less expensive space before you offer the business for sale. This is an extensive undertaking and can also be expensive in terms of moving costs, company downtime, and general disruption of the smooth flow of your operations. This is probably only a good strategic move in a very few cases. Nevertheless, if your company has a significant amount of excess space, you should do a cost-benefit analysis to determine if this option is viable.

If the excess space is relatively small (25% or less of the total space), it's most likely best to leave it as an area for expansion by a new owner. Do not forget that a potential buyer will be optimistic about the future and may see your excess space as a positive selling point relative to future business growth. There are two schools of thought about how to deal with the issue of significant excess space during the selling process. One position is that the business should "spread out" to fill the entire space and let the potential buyer know that the business space can be consolidated to allow for future growth. I favor leaving the space empty (clean and uncluttered) or used for orderly storage. Either way, the bottom-line profits of your company will not be affected, but I believe that the visual impact of the business's physical growth opportunity is a good selling point.

If you have excess space and cannot move to a smaller facility, you may want to consider subletting the extra space (if you lease) or renting out the excess portions (if you own the space). Many companies of all kinds—from office operations to manufacturing facilities, to retail locations—have done this very successfully. The added revenue to your bottom line will significantly increase the selling price of your business, and if you structure the lease/sublet correctly, you will still have the space as a future option for expansion. For example, I know of many restaurants that sublet a small portion of their entry area space to retail outlets of many kinds. Business enterprises such as gift shops (especially good in tourist areas), greeting card shops (or kiosks), and specialty packaged food sales all seem to do especially well and do not compete with the restaurant's primary business.

Some manufacturing or distributor companies with extensive warehouse and storage space have been able to lease space to parcel shippers (such as UPS or FedEx), paper record storage companies, and small start-up companies of all kinds. Use your own creativity and also talk to your local commercial real estate agent. They are sure to have some good ideas if this is an option you want to pursue.

When you rent or sublet a portion of your space, other cost savings/revenue opportunities will present themselves. Perhaps you can share the costs with the new tenant for the expenses of a receptionist, secretary, office equipment (copy and fax machines), and any other common business functions that make sense.

If renting or subletting your excess space is not an option, then consider consolidating into a smaller area and closing off that portion of unused space. At least you will not have to pay the utility costs for that portion of space. They can then go directly to your bottom line. A useful exercise for business owners is to calculate exactly what each square foot of space is costing them. This makes it very clear where costs might be reduced or eliminated for this frequently overlooked expense item. Add up all of the costs associated with your leased or owned business space. Include rental or mortgage payments, utility costs (heating, lighting, air conditioning, etc.), and maintenance and repair costs (janitors, repair trades, etc.). Divide these total expenses by the total square footage of your business operations. The result is the cost per square foot to conduct business for the space you occupy. Astute business owners ensure that each square foot of space is used wisely and contributes to the overall profitability of the business. If not, ways to minimize or eliminate this expense are pursued. When you do your calculations, you should categorize the space and related expenses according to major functions particular to your business, such as:

- Retail space.

- Office and administrative space.

- Warehouse space.

- Manufacturing space.

- Storage space.

- Order fulfillment space.

The following strategic move will be difficult to evaluate and even harder to implement. However, the potential increase in the profitability of your company could be significant.

Strategic Move #13:

"Evaluate every employee position relative to cost and the value added to your business."

Evaluate Your Employee Costs

You should examine every employee position in your company for need and the value added relative to the cost of the employee. In some businesses, this can be an extensive undertaking. In other less labor-intensive operations, it may be relatively straightforward. Whatever the case, you should carefully consider every employee position because labor and related benefit costs are very likely a significant part of your overall expenses. However, you must tread very carefully in this area because the success of many businesses are directly tied to their work force. It may be a false savings to reduce employees (or their related costs) in such a way that causes reduced productivity. This ultimately hurts the overall business. However, there may be many things you can do to reduce your total employment costs without adversely affecting your successful business operation. Before I talk about what you can do, consider the major components of your labor costs and what it all adds up to:

- Actual salary or payroll, plus bonuses.

- Workman's compensation insurance and social security taxes.

- Benefits including insurance, vacation, sick leave, holidays, company automobiles, and education.

- Professional and job-specific training.

- Pension plan expenses.

When you add up all of the employee costs, in even the most modest of businesses, you will quickly realize what a significant expense this is. Think about what value you can add to the selling price of your company if you can trim your employee costs even a little. If these cost cuttings are done without any loss in productivity or sales, you could realize approximately $4.00 in the selling price of your business for every $1 saved (based on my earlier example). This is because the reduced expenses will go right to your bottom-line profits!

In a perfectly run company, all employees' positions will be critical to your business operations or they would not exist. In my experience, though, most companies are not run perfectly. As time goes by and the company focus shifts, some jobs may become unnecessary or redundant and business owners are slow to react to this. Also, in this quickly changing technological age in which we now do business, some employee positions may become unnecessary almost overnight. This necessitates a frequent review of the value that your employees add to your business relative to their costs. One good way to begin to get your arms around understanding the relationship of your employees to their value added to your business is to develop a criticality matrix analysis that considers each employee. In some businesses with a large number of employees, it may not be practical to consider all employees. But for those several millions of businesses that have less than 20 employees, this is a very worthwhile exercise. As an example of how to do this, I suggest laying out your matrix in the following form:

Table 3-B

Employee Criticality Matrix

Employee Name	Principal Function	Annual Salary/ Total Cost	Person Critical/ Noncritical	Position Critical/ Noncritical
Anthony	VP/Marketing	$75,000/$100,000	C	C
Mary	Controller	$65,000/$95,000	C	C
Bill	Production Mgr.	$60,000/$90,000	C	C
George	Asst. Prod. Mgr.	$55,000/$80,000	NC	NC
Sheila	Exec. Secretary	$40,000/$55,000	C	C
3 Employees	Office/Clerical	$90,000/$108,000	NC	C
Tommy	Outside Sales	$75,000/$100,000	C	C
Connie	Outside Sales	$75,000/$100,000	C	C
Peter	Inside Sales	$65,000/$78,000	NC	NC
5 Employees	Shop Workers	$200,000/$240,000	NC	C
Tom	Shop Foreman	$45,000/$54,000	NC	NC

By quickly scanning the matrix, you will be able to identify some employees/positions which you can examine more closely for potential payroll expense savings. In the example above, there are three positions that are judged to be noncritical to the successful operation of the business. Even more importantly, the person in that position is also judged to be noncritical to the successful performance of the position. Clearly, these are the areas of "low hanging fruit" that might be ripe for the picking. Let's examine each one further.

- In the case of the Assistant Production Manager, George, it's not clear just what his principal role is. Most of the responsibility for managing the production is under the authority of Bill. It is also noted that George is the brother-in-law of the company owner and has been with the company for years.

- The Inside Sales position has become largely a position of order-taking as most sales not generated by the Outside Sales force are coming in through fax and Internet e-mail orders. Also, Peter's performance and work habits have declined as his traditional sales role has evolved from what it once was.

- The Shop Foreman position could easily be combined into one of the other shop positions. Improved automated equipment and the change to a profit-sharing system with the shop employees have increased

their motivation and responsibility and reduced this once largely supervisory role to that of a timekeeper. Tom's skills as a production worker
have eroded over the years since he shifted to a supervisory role.

There are a total of eight other positions that are critical, but the people in them
are not considered critical. Let's look at the characteristics of these people:

- In the case of the three Office/Clerical workers, their positions are
  extremely important to be accomplished, but the relatively low skill
  level of the job makes the individuals easy to replace.

- The five Shop Workers are extremely important functions relative to
  the generation of the company's product, but none of the individuals
  are of a high enough skill level to consider them to be critical to the
  business. If one of these employees were to leave, a replacement could
  be hired and trained without a serious impact to the overall production. During the employee search and training period, overtime could
  be used with the four remaining employees to pick up the slack until
  the new employee was able to be fully productive.

Now that the employee criticality matrix has been completed and a preliminary
assessment has been done, it appears that some employee payroll expenses
can be cut without hurting the business operation. It's now time to consider
the options of exactly what to do. Let's take each position that has been identified for possible savings and decide on a plan of action.

- The position of Assistant Production Manager is no longer needed (if it
  ever was). Upon reflection, it appears that George has gravitated into
  that position over the years after being hired at the urging of the
  owner's wife. Because George is "family," the situation is not as clear as
  it might otherwise be. Eliminating George's position could on the sur-
  face save the company about $80,000 per year. Bill feels that he can do
  his job without George, but would need to hire a low-level administrative assistant at a total payroll cost of about $35,000 per year to pick up
  some of George's work. The net savings then will be approximately
  $45,000 per year ($80,000 − $35,000 = $45,000). The owner quickly
  calculates that doing this will help to bring about $180,000 more in the
  selling price of the company, but may also get him in deep trouble with
  his wife and in-laws. The owner comes up with a plan to offer a $90,000
  cash settlement to George to accept early retirement which he agrees
  to. This turns into a win-win situation for George and the owner of the
  business who both gain $90,000.

- The Office/Clerical functions are put out to bid with a large national
  contract services company under the provision that if they get the con-

tract, they must hire the existing three clerical workers if they will accept the positions. The bid submitted is for $88,000. The clerical workers will have to take a 10% pay reduction which will bring them in line with prevailing pay scales, but their health and retirement benefits will be significantly better as the result of being employed by a much larger company that enjoys economies of scale. The owner accepts this approach and the three clerical employees are converted to contractors for a total payroll savings of $20,000 per year. Again, this is a win-win situation because the employees make up for their reduced pay scale with improved benefits and they get to keep their jobs.

- The Inside Sales person position is eliminated and Peter is laid off. He is replaced with another person from the contract employee firm with less skills, but well-qualified to handle the order-taking role that this position has evolved into. The new cost to the company is $40,000 per year for an annual net savings of $38,000 per year ($78,000 – $40,000 = $38,000).

- The company owner decides that there will not be any savings in trying to replace the noncritical Shop Worker employees. In fact, even though none of them individually are critical, the group taken together as a whole are essential. There are no savings to be gained here and in fact, a potential disruption to the business could occur if this was handled improperly.

- The Shop Foreman is due to retire in about a year and the owner decides to do nothing with this position until then. At that time, he plans to add the foreman duties to one of the five shop workers (with a significant raise in pay of about $10,000) and not replace the foreman. At that time, a payroll expense savings of $44,000 will be realized ($54,000 – $10,000 {increased pay to a current worker to assume the foreman's responsibilities} = $ 44,000).

Overall, these actions will reduce the total payroll expenses by about $192,000 within the next two years and should not hurt production or sales. Consequently, the owner is looking forward to increasing the profits of the business by $192,000 and the eventual selling price of the business by $768,000. The possibility of reducing the payroll costs by this amount is probably not as difficult as it may first seem to you. The total payroll costs in this example are $1,000,000 and a reduction of $192,000 is about 17% of the total. There are many business consultants who advocate that it is rare to find a mature business with 20 or so employees where payroll costs cannot be cut by 15–20% with aggressive management.

Even though the foregoing example is fictional, it presents some ideas and processes that you may want to use in your business as you prepare it for sale.

If nothing else, it should stimulate some constructive thinking on your part on how to reduce your overall payroll costs. Ultimately, it will be up to you to make these personnel changes and it may be difficult to look a long-time employee in the eye as you swing the ax. But keep this in mind. A new owner will most likely make these changes after the sale if you do not do it before-hand. If employee costs can be reduced, then you owe it to yourself to realize these expense reductions in a way that will maximize the selling price of your business.

There are many other things that can be done relative to reducing employee costs that are not discussed here. They may take a relatively long time to implement and the benefits may be much more modest and gradual. The entire area of fringe benefits, bonuses, and salary reductions could be explored. Generally, however, these are touchy areas that result in eroded employee morale and ultimately will directly and negatively affect the bottom line of the company, rather than improve it. As with any other cost-cutting initiatives you may take, be very careful not to end up hurting your overall business. A few of the negative results of employee cost-cutting initiatives that you must watch out for include:

- Decreased employee morale.

- Violation of union agreements.

- Charges of age discrimination and other EEO-based complaints.

- Creation of new business competition from discharged employees.

The next strategic move is more benign than the previous two, but it still presents a good possibility of producing an increase in your company's profitability.

Strategic Move #14:

"Evaluate all your business office equipment for efficiency, productivity, and cost-effectiveness."

Evaluate All Office Equipment and Computer Software

The efficiency and effectiveness of office equipment and computer software has exploded over the last few years, and the pace of new technology development continues to race onward. Even the smallest of businesses may be able to benefit greatly by evaluating the way they use office equipment and computers to conduct their business. Consider again the fictional company I described in the previous section relative to reducing employee costs. If the company has not updated office equipment technology in the last five years, it's very likely that an investment of a few thousand dollars in new equipment and software (and related employee training) will likely result in the ability of the company to eliminate one of the three office/clerical positions! This will produce an additional expense savings of about $29,000 per year. Even if the company's office operations are woefully behind the times, an investment of less than $20,000 will buy an extremely powerful, high-speed computer with two terminals, a high-quality 600-dpi, black-and-white laser printer that prints proof quality at the rate of 10 pages per minute, a good quality, color ink-jet printer suitable for printing trial quantities of marketing materials, a top-of-the-line fax machine with an automatic programmable send capability, and all of the latest software to make this highly efficient office suite work together.

The use of e-mail is an extremely low-cost way of communicating with customers, suppliers, and employees in the field. It's an absolutely essential capability for a business to have in today's world. Surprisingly, at this writing, not even half of the small businesses in the country use this simple, but powerful technology. The savings in telephone expenses, postage, stationery, and labor needed to communicate in the traditional way can be substantial. If your company is not yet using e-mail for communications, then you should implement this capability as soon as possible. It's relatively inexpensive and easy to implement. The increased efficiency benefits to your company can be extensive.

The fax machine has also become an office staple, not only for standard communications, but as a direct marketing sales tool. Your sales literature can be loaded into your fax machine and preprogrammed to automatically fax your material to your customers in the middle of the night or on weekends when telephone rates are the least expensive. Major savings are realized on postage, stationery, and printing costs. You use only one set of printed materials, but they will be duplicated at your customers' receiving fax machines hundreds, thousands, and even tens of thousands of times. You get all of this for the low cost of an off-peak telephone connection. And, since data transmits at a high rate of transfer, the telephone connection air time is relatively very short when compared with a voice call. With the proper computer software, you can even fax directly from your office computer and eliminate the need for any kind of paper at all! Also, your communication material can be changed instantaneously whenever you want, without waiting for printing suppliers.

Access to new customers via Internet marketing is advancing rapidly and you may be able to use this new and relatively inexpensive technology to add a quick boost to your sales and profits. However, Internet marketing can be tricky and is substantially different than the traditional ways you are most likely using. At this writing, the Internet has proven to be profitable for only a relatively few new enterprises, but it provides an excellent way to augment an existing business. For a relatively small fee, you can establish an Internet presence that can be accessed by your existing customers. They can easily learn about specials and sales that you want to offer without the expense of paper and postage.

Web sites have also proved very useful in answering customer service questions and providing technical product information. Some companies have been able to significantly reduce their cost of customer support by providing Internet sites with prepositioned answers to commonly asked questions and detailed e-mail information that can be requested by customers automatically without the need for a "real person" to field many of the inquiries. There are many books and other Internet-related information sources available to help you understand if this is a potential cost-saving or revenue-generating capability for your company.

Computer application programs for word processing, database management, inventory control, accounting, and graphic production are not only proliferating, but their functionality and ease of use has grown almost unbelievably. You should evaluate the latest software and computer hardware on the market to understand what applications your business should be taking advantage of. There are many sources of information and reviews of products are available in magazines and other periodicals. While you are considering your equipment costs, do not forget your production-related equipment.

Strategic Move #15:

"Evaluate all production-related equipment for cost-effective contributions to your business's bottom line"

Evaluate All Production-Related Equipment

If your business is equipment-intensive, such as a manufacturing company, machine shop, or construction company, you should carefully evaluate each major piece of equipment for its overall contribution to the expenses and profitability of your business. Some of the factors you should consider are:

- Maintenance costs and repair.

- Operator training costs.

- Energy costs.

- Set-up time and costs.

- Lost revenue due to downtime of the equipment.

- Potential increase in productivity or efficiency.

Sometimes a capital investment in new or upgraded production equipment to improve efficiency can return more than its cost in the sale price of the business by improving the business's bottom line. If your equipment is very old, or of poor quality, you may find that the maintenance and repair costs exceed the capital expenditure costs for new equipment! One small manufacturing company I know of had converted all of its multi-axis milling machines to CNC (computer numerically controlled) several years ago. The annual maintenance/repair contract costs ran into the tens of thousands of dollars, and they were still plagued with frequent downtime due to inherent software glitches and extensive set-up time for the equipment. A cost-benefit analysis by the business owner determined that leasing all new equipment to replace the milling machines would actually cost less per year than the current maintenance and repair costs. An added benefit was that the new equipment was much more "user-friendly" due to new technology. Consequently, the set-up time for jobs was significantly less than ever before. Productivity by the machinists soared and the annual operating costs declined, which resulted in a real winning situation. Although the principal motivation in this case was not a sale of the business, the resultant improvement to the net operating profits of the business greatly increased its value.

Other benefits of converting old and inefficient production equipment to new equipment often translates into lower savings than those in the earlier example, and these savings may occur over a longer period of time. But you should consider them as part of the overall plan of preparing your business for sale if time allows. Once you have determined the overall operating costs of each piece of your major equipment base and are satisfied that you understand its role in the profitability of your business, you may be able to have the rest of the analysis completed for you. Invite the salespeople for the companies that offer your kind of equipment to compare and contrast the operating costs for new replacement items for those used in your business. By going to various competing vendors and tasking them to do the same thing, you will get a completed analysis of the expense item savings that you might be able to realize. Then compare the savings you can expect to realize versus the capital cost of the equipment to make a determination as to whether it will make economic sense for replacement. Keep in mind the estimate of a $4 increase in the business selling price for every dollar of expense saved.

Strategic Move #16:

"Get rid of all those expensive owner "perks" that could rob your business of its selling value."

Evaluate All Owner-Specific "Perks" and Benefits

Some of the most immediate and significant things that many small business owners can do to dramatically improve the bottom-line cash flow and, therefore, provable profit of their business is to give up the perquisites (perks) that come with running a closely-held company. This will most likely be very difficult for many of you who have become used to benefits that help to shield your income from the IRS and enhance your quality and enjoyment of life. But remember, the value that you will be able to build into the business's selling price by increasing the bottom line over the one or two years before you sell the company can be significant.

You are the best judge of what is a "perk" and what is a necessary business expense, but I will list some items for you to seriously consider. Remember, you will only be giving these up for one to two years and the later return to you in the selling price of your business could be well worth it.

- *Unreported Cash Sales:* This is probably the most controversial, as well as illegal, perk that small-business owners have. I certainly do not advocate this practice and I (and any reputable business broker or other business consulting professional) always advise business buyers to completely ignore any claims of unreported income by a business seller. Unreported sales are not provable, will cast you in a bad light with a potential buyer as being a dishonest person, and could get you into serious difficulty with the IRS and others if the information became available to them. If you are skimming some cash from the business, stop the practice in stages and let the sales flow increase gradually over the business sale preparation period. A spike in sales (and profits) in one year may be difficult to explain.

- *Luxury Automobiles for Personal Use:* Many company owners require transportation in the course of conducting their business in order to visit and transport clients, travel to suppliers, deliver proposals, and so on. In very profitable companies, these vehicles tend to be Mercedes, Jaguars, and autos of that ilk. The business owner may claim a small amount of personal use of the auto, but the bulk of the costs are written off against the business. I recommend giving up the luxury auto and driving a Dodge Neon or similar type of car for a year or so. The annual difference in cost could be in the neighborhood of $10,000 per year, which could translate into an increase in your business selling price of about $40,000. You may also want to examine the use of your salespersons' vehicles and their related costs. Many times, the quality of the vehicle is higher than necessary and abuse of this perk by employees for personal use is not uncommon.

- *Company Aircraft and Boats:* As with luxury autos, these items may pass IRS scrutiny as "necessary" to the business operations, but you have to ask yourself if they are really needed. What are the savings if you and your staff fly commercially rather than maintaining a Leer Jet at your disposal? Do you really need that boat to entertain clients? On a more modest scale, many business owners are recreational pilots and have found that they can justify their Cessna or Beechcraft as a business expense because they use it occasionally to travel to business meetings. Ask yourself if this is really worth reducing your company's provable profit picture due to the added expenses of these luxury items.

- *Close Family Members on the Payroll:* Many business owners have found it advantageous to put Junior on the company payroll for after-school and summer work, but frequently Junior adds no value to the company. It may be a good way to transfer money to your offspring at a lower tax rate than if it went through your income process first and then to them. Also, many business owners have their spouses on the payroll for dubious or nonexistent work. In a C corporation, this is a way of getting profits out of the company and into the owner's hands without the disadvantage of double taxation (corporate income tax, plus dividend taxes). You must carefully consider your ability to convince a buyer that these salary costs are not really needed and should be considered as add-backs in an income and expense sheet reconstruction. How will the buyer know whether Junior really does a necessary job or not? How will the buyer know whether your spouse really does an important bookkeeping function that will have to be replaced and therefore expensed? As I have said, the best way is to eliminate these expenses ahead of time if they are unnecessary and let the increased profits flow to the taxable bottom line as proof of the income-producing capability of the business.

- *Personal Insurance Policies and Contributions to Retirement Plans:* Actually eliminating these expense items may not be wise or necessary because many buyers will allow these costs to be added back to a reconstructed income and expense statement. However, you should ensure that these expenses are properly considered in your financial statement reconstruction.

- *Extraneous Personal Expenses:* Does the building maintenance and landscaping crew also include your home in its normal services? What about fuel oil, vehicle repair and maintenance, utility costs, etc. Is the country club membership really absolutely necessary for your conduct of business? And what about those membership fees in tennis and other sports clubs, health and fitness facilities, fraternal and social organizations; the list goes on. It's best to carefully scrub your expense sheet to ensure you have not inadvertently combined some of your personal expenses with that of your business.

- *Travel and Entertainment Expenses:* Although the IRS has clamped down somewhat on these types of expenses, they are still a major perk for many business owners. It's no coincidence that many industry conventions are held in such places as Las Vegas, Orlando, Atlantic City, Aspen, Hawaii, and the Bahamas. You should carefully consider your need to attend these conventions during the years just before you plan to sell the business. Many times the expenses for a one-week junket of this nature are at least $5,000, or more if your spouse is a corporate member and can also have their expenses deducted. Although this is a generally accepted add-back to an income and expense sheet reconstruction, I have seen it challenged by some potential buyers. They may argue that it's a necessary expense to maintain the company networking among its clients, vendors, and suppliers; just as you would do with the IRS! If the trips are not necessary, it may be better to avoid them or pay for them personally (at least those costs that are truly personal).

- *Personal Lease-Backs to Your Company:* Some company owners have found it to be financially lucrative and a distinct tax advantage to own the business equipment and/or real estate in a separate entity and lease these assets back to the company at fairly exorbitant rates. For example, a business owner whose successful company is incorporated as a C corporation may find it difficult to extract all the funds they want from the business without a double taxation problem (corporate income taxes plus personal dividend taxes). Accordingly, the business owner may hold all of the business equipment in a separate sub-chapter S corporation which leases the assets at higher-than-fair-market rates to the primary business. This is an expense to the C corporation and income to the S corporation, but the funds pass directly to the shareholders of the S corporation with no dividend taxes (the shareholders are liable only for their personal income taxes on the flow-through of profits). Of course, this cost goes on indefinitely for the company that is to be sold, long after the equipment cost would have been paid off under a normal purchase or commercial lease arrangement. These recurring expenses may not need to be real expenses to the company. The owner should consider discontinuing this practice in the year or two before the sale and selling the assets at a nominal amount to the company to hold as an asset for the contemplated sale of the business. Or, the charges to the company can be scaled back to the level found in the open marketplace. Again, you may be able to convince a potential buyer to accept these expenses as add-backs to the income and expense sheet reconstruction, but why even cloud the issue if clarity will smooth the sale and enhance the value of the business?

Review All Products and Services

Review all products and services to ensure that everything contributes to the profitability of the business. Sometimes products and services are continued even though they lose money only because somebody has not looked at them for stand-alone profitability. It may make sense to eliminate them in order to enhance the bottom line. Consequently, I offer the next strategic move for you to consider.

Strategic Move #17:

"Remove all product and service dinosaurs that do not contribute to overall company profitability."

Examine each of your products and/or services individually and consider all costs associated with your production and sales. Now is the time to eliminate those items that are drains on the company's overall profitability. The challenge here is to properly allocate overhead costs to each product and/or service in a way that clarifies its true cost. As you go through this exercise, you will find that some expenses are fixed (like rent or mortgage payments), and some are variable (such as some utility costs, raw material, and production labor). I will use the following example for the fictional Grand Gadget Co. to illustrate a way of approaching this concept.

The Grand Gadget Co. produces five fabricated gadgets which it sells in the intermediate market (for use by their customers in producing retail products sold directly to consumers). The owner has decided to sell the business, wants to maximize the profitability of the company over the next two years, and has decided to carefully determine the viability of each of the company's products. The company's last full-year sales were $800,000, with a net pretax profit of $100,000. The owner first decides which of the company's expenses are variable and which are fixed:

Table 3-C

Fixed Versus Variable Expenses

Fixed Expenses	Variable Expenses

Real Estate Lease
Overhead Labor
Telephone
Miscellaneous Overhead
Utilities:
    Heat
    Water
Property Repair and
    Maintenance
	Utilities:
	    Electricity
	Production Labor
	Raw Materials
	Selling and Marketing
	Shipping
	Equipment Repair and
	    Maintenance
	Advertising

Total $250,000	**Total $450,000**

The owner takes the total of the fixed expenses and allocates them to each of the five product lines proportionately according to their percentage of the total sales dollars. For example:

Table 3-D

Allocation of Fixed Expenses to Product Lines

Product Line	Percentage of Sales Dollars	Sales	Allocation of Fixed Expense
1	10%	$ 80,000	$ 25,000
2	15%	$ 120,000	$ 37,500
3	15%	$ 120,000	$ 37,500
4	25%	$ 200,000	$ 62,500
5	35%	$ 280,000	$ 87,500
Totals	**100%**	**$800,000**	**$250,000**

Because the business owner uses a standard markup for each of the products, he believes that each one contributes approximately the same percentage amount of dollars to profit as it does to sales. For example, the owner believes that because product line #4 accounts for 25% of the sales ($200,000), it therefore accounts for 25% of the profits or $25,000 ($100,000 total profits x 25% = $25,000). This may or may not be a correct assumption for your particular business. Some products and/or services within companies typically have different markup structures and, accordingly, contribute differently to profitability. Be sure to use your specific situation as you do these calculations. You do not need to be 100% accurate in your allocations, but you should get as close as reasonably possible for a meaningful estimate.

The next step in the analysis is a little more difficult and will require the owner to approximate with some degree of accuracy the allocation of the variable expenses to each product line based on an analysis of actual expenditures. In this example, the owner finds that:

Table 3-E

Product Line Profitability Analysis

Variable Expense	Product Line #1	Product Line #2	Product Line #3	Product Line #4	Product Line #5
Utilities — Electricity	$ 1,500	$ 2,500	$ 8,000	$ 5,000	$ 10,000
Production — Labor	10,000	15,000	42,000	35,000	48,000
Raw Materials	6,000	10,000	37,000	17,000	30,000
Selling & Marketing	10,000	15,000	27,000	20,000	28,000
Shipping	2,500	3,750	8,000	4,250	6,500
Equipment Repair & Maint.	4,000	6,000	16,000	10,000	12,000
Total Variable Expenses	$34,000	$ 52,250	$138,000	$ 91,250	$134,500
Plus Fixed Expenses	25,000	37,500	37,500	62,500	87,500
Total Expenses	$59,000	$ 89,750	$175,500	$153,750	$222,000
Total Sales	80,000	120,000	120,000	200,000	280,000
Net Profit (sales less expenses)	$21,000	$ 30,250	$(55,500)	$ 46,250	$ 58,000

As can be seen by the above Product Line Profitability Analysis, product line #3 is losing $55,500 for the company and the owner should evaluate what can be done to turn this around. Actions that should be considered include:

• Reducing the variable expenses and/or,

• increasing the product price.

If neither one of these options are possible, then look at what happens to the profitability analysis if product line #3 is discontinued, and the variable expenses (and sales contributions) are eliminated.

Table 3-F

Reconfigured Product Line Profitability Analysis

Variable Expense	Product Line #1	Product Line #2	Product Line #3	Product Line #4	Product Line #5
Utilities — Electricity	$ 1,500	$ 2,500	0	$ 5,000	$ 10,000
Production — Labor	10,000	15,000	0	35,000	48,000
Raw Materials	6,000	10,000	0	17,000	30,000
Selling & Marketing	10,000	15,000	0	20,000	28,000
Shipping	2,500	3,750	0	4,250	6,500
Equipment Repair & Maint.	4,000	6,000	0	10,000	12,000
Total Variable Expenses	$34,000	$ 52,250	0	$ 91,250	$134,500
Plus Fixed Expenses	25,000	37,500	37,500	62,500	87,500
Total Expenses	$59,000	$ 89,750	$ 37,500	$153,750	$222,000
Total Sales	80,000	120,000	0	200,000	280,000
Net Profit (sales less expenses)	$21,000	$ 30,250	$(37,500)	$ 46,250	$ 58,000

This changes the overall profitability of the Grand Gadget Co. as follows:

New Net Sales	$680,000	($800,000 – $120,000)
Less New Variable Expenses	$312,000	($450,000 – $138,000)
Less Fixed Expenses	$250,000	
New Net Profit	$118,000	

The increase in profitability of the company is $18,000 (an 18% increase over the previous $100,000) which will likely translate into a net increase in the selling price of the business of $72,000 ($18,000 x 4 = $72,000). This may be well worth the trouble of shutting down product line #3. Of course, with any action, some caveats apply:

• To realize the savings in variable expenses, an employee or two will have to be discharged.

- Customers may rely on having product #3 available to them and without it they may not purchase your other products.

- The reduction in gross sales of the business, while improving the bottom line profitability, may hurt the attractiveness of the company to some strategic buyers who may be looking for increased market penetration, rather than having current profitability as a major concern.

Other Enhancements You Can Make

Here is a potpourri of other actions you can take to improve and enhance the value of your business before you begin the sales process.

Consider using outside consultants to help increase the business's profitability: Sometimes it's better to have a fresh, outside look at your business operations to help you get a handle on maximizing your company's profits. You may be too close to things to see various options, or you may not have the time (or inclination) to do some of the financial analysis necessary. The use of an outside consultant may also facilitate the releasing of unneeded employees. You may even be able to hire a good consultant on a contingency basis tied to the increase in profitability that they can bring to your company. Clearly, if you have to pay a $10,000 fee to a consultant who can increase your bottom line by even as little as the amount of their fee, you will be much further ahead when you actually sell the business due to the multiplier factor for the overall sales value.

Clean up the inventory to ensure that it's current: One of the biggest sticking points in the sale of a business with product inventory is how to value it. Typically, a value for a business is based on "everything else," plus the value of the inventory at the time of sale. Inventory varies due to quantity, age, and accounting price method (LIFO, FIFO, etc.). To minimize any disagreements with the potential buyer of the business, you should begin to clear out the old inventory (including work-in-process and completed goods) during the year leading up to the business sale. You may want to run a sale, offer premiums for purchase, sell material for scrap value, or just discard nonsalable material to ensure a clean inventory basis. Also, you may want to consider changing the inventory accounting method (from LIFO to FIFO) in the year prior to the sale for a quick boost to bottom-line profitability of your business. This is a practice of which most buyers (or their representatives) are aware. Expect them to want to discount the positive effects if they catch it.

Modify all leases, mortgages, agreements, and contracts so that they are assignable to a new owner: I discussed this earlier and I want to reiterate it here. This may be difficult for you to do, but if you start modifying these documents well in advance of the sale, it will save a great deal of time and trouble when the time comes to transfer ownership. If your business is incorporated and the documents are in the name of the corporation, then this process may not be necessary. But many businesses are operated as sole proprietorships or partnerships, and all of the legal documents that you may want to transfer to a new owner will most likely not be assignable without specific action on your part to make the necessary modifications. Even in many incorporated small businesses, leases and mortgages are required to be personally guaranteed by the principal(s) in the company. Without specific language allowing it, these documents cannot be assigned.

Have your financial statements professionally audited by a CPA for the one or two years before you plan to sell the business: This process may be fairly expensive based on your type of company, the quality of your record keeping, and the capability of the firm that you hire. For a very small business, this action most likely will not be necessary. But for larger companies with many product lines, various physical locations, diverse inventory, international sales, and a host of other considerations, audited financial statements will greatly help establish the value in your business. There is a caveat here that I want to let you consider. Some business brokers/investment bankers do not feel that this is a worthwhile expense for a business seller for the following reasons:

- A sophisticated buyer knows that if a seller with larceny in their heart wants to fool an auditor, they can.

- The buyer will be conducting their own due diligence in pursuit of understanding the business that is for sale and, in essence, will be accomplishing their own independent audit of the seller's claims about the business.

Accordingly, you may want to carefully consider whether you want to incur the expenses for auditing your financial statements before a specific buyer is identified. You may also want to offer to have this done at your expense (or on a shared expense basis with the buyer) using an accountant of the buyer's choosing once a serious interest in your business has been expressed.

Bring the accounts receivable up to date: Even though you will most likely sell the business with some adjustment to the accounts receivable, it's a good idea to ensure that they are as current as possible. Many business buyers will pay 90% of current accounts receivable (or more depending on demonstrated customer payoff history), but will only pay 50% for 60-day past due accounts, 25% for 90-day past due accounts, and nothing for any older accounts. Of course, this will vary depending on your type of business, the quality of the accounts, your payment policies, the attitude of the buyer, and other considerations. Your goal should be to have only current 30-day accounts receivable to transfer at the time of business sale. However, in many business sales, the accounts receivable are not included in the sales price and are left for the seller to collect. Another alternative is for the buyer to hold back payment for the accounts receivable and pay the seller only as the receivables are collected. No matter how the accounts receivable are ultimately structured in the sale, it's better to have them as current as possible when you offer the business for purchase. This will help to demonstrate good management practices and a high-quality customer base.

Settle all outstanding lawsuits, tax liens, employee disputes, and union grievances: Now this is something that is definitely easier said than done. Lawsuits and other related disputes tend to take years to resolve. You probably have good reason for arguing the appropriateness of any tax liens and employee disputes, and union grievances tend to also stretch on "ad nauseam." Even if you cannot reach reasonable closure to all of these issues before you begin the selling process, the issues should be carefully documented and disclosed to the potential buyer. You may want to estimate a potential downside to any of these issues. If they are substantive in nature, you may have to personally indemnify the business buyer against any future losses as a result of the resolution of the issue. If this does not sound attractive to you, I am not surprised. It's very disconcerting to sell a business subject to a possible contingent liability over which you no longer have any control. Do your best to resolve all of these serious outstanding issues before you put your business on the market and certainly before you sell the company.

Resolve all partnership or shareholder disputes: If you have a partner(s) or are incorporated and have equal or minority shareholders, it's in your best interest to make sure you are all singing from the same sheet of music when it comes to selling the business. Squabbling partners and shareholders have killed many deals that would have been good for all involved. When you decide to sell your business, one of the first things you should do is ensure that your partner/shareholders are in agreement. Work to resolve any concerns they have. In the case of a partner, you should put into writing certain issues and agreements relative to selling the business. Even the threat of legal action by a disgruntled minority owner in a company can cool the enthusiasm of even the most ardent potential buyer.

Ensure that you have replacement corporate management: Many small, closely-held companies are run almost exclusively by the primary owner (including being the decision-maker) for all the important management issues. It's been said that if your company cannot continue without you, you do not have a business. You have a job. A buyer may have a legitimate concern that when you leave the company, the business will suffer without you. One way to alleviate this concern is to begin bringing your subordinates into the senior management issues of the company well in advance of a sale. Be sure to include them in negotiations for the sale of the business so the buyer will see that there will be a "corporate memory" after you leave the company. This process will certainly take time to accomplish. You will need to start it at least a year in advance of the sale to be really effective.

Do not take on any new debt: It's best to avoid taking on any new long-term liabilities for the company in the year or two before you plan on selling. Additional debt service (the interest and other charges) will deflate your net profit, and the principal payments will reduce the company's available cash flow. This is just the opposite of what you want to do at this point. You may want to defer things like new product initiatives, new physical facilities, increased R&D expenses, etc. that may have a high front-end cost with an expected payoff several years later. Leave these items for the new business owner to pursue. In fact, a bona fide, high-probability new product initiative may be an excellent selling point with a potential buyer.

Defer all major facility improvement or expansion programs: Even if you are able to finance these initiatives with available cash, they are best deferred until after the business sale process. Any major perturbation to your company's normal operating procedure will unnecessarily complicate the picture for a potential buyer. You may find that you have committed a significant amount of funds to a project that a buyer has no interest in or one in which the buyer does not believe to be practical. Consequently, you will have effectively reduced the net proceeds you will receive from the sale of your business, because many buyers will not pay for this kind of potential. It is usually better to fully document your improvement or expansion plans as future possibilities for the company and offer them as part of the sale process.

Separate the real estate from the business: If you own the physical real estate associated with the business under corporate ownership, it may be wise to separate it from the business for several reasons before you begin the sale process:

- You may find it easier to sell the business separate of the real estate because the total cost of the business will be lower. This may increase the quantity of potential qualified buyers with whom you can negotiate.

- It may be a tax advantage for you to have the corporation sell the real estate to you personally and then you lease it back to the new owner. You may be able to shelter a significant portion of the business sale income through the depreciation charges you will be able to take against the real estate. Of course, the business will have to pay capital gains taxes on the sale of the real estate and recapture the depreciation expenses as ordinary income.

- If the new business owner does well with the company, you may also be able to directly benefit, especially if you tie the lease terms for the property to performance factors for the business (such as gross sales).

- Ultimately, you will probably be able to sell the real estate for a better value to a successful operating business at a later time than to a new owner who may initially have concerns with very tight cash flow.

If the real estate is owned by the corporation and it's a significant portion of the overall business value, there may be a way for you to improve the opportunity for selling the business and to minimize your tax exposure regarding the real estate. For example, a buyer could buy all of the assets of your corporation except for the real estate. You keep ownership of the real estate through the corporation and lease the property to the new owner. The buyer is able to purchase the business at a much reduced price without the real estate and you have a better chance of selling the business (the smaller the cost, the greater the pool of potential buyers). In addition, you avoid the tax consequences of selling the real estate. To enhance the deal in the buyer's eyes, you may have to agree to a priced option for the new business owner to purchase the real estate at some later date. This should not be a problem for you because you probably do not want to be a landlord for very long and pushing the sale of the real estate into later years may significantly reduce your overall tax exposure.

Be prepared to stay with your business, after the sale, for a set period of time: Many business sellers agree to stay on with their company for a period of time after it is sold to assist in the transition process. In addition to smoothing the leadership transition, you can take part of the selling price as your salary. This could help to justify your desired sales price or even increase the total compensation you will receive. If you are able to do this, it may be a good selling point if the buyer is interested in your services. It also gives the buyer a way to write off, as a current expense, part of the purchase price of the business which might otherwise have to be capitalized and depreciated over a long period of time. Of course, in this arrangement, you will be receiving ordinary income versus capital gains which could increase your tax liability. However, it may be a way to make an otherwise shaky deal work successfully.

Ensure that you have an impressive and active Board of Directors: If your business is incorporated, you must have a Board of Directors in accordance with your particular state requirements. Many closely-held small businesses fail to make full use of the benefits that a Board can bring to the company: Good advice, guidance, access to capital sources, and new customers, to mention a few. As you begin preparing your business for sale, you may find that you want an active Board to use as a "sounding board" as you entertain offers, consider options, and make tough negotiating decisions. A strong Board comprised of members with impressive credentials may also be a selling point to a buyer. The potential buyer may see value in the Board and consider it an additional asset that may (at the buyer's option) come with the company.

Make sure that all of the company's product/service liability coverage is in place: In today's litigious society, nothing can put a cloud on the sale of a business like potential contingent liabilities associated with the company's products and/or services. You may have to provide indemnification for the buyer against hidden liabilities, but you should also make sure that the company has all the right product liability insurance policies in place as well as professional errors and omissions insurance if applicable to your type of business. You will also want the buyer to certify that they will continue these policies in force when they take over the ownership of the company with you named as a covered party.

Upgrade all of the company's sales and marketing literature: Do not forget that in addition to maximizing the provable profits in the business, you also should put a high quality face on everything in the business. This includes ensuring that all of your sales and marketing materials are current and accurate.

Ensure that all of your copyrights, trademarks, service marks, trade names, and patents are fully documented. This is extremely helpful in establishing a sense of value in the mind of a buyer. All of these items are unique assets of your company which, taken together, help to establish the continuing revenue-generating capability of your business.

Miscellaneous: There are many small things that you can do to enhance the outward appearance of your company that will help to create a good first impression for a buyer. None of these items by themselves are significantly important, but taken together, they can help to create a positive atmosphere for your company that could help sway a buyer to want to own your company. Here are some examples:

- Modern, up-to-date signage clearly visible to clients and customers.

- Company employee uniforms in certain types of businesses convey a sense of orderliness and team work on the part of the employees.

- Cleanliness and neatness of the premises.

- Well-stocked supply rooms indicate a robust, forward-looking company.

- Prominently displayed business community citations such as vendor awards, and fraternal and social organization recognition for contributions of any kind.

- Membership in organizations such as the Better Business Bureau and the Chamber of Commerce.

- Busy employees when the potential buyer visits and tours your company.

- Cheerful employees who appear to enjoy their work and are customer-oriented.

- Municipal recognition of your company as an important economic part of the local community.

- Ample customer and employee parking.

- Public and private grounds in good condition and visually inviting (grass cut, plantings trimmed, pavement patched, fresh paint inside and out, etc.).

Although there are many things you can do to enhance your business value in the eyes of a potential buyer, there may be some negative items remaining which you cannot affect. Sort of the warts and wrinkles that will not easily go away. You should try to identify these concerns by putting yourself in the buyer's shoes. This leads to the next strategic move.

Strategic Move #18:

"Put yourself in a buyer's shoes to anticipate, eliminate, or neutralize any concerns that they may have about your business."

Anticipate Buyer Concerns

You should ask yourself: "If I were a potential buyer for this company, what would I be most concerned about?" It's very likely that many of your concerns will also be shared by a would-be buyer. If you can anticipate these concerns in advance you will have time to effectively prepare for them. You will have several choices for action:

- Change or eliminate the issue of concern.

- Develop a plausible explanation about why the concern is not significant.

- Address the issue head-on to diffuse it as a major concern.

For example, when you review your income and expenses you may find that your profit margins are not up to those experienced by similar companies or consistent with your industry in general. It's very likely a buyer will be concerned about this and you may find it difficult to deal with this issue during negotiations. But before you ever talk with a potential suitor, you should know that your profit margins need improvement and analysis may determine that the problem is in the level of employee payroll. You can take steps to eliminate this concern by appropriately trimming your payroll expenses. Refer back to Chapter 1 and the discussion concerning business operating ratios.

Let's say that you anticipate a buyer being concerned with the new mega-mall planned to be built down the road from your retail store. You may be able to address this issue as a positive situation because it will increase the traffic that travels past your business site. You may also point out that because your business serves a niche market, it is not likely to be affected by any possible store that could open in the mall.

Some concerns are potentially real hard problems but it's always better to address them head-on in the discussions with the buyer. Let's say you have a marketing and advertising design company that you started 30 years ago and your last three years of financial statements show eroding sales revenues. Perhaps the problem has been your reluctance (fear?) of converting to full-scale use of new technology and you still do manual layout and paste-up of your ad work. You cannot recover the lost revenues and it does not make sense to throw a whole bunch of money at trying to bring yourself into the 21st century in a few months. The financial payoff may take years to realize. It's usually better to confront this issue directly with a serious buyer and point out the changes the buyer can make to improve the business and recapture the market you once had.

Make a list of your areas of vulnerability for your business's continued success. You can be sure a buyer doing their due diligence will do this as well. Once you have made this list which will be very specific to your particular business, you need to develop an approach and take action to eliminate or minimize the risk associated with each area of vulnerability. By doing this, you will enhance the overall value and salability of your business. To start you thinking, here are a few areas that you should consider:

- Product/service obsolescence.

- Extraordinarily large potential increases in taxes on real estate, inventory, equipment, etc.

- Noncompliance with state and federal environmental issues.

- Potential loss of customers who may be loyal only to you personally.

- Declining business trends in your company's particular industry.

- Expiring licenses, patents, contracts, or agreements that affect the successful operation of your business. For example, patents have a life of only 17 years and you may have one or more expiring that are crucial to your business.

- Changing franchise terms that will increase the operating expenses for your business.

- Increased difficulty or expense in obtaining raw materials, products, or services. For example, a recent increase in coffee prices has severely curtailed business at the many coffee shop businesses around the country.

- Significant increases in business location lease costs. For example, you want to keep in mind that many landlords use the occasion of a business sale to increase the rent on the property if there is no prepriced, long-term assignable lease in place.

- Any pending litigation against your company. For example, what if a supplier or customer, with whom you are having a major disagreement, has placed a lien against your business assets?

- Inability of your company to keep its key personnel during or after the business sale transition For example, how will you convince a buyer that your star salesperson will stay on with the company after the sale?

Whatever the potential buyer's concerns might be, if you can anticipate them and develop a plausible explanation or possible work-around before they become major issues in negotiations, you will have a much better chance of diffusing them as deal-killers. You will have to use your best judgment as to which ones you disclose early in negotiations, and discuss right away, and those you hold in abeyance in the hopes that the buyer does not bring them up. In general, it's been my experience that serious problems discovered by potential buyers during due diligence tend to be deal-killers no matter how good your explanation. You will be the best judge of what serious potential problems should be disclosed early, and those that are relatively minor and can be addressed as they are raised. However, you may want to discuss all of these issues with your broker/investment banker to develop a consensus plan of how they should be handled.

In addition to maximizing your financial bottom line and making all of the other improvements and enhancements suggested, you will probably still need to sell a prospective buyer on the overall desirability of purchasing your business. Such a need leads to the next section and strategic move #19.

Give a Buyer a Good Reason to Buy

Strategic Move #19:

"Remember Sales and Marketing 101: Be sure to give a potential purchaser a good reason to buy your business."

It's absolutely essential that in addition to all of the financial preparations and other business enhancements you will make, you must also provide the buyer with a good overall reason to buy your business. While this is less important for strategic and other types of buyers who will most likely have their own motivations, it's very important in the case of a financial buyer. What you should do is develop an encompassing theme to the way your business is presented that will appeal to the emotions of a prospective buyer. To do this, it is helpful to consider the primary motivations and characteristics of a financial buyer and relate them to your particular business attributes. Most financial buyers are private parties (rather than other companies) and will fall into one of these categories:

- Individual.

- Partners.

- Husband/wife teams.

- Employees (other than through a formal ESOP).

There are many varied reasons why private parties seek to buy businesses with the predominant reason being to make money. By far, their principal concern will be with the investment value of your business. But they have other motivations, some of which are also related to making money and you may want to address these as you develop a strong overall reason for a buyer to purchase your business. Some of these motivations include:

- Buying a job to earn a living. (Many potential buyers have recently lost their job.)

- Buying prestige. (Some buyers are motivated by their desire to become prominent and respected community figures.)

- Buying a hobby or retirement occupation. (Quite a few buyers purchase a business as something to do after their primary career is over.)

- Buying self-fulfillment. (There are a substantial number of potential buyers earning a good living in a particular job who are not happy and are seeking personal fulfillment by being their own boss in a field they want to pursue.)

After you have followed the advice in this book on how you can improve the profitability of your business as well as made the other enhancements recommended, make up a list of the emotional and financial selling points that you or your sales representative will want to make to a prospective buyer. These will help to create expectations in the buyer's mind and aid in creating value for your business. Some of the emotional selling points you may want to make are:

- You have made an excellent living from your business over the years, including being able to own a beautiful home, take great vacations, afford to send your children to college, etc., etc.

- You enjoy the respect and admiration of many people in the business community because of your business ownership and management. Be sure to stress all of the business and fraternal organizations of which you are a member.

- You greatly enjoy running the business with its diversity of tasks that are always challenging and personally rewarding. No day is ever the same as another and you look forward to coming in to your business every day.

Some of the related financial selling points you or your sales representative may want to make are:

- Strong sales and earnings growth.

- Declining operating expenses.

- Potential new markets to be tapped.

- Upward trends in your industry segment.

- Excellent management and sales force.

- Well-maintained facilities with room for expansion.

- New products in development.

Many of these financially-oriented expectations can be addressed with a well developed pro forma income and expense financial projection. The challenge for you is to be optimistic without being unrealistic. If you do not have upward trending sales and/or profits, or downward trending expenses over the last two to three years, it will be very difficult to convince a buyer that they can expect to enjoy these positive trends if they buy your business. In Chapter 7, I will cover the preparation of a pro forma that will address these issues and tie everything together in a sales prospectus for your company.

The last section of this chapter deals with ensuring that your company is properly organized so that you know what you are selling and the buyer knows exactly what they are buying. This gives rise to the next strategic move.

Strategic Move #20:

"Make sure that your company is properly organized to facilitate the sale process."

Properly Organize Your Company

Having a properly organized company to offer for sale is very important in helping the buyer to understand what your company does, what exactly is for sale, and why the business is valuable. A well-organized company will have the following characteristics:

- The complete corporate stock ownership status will be clear. In many small companies not properly prepared for sale, there are sometimes vague stock purchase options, undocumented stock held in retirement plans, out-of-date family member trusts, unrecorded stock pledged as collateral against loans, etc.

- If the company is a partnership, there will be a properly-executed partnership agreement in place which formalizes the relationship between the parties as to ownership percentage and divisions of responsibility and authority.

- The company debt structure will be clear and well documented. In addition to all mortgages, promissory notes, and other debt instruments, all officer loans will be properly recorded in the financial records of the business.

- All retirement plan documentation will be up-to-date and fully described. For example, Simplified Employee Pension (SEP) plans, Keogh plans, 401(k) plans, and Deferred Benefit Plans will be clearly documented and their possible impact on the sale of the business identified.

- All information concerning subsidiary operations, joint-venture agreements, and similar business arrangements will be fully described and documented.

- If the company is a sole proprietorship, there will be a record of ownership of the corporate assets, a properly executed agreement by the owner's spouse authorizing the sale of the business assets, and a record of all municipal and state filings such as d/b/a's and fictitious names.

- The management hierarchy and roles and responsibilities of all the principals will be clearly defined no matter what the legal form of the company.

- A comprehensive operations manual that covers all aspects of the day-to-day running of the business, including procedures for compliance with EEO, EPA, OSHA and other applicable government regulations.

- A comprehensive human resources manual that covers job descriptions, safety procedures, vacation, holiday, and sick leave rules, hours of work and overtime, and compensation.

In Summary

This chapter has presented many different recommended actions that you should consider in preparing your business for sale. Some are financial in nature and geared toward maximizing your company's bottom-line profits on the premise that most buyers will be very concerned about this aspect of your business. Others are directed more towards putting the best possible outward face on your business, so that the physical appearance is complementary with your goals. Still other suggestions are aimed at clarifying what you actually have for sale in terms of who owns what and how it is owned. Some of these concepts and suggestions may not apply exactly to you and your particular type of business. Some may apply but you may not have the luxury of the necessary time to fully implement them. However, I recommend that you consider each and every one of them. Your thinking may spur you to come up with other things that you can do which I have not covered. They, too, will help you to maximize the selling price of your business.

A discussion about short-run gains in profitability at the expense of long-term profits is in order here. When you take the actions recommended in this chapter, be sure to weigh the long-run implications of them on the company. Even though your plan is to sell the business as soon as possible, you should not anticipate passing any newly created problems off to the new owner. For one thing, it may take a great deal longer to sell your business than you expect and the chickens may come home to roost on your doorstep. For another, you will most likely be holding some amount of financing as part of the business sale terms. If the business suffers financially from poor decisions you may have made to increase the short-run profits, you may find that the buyer is reluctant to honor the payout agreement with you.

In the next chapter, I will cover the key financial and tax consequences relating to selling your business that you will need to consider in structuring the business sale. You will want to minimize the tax consequences and maximize the money that flows to you within the time frame you desire.

Financial and Tax Consequences of Selling Your Business

- *Introduction*
- *Financial Considerations*
- *Tax Considerations*
- *Real Estate Considerations*

Introduction

As with the sale of any investment asset, there will be financial and tax consequences to deal with when you sell your business. This applies whether you sell the business at "arms-length" to a stranger or to a close family member. You will need to have a basic understanding of how these issues affect your business in particular. This is where a good certified public accountant (CPA) will be able to provide you with much needed advice as to how to structure the sale for your particular circumstances. Because each business is as uniquely individual as any person, this book cannot cover every situation. What I will do is give you an overview of how the financial and tax issues could affect your business sale. Once you have determined how these issues affect your particular business sale, you should incorporate them into your exit plan discussed in Chapter 7, "Putting It All Together: Preparing an Exit Plan."

An important strategic move that you need to implement is to decide early upon the form in which you want to take the proceeds from the sale of your business. There are many possibilities, but generally your safest approach is to strive for an all-cash deal. Of course this is not always possible or even desirable, and realistically you will most likely need to provide some financing for the buyer of your business.

Strategic Move #21:

"Work toward an all-cash deal if possible, but be willing to finance the sale if necessary."

There are basically four different ways that you can be compensated in the sale of your business:

- Cash.

- Promissory notes.

- Corporate stock.

- Earn-out.

It has been said that cash is king and that all other forms of compensation are just different forms of higher risk. This is true for the most part but taking all-cash has its own problems which I will discuss later. Typically, most business sales involve some combination of at least three of the four forms of compensation.

Financial Considerations

There are many issues and concerns that you will need to consider relative to the financial consequences of selling your business. I will list them here and then cover each of them in more detail:

- Cash required at the time of closing.

- Personally financing the sale through promissory notes.

- Taking corporate stock in payment.

- Taking an earn-out.

- Assisting with third-party financing

Cash Required at Time of Closing

Strategic Move #22:

"Carefully estimate the amount of cash you will need to take as a minimum at the time of closing."

It's very important to estimate the amount of cash that you will need to receive at the time you sell your business. You will be responsible for many financial requirements at the time of sale, so you need to carefully calculate your needs if the sale is not an all-cash transaction. Some of your funds requirements will be:

- Capital gains taxes.

- Fees to professional advisors.

- Business broker fee/investment banker fee.

- Payables not being assumed by buyer.

- Personal requirements.

- Selling your business for all-cash.

Capital Gains Taxes

Capital gains taxes will have to be paid on the gain that you realize from the sale of your business. No matter how you feel about it, you will most likely have to pay state and federal income taxes, although there are various financial planning strategies that can reduce or even avoid these taxes. The actual amount will be very specific to your particular personal and business tax requirements. Consequently, there is no simple formula to help you calculate the actual amount, although many advisors use a figure in the 30% to 40% range for general planning purposes. You will need to consult closely with a CPA to determine your personal tax obligation. The actual amount of taxes could be significant depending on the cost basis in your company relative to the selling price. If you have owned the business for a lengthy period of time and the sale will involve the transfer of real estate or other depreciated assets, it's a good bet that your basis is very low and, therefore, the tax will be relatively high. You may want to carefully consider the discussion contained later in this chapter in the section titled "Estate Planning." The key point to remember as you outline a preliminary sale structure is that you will need up-front cash to cover your income tax payment requirements.

Professional Advisor Fees

The *fees due to your professional advisors* may be relatively high depending on the method of business sale that you pursue. If you own a larger company and are considering an ESOP, fees can run anywhere from about $10,000 for a very simple situation with just a few employees up to $50,000 or more, depending on many variables. So, too, with an IPO. Even a simplified and limited IPO can cost about $20,000 with a full-blown IPO running sometimes into the high six figures. In a relatively simple sale to a private buyer, the attorney and accountant fees will usually run several thousand dollars once the business sale is finally closed. Early in the sale process, you should ask for a solid estimate of costs from the advisors that you plan to use. This may be difficult for them to do because of their hourly rate fees and the uncertainties inherent in the overall task. Some professionals may be willing to negotiate a "fixed price" fee where they will see you through the entire process for an agreed-upon amount. If you can negotiate this type of arrangement, you will be able to pin down one of the significant variables in determining your overall cash requirements. Even if you cannot agree to a fixed price for professional fees at the start, you will most likely find a point in the sale process where the final costs can be reasonably estimated and you can then factor these into your cash requirements.

For traditional sales of operating businesses to arms-length buyers, whether corporate stock sales or asset sales, I usually advise sellers to budget approximately 2–3% of the gross estimated selling price of the business for professional fees if the selling price is $500,000 or more. The difficulty in trying to estimate professional fees is that frequently a "small" business sale will require almost as much legal and accounting help as a "large" business sale. Generally speaking, all of the legal documentation and tax and financial accounting requirements are the same for small or large businesses; only the dollar amounts on the paperwork are different. Accordingly, the fees for a small-business sale, as a percentage of the total dollar transaction, will be significantly higher. Even if you expect your business to sell for only $100,000 or so, it's not unrealistic to plan for about $5,000 in legal and accounting fees for even the simplest of transactions.

Business Broker Fee

The *business broker fee* will also be due and payable at the business closing and enough cash will have to be allocated to cover this significant cost. The actual amount will, of course, depend on the terms of your agreement with the broker, but typically it will run to about 10% of the gross selling price of your business. The fee could be an even higher percentage if your business sells for less than $150,000. Some business brokers charge a minimum fee of $15,000 or more. A typical fee schedule may look like this:

> 10% of all business value up to $500,000
> plus 9% of all business value on the next $100,000
> plus 8% of all business value on the next $100,000
> plus 7% of all business value on the next $100,000
> plus 6% of all business value on the next $100,000
> plus 5% of all business value over $1,000,000

Investment bankers and M&A specialists usually represent much larger transactions than do business brokers, and accordingly have a different fee structure. They almost always require an up-front retainer fee and then work to a commission structure. The most frequently used commission basis is referred to as the Lehman formula (after the investment banking firm by that name). This sliding scale formula is calculated as follows:

> 5% on the first $1 million of sales price
> 4% on the next $1 million of sales price
> 3% on the next $1 million of sales price
> 2% on the next $1 million of sales price
> 1% on $5 million and up

One of the most misunderstood issues and, therefore, one of the biggest problems between brokers and sellers at the time of the closing, is the basis for the business selling price upon which the commission is to be based. This should be clearly spelled out in your listing contract with your business broker, but it is sometimes not made as clear as it should be at the time. As you plan your cash requirements at the time of sale, make sure that you take into consideration the total amount of the commission that will be due. In fact, once you have a preliminary outline of a deal with a prospective buyer, you should ask for and receive from your broker an estimate of the commission that will be due if the transaction takes place under the planned structure.

The following is a representative listing of the terms and items that usually make up the basis on which a commission fee is based:

• The total consideration involved in the business sale whether paid at the closing or deferred to a later date including all payments to the company, its principals, or members of the principal's immediate family.

• The total consideration will typically involve all aspects of the transaction's value including such items as:

- Corporate stock (to include all categories; common, preferred, etc.).

- Tangible and intangible assets.

- Any and all products and/or services.

- Covenants not to compete.

- All current assets retained in the company or distributed to the sellers, including cash, inventory, and accounts receivable.

- Repayment of officer's loans.

- Liabilities assumed or paid off by the buyer.

- Management, consulting, or employment contracts/agreements for the full term of the arrangement.

- Payment of rent for or sale of real or personal property associated with the sale of the company.

- Interest on any promissory notes made by the buyer.

- Dividend payments made by the company in association with the business sale.

Unassumed Payables

If the business sale is going to be structured as an asset sale, *the buyer will most likely not assume any of the debt or current payables of the business.* Even in a corporate stock sale, the terms agreed to may stipulate that certain current and long-term liabilities be retired before or at the closing. You must ensure that enough cash is allocated for this contingency, if appropriate. Some examples of liabilities that you may have to retire before selling the business include:

- Any promissory note or other debt instrument for which you have agreed to be personally liable.

- Any unfunded portions of an employee retirement program from which the company may have borrowed.

- Any mortgage obligations that are not assumable by a new party.

- Any officer loans on the books.

- All current liabilities.

In many business sale transactions, the following cash adjustments are usually made at the closing:

> The agreed upon price for the business corporate stock or designated business assets:
>
> *Plus*   the negotiated value of the inventory as of the day of the closing,
> *Plus*   the negotiated value of the real estate (if applicable),
> *Plus*   the cash and cash equivalents in the business,
> *Plus*   the accounts receivable at a negotiated amount to account for uncollectables,
> *Minus*   the accounts payable,
> *Minus*   the long-term or other debt not being assumed as part of the negotiated agreement.

There are many variations to the above listing of adjustments, but they will all have been negotiated and agreed to well before the closing date. Some buyers will want a "clean slate" deal where all receivables and payables are resolved by the seller before the sale or collected/paid right after the sale. Many times the seller takes responsibility for collection of the receivables after the sale (especially if there are some aging, substantial accounts). Whatever your arrangements, make sure that you accurately estimate the amount of cash that you will either receive or pay in accordance with these adjustments.

Personal Cash Requirements

Last, and certainly not least, is the *amount of cash that you will personally require for the next phase of your life.* Even if you have agreed to a payout over some period of time, you will most likely require some cash at the closing for personal reasons. It may also be wise to insist on a significant amount of cash from the buyer to ensure that they are personally and financially motivated to make the business succeed. Even if you are the seller of a very profitable, cash-rich business and do not need much up-front funds from a buyer, you are well advised to seek at least 25% of the selling price in cash from the buyer at the time of sale. This is especially true if the buyer is an individual who will be using the business as the primary source of collateral. The last thing you want to do is to take back the business after the buyer has defaulted on their obligation to you. Most likely, the business will be so far gone and you so removed from it that your remaining equity in the business will be worthless.

Many business sellers want enough cash to retire all of their personal debts, such as their home mortgage, personal car loans, credit card debt, and perhaps any lingering loans for such things as their children's college education expenses. Additionally, you may be looking forward to a long (and expensive) vacation or a condo in Florida for the winter. Whatever your personal needs, be sure to estimate the amount of cash you will need for them and include it in the total cash you are to receive from the business sale.

To satisfy the above needs, you may require a significant amount of cash as a minimum in the sale of a business for which you agree to provide financing. Typically, cash requirements range from a low of 25% up to 50%, and sometimes even higher. A problem could develop in finding a financial (versus strategic) buyer who is capable of coming up with this amount of cash. Do not forget that the buyer will still have to provide operating capital for the business plus pay their own professional advisor fees, not to mention other ancillary costs associated with the takeover of an operating business (new advertising, signage, transfer taxes, etc.).

Even if the cash requirements are high, it's better to estimate them early so as to avoid dealing with a potential buyer that does not have access to the necessary funds. For example, if you thoughtfully estimate your cash requirements to be $500,000, then whether this is 25% or 75% of your expected selling price does not really matter. That is your cash requirement. Accordingly, you and/or your broker can limit your search for a buyer to only those who can demonstrate an ability to come up with a minimum of $500,000 plus their own expenses and operating capital requirements.

Selling Your Business for All-Cash

One of the downsides to accepting an all-cash deal for the purchase of your business is that all of your profit from the sale will be taxed in the year in which you receive the funds. This will put many of you in the highest tax bracket possible and basically serve to maximize the tax impact on you. Taking deferred payments of any kind, whether as an installment sale or an earn-out, will spread your income over several tax years and may help to minimize your tax exposure by moving your income into later years when your total income and consequential tax exposure may not be as large. Even by structuring the sale to receive the proceeds over just two tax years may prove beneficial.

For example, you may want to schedule the business sale closing as close to the end of a calendar year as possible and take half the proceeds in December and the other half in January. For personal income tax purposes, this will spread your income into two tax years. This could be a significant tax advantage to you. The added benefit is that you will essentially receive all of your business sale proceeds at once (just spread over a short period of about a month).

However you structure the sale, remember that it will trigger a "tax event" of some magnitude for you, and you will want to be sure that the payments you will be liable for to the state and federal tax authorities are fully covered.

One other downside to an all-cash deal is that you will probably be offered less money for your business than if you accept any kind of deferred payment arrangement. The main reason for this is that money today is perceived to be more valuable than money in the future. Anyone who accepts future payments takes a greater risk of not being paid. Even though interest rates are applied to compensate you for taking future payments and, therefore, are intended to cover the issue of risk, experience has shown that buyers will usually want a price concession if they pay all-cash for your business. Typically, this will run as a discount of from 5% to 20% of the value they may otherwise pay through a promissory note or other kind of deferred payment schedule.

Another problem with requiring an all-cash sale is that you will certainly reduce the available pool of potential buyers for your business. The vast majority of prospective business buyers expect to leverage their cash as much as possible. Most financial types of buyers will not even consider the purchase of a business that does not offer some amount of purchase financing. By requiring all-cash, you may be restricting the potential sale of your business to a very narrow field of strategic buyers only.

Personally Financing the Sale

Strategic Move #23:

"Accept the fact that you will most likely have to finance at least part of your business sale and plan accordingly."

No matter whether you like the idea or not, you will most likely have to take a promissory note ("hold paper") to complete the sale of your business, especially if you are selling to a financial buyer. I know most sellers just want to sell their business and be done with it, but it usually does not work like that, especially with smaller businesses. Unless your company is extremely profitable, very well established, has a strong, consistent, and loyal customer base in a growing market, most banks and other lending institutions will loan only a relatively small portion of the business value, if anything at all. This is especially true if a significant portion of the business value is in "goodwill." In fact, many lending institutions will not loan more than 70% of the fair-market value of the tangible assets, and will not loan any portion of the goodwill at all. So, unless the buyer has a significant amount of cash, you should think about how much, and under what conditions, you will take back a promissory note against the sale of your business.

Some other points that you should consider regarding this topic of seller financing are:

- Most sales of small closely-held businesses are primarily financed by the seller. Some business brokers estimate that at least 75–85% of all small businesses that sell for under $1,000,000 involve the seller "holding paper" to one extent or another.

- Most buyers just do not have the entire amount of the business selling price in cash. There are also many other demands for the buyer's money at the time of transfer of ownership of the business, such as professional advisor fees, transfer taxes and related expenses, as well as operating cash requirements. The buyer also needs to hold a certain amount of ready cash in reserve to cover surprise expenditures and other contingencies.

- Even if the buyer has the available cash at their disposal or is able to obtain outside financing, they will usually want to see a continued financial involvement by you. This serves to establish some confidence on the part of the buyer that your sales and profitability claims about the business they are buying are true. I liken the thinking here to our national defense policy during the years of the cold war: "mutually assured destruction." Most buyers want to enter into a transaction with the feeling that if they fail, you will be significantly hurt as well, without them needing to take legal action against you. They feel that this arrangement helps to ensure that they pay a fair price for a good business. In other words, you both have a strong interest in seeing that the business continues to succeed.

- It's very difficult to obtain third-party financing for the purchase of an operating business. Commercial banks, venture capitalists, and other sources of funds are very wary of financing a transaction of this nature because of the many things that can go wrong under a new owner. Most of the potential problems are extremely difficult to evaluate effectively before the sale of the business. Accordingly, any outside financing may carry such a high interest rate (to cover the risks involved) that the debt load may make the purchase impossible.

- You will usually receive the highest price for your business if you provide the financing for the buyer. That is because you can provide the best terms. You have a great deal more latitude in selecting an interest rate and a payoff period than a conventional lender. Consequently, you will be better able to ensure that a successful sale of the business takes place at the highest reasonable price.

Financing with Promissory Notes

This issue of accepting a promissory note for some portion of the business sale price bears a little more discussion. The promissory note can be a form of deferred compensation from a tax perspective, and may have positive tax benefits for you. You will want to explore this issue with your accountant. Beyond the tax considerations, there are several other variables that need to be considered from both the buyer's and seller's perspectives:

- Amount of the promissory note.

- Interest rate and period over which it is to be paid.

- Security for the promissory note.

Amount of the Promissory Note

The *principal amount of the promissory note* (the amount of money owed) is usually not as flexible as is the interest rate and period of time over which payments are to be made. If the business has been fairly valued, there should be enough cash flow from the business operations to cover the payments the buyer must make to you. Remember, the business must be able to pay itself off through cash flow over a reasonable length of time. You will want to ensure that the amount of the note does not exceed the fair-market value of the assets in the business that are being used as security for the note. Sometimes a buyer will need to provide more cash down (25% to 50% of the purchase price is usual) to lower the amount of money owed, thereby lowering the amount of the payments.

Interest Rate and Time Period

The *interest rate and time period* of the note are key factors in determining whether the business can afford to pay for itself. The interest rates charged by you should be pegged to the prevailing best bank loan rates, or even somewhat lower. You have to be careful about setting the interest rate too far below bank rates because the IRS has the ability to "impute" a fair market interest rate if they determine that the interest rate is too low. Impute means that they will tax you, for example, as if the rate was 8% rather than the 4% rate actually being charged. However, there's usually a wide latitude for negotiation here. For example, at the time of this writing, the best bank rate (prime rate) is about 8% whereas many commercial loans are being written at rates up to 12% and higher. The current SBA-backed commercial note carries an 11% interest rate. To give you an idea of the difference that the spread of interest rates can make in the amount of a $500,000 note amortized over seven years, consider the following:

$500,000 for 7 years @ 4% is $6,834 monthly
$500,000 for 7 years @ 7% is $7,546 monthly
$500,000 for 7 years @ 10% is $8,301 monthly
$500,000 for 7 years @ 12% is $8,826 monthly

The time period of the note is also a key factor when considering the financing of a business sale. You and the buyer will both usually want the note paid off as soon as possible for different reasons. You will want to collect the money for the business to "cash-out" as soon as possible in order to minimize the risk that the money would not be paid. As a seller, your biggest fear in accepting a note for the business is that the buyer will run the business into the ground, effectively making the business assets worthless, and then will not pay the promissory note. You would then recover a business with little or no value, having received only a portion of the business's original value. The buyer wants to pay off the note as soon as possible within the constraints of the business's cash flow so that they can realize the maximum financial benefits as soon as possible. For these reasons, most business sale promissory notes have a time frame in the three- to seven-year range, with a tendency towards the shorter time periods. To see the effect that the different time frames have on payments at a particular interest rate, the following calculations are offered. I have picked 10% as a representative interest rate for illustration purposes:

$500,000 @ 10% for 7 years is $ 8,301 monthly
$500,000 @ 10% for 6 years is $ 9,263 monthly
$500,000 @ 10% for 5 years is $10,624 monthly
$500,000 @ 10% for 4 years is $12,681 monthly
$500,000 @ 10% for 3 years is $16,134 monthly

Obviously, from the data presented above, the interest rate and payment period of a promissory note can have widely different effects on the business's ability to pay the note off. Herein lies fertile ground for negotiations of the business price between the buyer and yourself. For example, if you hold the interest rate and monthly payment amount constant, but vary the payment period between three and seven years, the face amount of the note, (the "amount paid for the business") can vary widely:

$8,301 monthly @ 10% for 3 years = $257,258 promissory note amount
$8,301 monthly @ 10% for 4 years = $327,293 promissory note amount
$8,301 monthly @ 10% for 5 years = $390,690 promissory note amount
$8,301 monthly @ 10% for 6 years = $448,077 promissory note amount
$8,301 monthly @ 10% for 7 years = $500,024 promissory note amount

As you can see from the above example, the choice of the financing terms can change the face amount of the promissory note, and thus the price that the business sells for by about $250,000!

Security for the Promissory Note

Another point to consider is that the *security for the promissory note* from the buyer to you can be a difficult issue to resolve. The buyer normally wants to secure the note with the business assets (after all, didn't you and the buyer just agree as to what the business is worth?). On the other hand, you probably want to secure the note with the personal assets of the buyer (because the buyer could mismanage the business and leave no assets for you to recover in the event of a default). This is a dilemma! The problem here is that both you and the buyer are right to some extent, which in itself suggests the solution. The best approach here is for a 50-50 compromise between you and the buyer. Half the note amount could be secured by the buyer's personal assets and half could be secured by the business assets. This results in the buyer assuming somewhat more risk than you since the buyer has already provided cash as part of the purchase. This is generally seen as fair by a buyer because they control the business assets, and therefore should accept greater risk. This does not always work out quite so neatly, so you and the buyer may want to address this issue early in negotiations to make sure that it will not ultimately be a deal killer.

Taking Corporate Stock in Payment

Strategic Move #24:

"Consider taking the buyer's corporate stock in partial payment for your company."

In a merger or acquisition purchase of your business by another company, you will most likely be asked to accept stock in the merging/acquiring company as part of the transaction terms. After first ensuring that your immediate cash needs are met, accepting stock for the balance of the purchase price may be an excellent decision. This is especially true if the stock is in a publicly-traded corporation where you can evaluate the stock price as a multiple of its earnings. The acquisition of your company could well push the price of the acquiring company's stock up to at least reflect its traditional multiple. In this case, you may receive a bonus over what you otherwise expected from the sale of your business. Consider this example: You sell your privately-held regional distribution business for $4 million which turns out to be eight times your net operating profit of $500,000. You accept cash in the amount of $1 million and stock in the acquiring corporation of $3 million. The acquiring company is a national distributor that is currently selling on the NASDAQ for 15 times earnings.

The addition of your company's earnings of $500,000 will go right to the acquiring company's bottom line and will tend to drive up the share price to maintain their traditional multiple of 15 times earnings. Your $3 million of stock (valued at the price before the purchase of your company) could be worth significantly more based on the new earnings of the acquiring company. The actual amount will be based on many factors, including the size of the acquiring company, the number of shares outstanding, and the vagaries of the stock market in general. But the potential is there for you to make even more money than you anticipated. Of course, stock prices have a way of going down as well as going up and this is a risk that you will want to consider carefully.

Other considerations in accepting corporate stock are:

- Will you be required to hold it for a specific period of time before it can be sold?

- Is the stock designated as common or preferred stock, or some other special class of stock that contains certain restrictions?

- Is it voting stock and, if so, what percentage ownership will you hold in the company?

- Will you be offered a seat on the Board of Directors of the acquiring company as a way of looking out for your investment?

All of these considerations are some of the factors that you should carefully evaluate and negotiate in accepting corporate stock in payment for the purchase of your company.

Taking an Earn-Out

Strategic Move #25:

"Consider taking an earn-out to boost the ultimate sale price of your business or to resolve a negotiation impasse."

An earn-out is additional or deferred compensation paid to a seller based on the future profitability (or other criteria) of the company being purchased. This is especially useful in selling a company in a turnaround situation or one that is in a temporary business downturn, but must still be sold now. An earn-out can be a portion of the agreed-upon purchase price or it can be an amount over the sales price which is paid as a bonus to the seller as an incentive to stay with the company in order to help maintain management continuity and/or to increase sales and profits. However, you should never agree to take an earn-out that is based on profits, unless you are selling to a publicly-traded corporation where standard accounting practices are established by the SEC. A wily business operator of a private company can manipulate the profit picture in such a way as to not show an increase in profits during your earn-out period, even if the business climate is dramatically improving. It's much better to tie an earn-out to gross revenues or to the number of units sold. The formula should be simple and easily verifiable such as: $1.00 per unit sales of item "x" over a base quantity of 25,000 through a specified number of fiscal years, or 5% of all gross revenues over the base amount of $500,000 for a certain period of time. You can also take an earn-out in which you receive corporate shares, or even options to purchase shares, at attractive prices in the acquiring company instead of cash payments. There are many possibilities to structure an otherwise impossible deal by using an earn-out strategy.

A Word About Voting Seats on Your Board

If you decide to sell your business by holding all or part of the financing, I strongly recommend that you receive a voting seat on the Board of Directors. Of course, you will have to stay current with what is going on with the company in order to provide broad guidance as to new directions the company may want to take. This may be very important to protecting your investment in the funds that are owed to you. If you envision spending all of your time on the golf course or some other form of leisure retirement, you may want to consider a method of sale that results in an all-cash buyout. Frequently an all-cash purchase will mean a lower sale price and a greater tax exposure to you but may well be worth the peace of mind that this brings.

Even in the case of the sale of a non-incorporated, sole proprietorship business, if you are going to hold financing as part of the sale terms, you may want to insist that the buyer operate the company as a corporation. This way you will be able to have a seat on the new corporation's Board of Directors (even if there are only two or three members). This will allow you to have an insight as to how the business is progressing and have a say in new or changing approaches to the way things have normally been done.

A savvy buyer of your business will probably not object to your serving as a Director. Having your experience and knowledge on a continuing basis may be very important to the overall success of the business under its new ownership. Often, you can provide the rationale behind past business decisions that may save the new business owner from making mistakes already experienced by you in the past. So if you are up to it and are financing some part of the business sale, ensure that you are appointed to the business's Board of Directors for the period that covers your payout or earn-out agreement.

Third-Party Financing

Strategic Move #26:

"Assist the buyer with third-party financing in order to help sell your business for cash."

If you require an all-cash purchase of your business, you may have to consider assisting with third-party financing. The buyer may have a significant amount of cash, but not enough to complete the entire deal. In some cases, the buyer may find a lender who will advance the remaining funds, but a security guarantee will be required from you, as the business seller. In this case, you may be asked to escrow a certain portion of the business sale proceeds for a period of time or grant a first mortgage position on the separately owned business real estate. If you accept any of these conditions, then you effectively do not have a complete cash deal that takes you entirely out of the picture. However, this may be an acceptable compromise for you that lies between the all-cash deal and the seller financing alternative.

However, there are some reasons that you may not want a bank to participate in the financing of your business sale:

• A bank loan will take a substantial amount of time to arrange and the costs of the overall business sale transaction will increase (appraisal costs, origination fees, points, etc.).

• The bank will most likely want to structure its payment terms ahead of you (if you are participating in the financing). This means the bank will want to be paid entirely before any payments flow to you.

• The bank may require a security guarantee for its funds backed by your personal assets in addition to the business assets. You may not want to tie up your personal assets in this way.

There are third-party financing options other than banks, such as venture capitalists and finance companies of all sorts. The financing terms of any of these entities are bound to be less attractive than those the buyer will get from a bank, but are another source of financing that should be explored, if a bank loan is not available.

The best bank financing arrangement for both you and the buyer may be a loan backed by the Small Business Administration (SBA). Although the SBA generally secures only bank loans for startup or expanding businesses, it is possible for the buyer to obtain a loan to buy your company assets under certain conditions. If you have a well-qualified buyer in all respects other than cash, and you absolutely will not or cannot finance the purchase yourself, it may be worth working with the buyer to structure your business sale in such a way that they will qualify for an SBA guaranteed loan.

Tax Considerations

Strategic Move #27:

"Carefully plan your business sale structure to minimize the income taxes you will pay."

As with almost every other business transaction in life, Uncle Sam will be right there when you sell your business, looking for a cut of the proceeds. You and your accountant can minimize your tax exposure by carefully structuring the business sale and by having a well-crafted estate plan. Sometimes this will present a problem to the potential buyer because what may be an advantageous business sale structure to you may not be such a good deal for them. However, if you have structured the sale the way you want it in advance and present this as a "fait accompli" to the buyer, you will have a better chance of completing the sale on your terms. Some issues you will need to consider are:

- Structuring the sale in relation to your estate plan.

- Recapturing past depreciation of assets as current income.

- Selling the assets or the stock if your business is a corporation.

- Installment sale considerations.

- Converting a regular corporation to a sub-chapter S corporation for sale purposes.

- Sole proprietorship/partnership versus corporation.

- Capital gains versus ordinary income tax.

Business Sale Structure Relative to Your Estate Plan

You will want to *structure the sale of your business in relation to your estate plan* if you have one. In the next section, I will address the issue of estate planning in more detail. For now, keep in mind that you will want to mesh as closely as you can with your estate planning process in order to minimize or even eliminate future estate and, perhaps, current income taxes. If you are selling a family-owned business to a family member, this may be of more importance than if you are selling to an outside person or entity. Even if your estate plan does not play a role at this point, you should be aware of how you want the proceeds from the business sale to flow to you now and in the future with respect to your overall estate plan.

Recapture of Depreciation

When planning for the income tax consequences of selling your business, you should be alert to the IRS requirement to *recapture the past depreciation of assets as current income.* This means that the assets are therefore subject to ordinary income taxation upon the sale of your business. For example, much of the machinery, furniture, fixtures, automotive, and other equipment will probably have been depreciated down to a salvage value which can be as little as 10% (or even less) of its original value. Many times, the depreciation expense that your business has taken for the asset is only a bookkeeping expense which does not reflect the true value of the asset as it exists today. For example, if you purchased a piece of production machinery ten years ago for $100,000, chances are that you have depreciated that asset down to a residual or salvage value of $10,000. In reality, the equipment may still be worth nearly as much as what you paid for it ten years ago! Many pieces of production equipment such as machine tools, heavy construction equipment, and the like, do not devalue very rapidly if they are maintained properly. In the example of the production machine that you depreciated down to $10,000, the current market value may well be $75,000. If you allocate this amount of the sale price of the business to that asset, you will have a taxable ordinary income of $65,000 ($75,000 allocated sales price less $10,000 salvage value).

Asset or Corporate Stock Sale

The issue of *selling your business corporation as an asset or stock sale* will have tax implications that you need to consider. For reasons other than just tax issues, the buyer will most likely want to buy the assets of your company and form their own new corporation to operate the business. You, on the other hand, will most likely want to sell the corporate stock. The buyer usually does not want to buy the corporate stock of your existing corporation for at least two reasons:

- The potential for hidden contingent corporate liabilities that may come up at a later time, and

- The ability to buy the business assets separately and assign a new, non-depreciated value to them (establish a new depreciation basis). They will then be able to begin their own depreciation schedule and realize a tax shelter benefit against their future earnings.

Installment Sale

In many sales of small businesses, the seller takes a promissory note for some portion of the overall business sale price and elects to have it treated as an installment sale by the IRS. The following is a simple example of an installment sale to demonstrate the concept. Assume that you sell your business on June 30 for $1,000,000. The primary company assets consist of machinery and other equipment with a depreciated tax basis of $400,000. The buyer agrees to pay you $200,000 in cash and the balance of $800,000 in a promissory note with a 6% interest rate payable in eight equal annual installments of $100,000 plus accrued interest. You would calculate your taxable gain as follows:

Cash received (in year of sale)	$ 200,000
Promissory note (principal amount)	$ 800,000
Business selling price	$1,000,000
Computation of taxable gain	
Selling price	$1,000,000
Less adjusted basis	$ 400,000
Gross gain	$ 600,000
Gross percentage profit	= Gross gain/Business selling price
	= $600,000/$1,000,000
	= 60%
Payment received in year of sale	= $200,000
Reportable gain in year of sale	= gross percentage profit x cash received
	= 60% x $200,000
	= $120,000

Reportable gain in first year of installment period = (Annual payment x gross profit percentage) + interest

$$= (\$100,000 \times 60\%) + \$48,000 \text{ (interest)}$$
$$= \$60,000 + \$48,000 \text{ (interest)}$$
$$= \$108,000$$

Note: The actual tax due will be dependent on the allocation of the income between ordinary income and capital gains. The interest paid will be taxed as ordinary income and a portion of the $60,000 may be taxed this way as well due to the requirement to recapture depreciation expenses as ordinary income. These issues will be very specific to your particular business and personal circumstances.

Converting a C Corporation to a Sub-Chapter S Corporation

You may want to *convert your C-type corporation to a sub-chapter S corporation* prior to the time you plan to sell your business. This will allow you to sell the assets of the corporation and pass the gain to the individual shareholders. They will in turn be taxed at their personal rate and there will be no corporate level tax. This process will avoid the double taxation problem of both corporate taxes as well as personal taxes. However, not every corporation can convert to a sub-chapter S status because of various restrictions that are applied by the IRS. For example:

- There is a limit on the number of shareholders allowed in a sub-chapter S corporation.

- There is a restriction on the type of voting stock that is allowed.

- There is a minimum amount of time that must elapse after conversion to a sub-chapter S corporation before the business can be sold or liquidated. Otherwise the taxes will be assessed as they would be for a regular corporation.

- If the company was once a sub-chapter S corporation and then changed to a regular corporation and you now want to change it back, even more requirements apply.

Although the process of converting to a sub-chapter S corporation for the purposes of selling your business is long and cumbersome, the tax savings may be worth the effort. Long lead-time planning is definitely required and you should seek the advice of your corporate accountant and attorney to see if this option makes sense for your business.

Sole Proprietorship Versus a Corporation

If you are operating your business as a *sole proprietorship or partnership* at the time you begin planning to sell, there is no tax reason or other benefit to convert to a corporation in anticipation of the sale.

Capital Gains Versus Ordinary Income

There is a significant difference in tax rates under the most recent (1997) tax law changes regarding *capital gains and ordinary income.* The federal capital gains tax rate has now been changed back to 20% from a previous level of 28%. This compares with a top ordinary income tax rate of 31%. Clearly, as a seller, you will want to allocate as much of the business sale price to capital gains as you can, but this will usually set up a conflict with a business buyer. The buyer will most likely want to allocate as much of the business purchase price to a current expense as possible in order to take advantage of the immediate tax shelter opportunity. As an illustration, let's say that you sell your company for $1,000,000 (as in the earlier example), but the buyer offers you $400,000 for the business and a consulting contract for $600,000 ($125,000 per year for five years). This allows the buyer to write off, as an expense, the $600,000 against the business over the next five years. This shelters the buyer's taxes on the $125,000 of profit the company is making. This is a pretty good deal for the buyer, and you as the seller must take $600,000 as ordinary income at a 50% higher tax rate (31% versus 20%). Not to mention there is no interest on the $600,000 or security arrangement to protect you in case of a default! This is an extreme and very simple example, but it shows you the differences that can result from the buyer and seller trying to best position themselves within the U.S. Tax Code.

Estate Planning

Strategic Move #28:

"If you do not already have an estate plan, you owe it to yourself, your business, and your family to put one in place now."

For most business owners, the prospect of estate planning is something they do not want to even think about. Perhaps it's the fear of facing your own mortality or maybe it's because the whole subject is so darn complicated! I accept the broad economic concept of a need for wealth redistribution in a free economy society. Clearly, if there were no inheritance tax provisions, then in a relatively short time 99% of the nation's wealth would be concentrated in 1% of the population. Of course, as history teaches us, this would lead to an ultimate conflict between the "haves" and the "have nots" long before those percentages were reached. So, to avoid the creation of a privileged aristocracy and the ultimate resulting anarchy on the part of the "have nots," the government has imposed an inheritance tax requirement. The problem comes in as a result of the complexity to which our lawmakers have allowed this basically simple concept to evolve. The rules are so complicated and the jargon so foreign, that the ordinary person cannot even begin to understand the ins and outs of the tax code. Enter the financial and estate planners. A multibillion dollar industry exists just to tell us how to pay our taxes, because even the IRS cannot explain it to the taxpayer! Notwithstanding all of the faults with the process, you and I are caught up in it and must find a way to effectively deal with it, or suffer the financial consequences. You will most likely need an estate plan as part of your early preparations for selling your business and will have to deal with one or more of the specialists in the field.

Most small-business owners are very busy running their companies and have little or no time for the education, effort, and expense it takes to set up a proper estate plan for themselves. As I have already said, you need an estate plan to protect your heirs and business in the event of your untimely death or disability. An estate plan can also be very useful while you are alive and in the process of selling your business to a family member or a close business associate. I will discuss the issue of estate planning in more detail as it relates to the transfer of ownership within a family-owned business in Chapter 5, "Succession Planning for the Family-Owned Business." Here I will describe the broad concept of estate planning for you and relate it to what you need to consider in the business sale process. This is intended to be an overview of the estate planning field with enough information to get you thinking about what you might need as you prepare your business for sale.

What Is Estate Planning?

Just what is estate planning and how does it affect you relative to preparing your business for sale? Estate planning is the legal and financial process by which you lay out a clear succession framework for your business and other assets in ways that protect your family and heirs from a potentially devastating tax situation and which ensures that the process is carried out in accordance with your wishes. It can also lay out the guidelines for the transfer of ownership in your company so that it will continue to operate in the way you envision for it. You cannot rely on your will alone to ensure an orderly conveyance of the business to your spouse, children, other family members, partners, shareholders, or long-time employees.

Family members who inherit a family business face a significant challenge; not only must they have enough cash (or access to it) to buy the business from the remaining shareholders or partners, but frequently they must pay estate taxes that can be devastatingly large. There is some good news for small-business owners that is evolving as this is written. The newly revised tax code in 1997 allows the owners of closely-held businesses a "qualified" estate tax credit of $1.3 million rather than the $600,000 that was the past rule for many years. A "qualified" business must meet certain requirements established by the U.S. Tax Code. For example, the business must be at least 50% owned by one family member or 70% owned by two. The total value of the business must also be at least 50% of the overall value of the total estate. This increase in exemption is available immediately to all qualifying closely-held family business owners and farm owners and is to be gradually phased in up to $1 million to other taxpayers over the next several years. By then the business tax credit will only be worth $300,000 (the amount greater than a nonbusiness owner would receive). What this means is that you are better off dying now from a tax perspective, but I do not recommend this as an estate planning strategy! Although this is excellent news and will help a great deal of small businesses stay in the family and avoid liquidation upon the demise of their owners, it certainly does not eliminate the need for estate planning for most small-business owners. In fact, there are a great many businesses with valuations well in excess of the $1.3 million. Or, the valuation may be smaller, but when it is combined with the business owners' other assets, the total exceeds the new exemption amount.

Let's look at an example to understand the implications of no estate planning if you suddenly pass away. If you are an unmarried business owner with almost everything you own tied up in your business for a total estate valuation of say $5 million, the tax (with the new credit of $1.3 million) will still be about $2 million. Does your business have enough free cash to cover this? Does your business successor or heir have enough to pay this sum of money or will the business perhaps have to be liquidated (or sold under pressure) to pay these taxes? The answer is most likely no; there is not enough cash to pay the taxes. Even if you are married and intend to pass the business along to your spouse and/or children, the tax implications may be so substantial as to force a liquidation of the business to satisfy the tax requirements. A properly prepared estate plan will help ensure that this does not happen.

The basics of estate planning include the following major objectives:

- Legacy planning to build wealth for future generations.

- Business succession planning to allow for the successful transition of a family-owned business to the next generation.

- Probate avoidance to eliminate the costs and delays associated with probating a will.

- Tax planning to save a significant amount of taxes on your personal estate.

- Longevity planning to provide health care, powers of attorney, and medical instructions in the case of incapacitation.

- Protection of assets from liability through the use of a family limited partnership and certain trusts.

- Pre- and postnuptial agreements to keep business and other assets in the family.

- Pension planning to maximize the gain and minimize the tax on your Keogh, 401-K, or other pension planning mechanism.

Your estate plan will most likely include these basic components:

- A will.

- One or more trusts.

- Tax planning strategies.

- Gift planning strategies.

- Competency contingencies.

Your Will

A *will* indicates who, according to your wishes, gets what parts of your estate, may provide some tax planning, and will name the executors, trustees, and any other fiduciaries who will administer the document.

Trusts

A *trust* allows you to put certain assets (including stock or partnership shares in your business) into the control of a second party in order for them to be used for the benefit of a third party. A "party" can be a person, a bank, a corporation, or any other legal entity. Trusts can be made to be revocable or irrevocable. If properly drafted and funded, trusts offer the following benefits:

- Professional management of your assets.

- Tax savings because trusts have their own tax bracket that may be lower than your personal tax bracket.

- More tax savings if the trustee distributes the assets to a beneficiary who is in a lower tax bracket than yours.

- Even more tax savings potential if your assets are completely out of your ownership and control because they will not be counted in your estate for inheritance tax purposes.

- Avoidance of probate because the trustee can distribute the trust's assets upon your death without probating a will if properly funded.

One important point to keep in mind about the tax savings advantages of trusts is that they generally must be irrevocable to save estate taxes.

Tax Planning Strategies

There are many *tax planning strategy* possibilities within the estate planning framework. Trusts, in and of themselves, can be significant tax planning tools. There are also many different kinds of trusts, depending on your particular situation. Three trusts that may be of special interest to the business owner are GRITs, GRATs, and GRUTs. These trusts give you the power to use the income (taxable) from the trust funds for some period of time. They also provide the maximum amount of estate tax savings.

- A GRIT is a Grantor Retained Interest Trust in which you, as the grantor, can transfer the shares in your business to someone for a specified period of time. During this period, you can receive income. At the end of the period, the trust terminates and your beneficiary (family member, business partner?) receives the ownership of the shares of stock in your business. No tax is paid at that time. If you outline the time frame of the trust, the assets will not be counted in your estate, but if you die before the trust concludes, the assets in the trust will be counted in your estate.

- A GRAT is a Grantor Retained Annuity Trust which is basically the same as a GRIT except that you must receive a specified fixed percentage of the value of the assets in the trust for a certain period. If you survive the trust period, the total trust amount is excluded from your estate. If you die before the trust time frame expires, the amount remaining in the trust is added to your estate.

- A GRUT is a Grantor Retained Unit Trust and is the same as a GRAT except that the income as a percentage of the trust varies annually. A GRUT is good for you to use if you want flexibility in the amount of income you will receive each year.

Gift Planning Strategies

Gift planning strategies also abound in the world of estate planning. I have discussed two charitable trusts in Chapter 5 that are especially useful for business owners planning to transfer ownership of their company within the family. But there are many other aspects to be considered relative to gifts in estate planning. For example, there are the following:

- The gift tax exclusion.

- The so-called Kiddie Tax.

- The Uniform Gifts to Minors Act.

- Spousal gifts.

- Joint ownership gifts.

Gift Tax Exclusion

The *gift tax exclusion* allows you to give $10,000 per year per person without paying a gift tax and without including this amount in your ultimate estate for estate tax purposes. You can give this gift annually to anyone, family or not, and you can give as many total gifts annually as you want, as long as the amount does not exceed $10,000 per person. If you are married, you and your spouse can each give $10,000 ($20,000 per couple) to an individual. As an example, let's say that you want to leave a large portion of your incorporated business to your family. At some point, you can begin gifting shares in the company valued at up to $10,000 to each of your children, and your grandchildren as well. If you are married with two children and five grandchildren, you could gift $140,000 per year of stock in your company tax-free. All of this would be outside of your eventual estate. You should note that the above amounts are approximate. The Tax Reform Act of 1997 allows escalation of the gift amounts tied to an inflation index. For example, if the inflation rate is 3% in 1998, the gift tax exclusion will rise from $10,000 to $10,300. It will continue to increase in relation to inflation for each year thereafter. Depending on the size of your estate and your timing, you could eventually transfer the entire ownership of your company to your family tax-free! Of course, the problem of control of the company comes into play, but by using trusts and/or family limited partnerships, you can find a way to "have your cake and eat it, too!" See Chapter 5 for further discussion of these estate planning techniques for family-owned businesses.

Kiddie Tax

The *Kiddie Tax* allows you to transfer income-producing assets to your minor children who most likely are in a lower income tax bracket than you. They will own the assets and pay a lower tax, but you will control the assets as the legal guardian. There are age rules and exemption issues to check out here, but this is another way of gifting your assets in order to lower or avoid ultimate taxes.

Uniform Gifts To Minors

The *Uniform Gifts To Minors Act* is an alternative to giving gifts outright or in trust to minors under the age of 21. To make a gift, you give the funds to a custodian for the benefit of the recipient. The custodian can be an adult in the minor's family, a legal guardian, a trust company, or other legal entity. If the gift is in the form of money, you can be both the donor and the custodian. As the custodian, you have broad authority to hold, manage, and invest the funds, and use the proceeds for the benefit of the minor. At the age of 21, all the money goes to the minor and becomes part of their estate. You should note that once you give a gift under this act, it is irrevocable. Even if you are the custodian for the minor, the money earned is taxed only at the minor's tax bracket rate. So you have control over the money that you intend to eventually give to the minor anyway (for college expenses for instance), and the money's earnings are taxed at a much lower rate. In addition, it is out of your estate for estate tax purposes (unless you die before the minor reaches 21).

Spousal Gifts

Spousal gifts are unlimited and there is no gift tax to be paid no matter how much is given. This is a very powerful opportunity that, if planned correctly, can save up to about $200,000 in estate taxes! This involves the use of a clause known by several different names including the "credit shelter clause," the "unit trust clause," and the "federal exemption clause." If you do not have an estate plan and your estate exceeds $1.2 million (or $600,000 if you do not have a spouse), then don't walk, but run to a competent estate planning attorney to take advantage of this opportunity for estate tax shelter. Take this action independent of your plans for selling the business or transferring business assets within your family. You should note that the above amounts are approximate. The Tax Reform Act of 1997 provides for an escalation of these amounts up to approximately $2 million (for a married couple) by the year 2006.

Joint Ownership Gifts

Joint ownership gifts can be made in many different ways with various advantageous tax implications. For example:

- You can add someone's name as joint owner on real estate and file a new deed.

- You can add another person's name on U.S. Savings Bonds and a tax will not become due until that person cashes in the bonds.

- You can buy shares of stock and designate another person as a joint owner.

- You can open a joint bank account with another person and there will be no tax incurred until they make a withdrawal.

There are also some downside issues with joint ownership gifts which you should consider. For example:

- You may need to file a gift tax IRS return on any amount over the exclusion.

- You may be exposing the giftee to possible creditors in the case of real estate or similar assets.

Competency Contingency Planning

Competency contingencies include such things as living wills and health-care powers of attorney. They are legal documents that spell out, for the fiduciary you select and/or the physician who is caring for you, what to do if you become incompetent or incapacitated.

As you can probably tell by now, there are many facets and nuances to estate planning. It's a complicated field that is very specific to your particular situation and only a professional planner can really help you. The specific application to you as a business seller tends to blur at times, but there is clearly a need for you to have an estate plan in the larger picture of life. Hopefully, this overview has given you enough ideas to decide to set up an estate plan, even if you are going to sell your business to someone other than a family member. Even if you don't transfer the business within your family, you most likely will realize a significant amount of wealth from its sale. You will want a plan on how to keep as much as you can for yourself at the time of the sale. And you will want a plan that passes along as much as you can to your heirs when you go to your larger reward in the hereafter.

Real Estate Considerations

Strategic Move #29:

"Consider selling your business real estate separately from your company."

In almost all cases in privately-owned, closely-held corporations, it is better for the business real estate to be owned separately by the business owner. The real estate is then leased to the corporation for its business purposes. There are very good reasons for this from a tax and potential business sale point of view.

If your corporation owns the real estate and the real estate generates an operating loss (which the real estate often does when considering the allowable depreciation expenses), the loss can only be used to offset the corporate income. If the corporation is operated (intentionally or unintentionally) to show little or no profit, then the real estate losses as a tax shelter will be of no value. If you own the real estate personally outside of the corporation, then the losses (within limitations, of course) can be applied against your income for personal tax savings.

If your corporation owns real estate which generates an operating loss and your corporation shows a profit, then that profit can be reduced by the amount of the real estate loss, thereby saving corporate taxes. But, unless you operate the corporation as a sub-chapter S, the only way to personally receive the benefits of this real estate tax shelter is to take the proceeds in the form of dividends which are themselves taxable to you personally and are a nondeductible expense to the corporation.

Another way you can benefit by owning the real estate outside of the corporation is when improvements are to be made to the property. In addition to the tax deductible lease payments made by the corporation to you, the company can pay for all improvements as expense items. The income from the rental of the property is taxed only once to you and the improvement expenses will shelter income from taxes within the corporation.

If the corporation owns the property when you sell the real estate as part of the business sale, it may face double taxation as corporate profits and then again as dividends to you. By owning the real estate outside of the corporation when you sell the business, you can sell the real estate separately. The gain on the real estate will be taxed only once to you. You may be able to allocate a higher than normal value to the real estate as part of the overall business sale. This, in turn, may lower the overall tax payment you have to make. This arrangement may also be attractive to the buyer since they will receive a depreciable asset they can readily use to offset income for tax purposes. In fact, some sellers have arranged for all or most of the business sale value normally attributable to goodwill (a nondepreciable intangible asset) to be allocated to an inflated value for the real estate (which is a depreciable asset).

One other good reason for personally holding ownership of the real estate outside of your business is that you will increase the number of potential qualified buyers. The reason for this is that you will be able to offer the business for sale at a lower price, separate from the real estate. This will help to overcome part of the biggest obstacle to business buyers; the amount of cash required. Of course, you will have to provide an acceptable lease to the business buyer, both in rental fees and length, but you can then handle the real estate separately. You may choose to hold the real estate yourself for income purposes, sell the real estate to a third party, or transfer ownership to your family heirs by any number of ways including a family limited partnership or a family real estate corporation. Either one of these last two approaches is a good tax planning strategy if you are planning to leave the real estate to your heirs, but want the income that the real estate will provide to flow to you during your lifetime.

In Summary

This foregoing discussion of the real estate issue and all of the other discussions about tax and financial implications are necessarily general in nature. They are intended to spur you to start planning with your professional tax advisor and estate planner as to how best to structure a business sale arrangement for your personal circumstances.

In the next chapter, I will cover the subject of succession planning for the family-owned business. Although many businesses may not consider themselves as family-owned, you fit the loose definition of "family-owned" if you have children or other close family members (including your spouse) that could possibly take over the business from you. Even if you are not planning to transfer your business ownership to a family member as a way of selling your business, you should read this next chapter. It will provide information that you may want to use on an interim basis as you prepare to sell your business to an entity outside of your family. Do not forget that if you die or become incapacitated before you are able to sell your business, your company ownership will pass to your heirs. Whether you intended it or not, your business will become family-owned. Our untimely death is not something that any of us relish thinking about, but it is always a possibility. An astute business owner will plan for this eventuality to protect family and employees by ensuring an orderly transition of the ownership of their company upon their passing.

5

Succession Planning for the Family-Owned Business

- *Introduction*
- *Personal Issues*
- *Strategic Issues*
- *Financial Issues*
- *Developing a Succession Plan*
- *Developing a Financial Transition Plan*
- *Succession Plan Checklist*

Introduction

A family-owned business is an operating company in which more than one member of the immediate family has ownership, control, or other significant involvement in the running of the business. A family-owned business can also be defined as a company with second- or later-generation ownership, independent of whether there is more than one immediate family member involved. Sometimes it's not clear just what constitutes a family-owned business, especially in the first generation. The founder/owner of a first generation business needs to decide whether they want—and are able to—pass control of their business to a family member. If they have a son or daughter or other close family member to whom they hope to pass the business, they should consider themselves a family-owned business and pay particular attention to the issues and concerns raised in this chapter. If the business is already second-generation (or later), and the owners wish to maintain family ownership from one generation to the next, then this is clearly a family-owned business.

Family-owned businesses are a major economic force in the United States. There are over 12 million of them and they account for about 50 percent of the country's gross domestic product and 65 percent of all wages paid. However, only about 30 percent of family-owned businesses make the transition from the founders of the business to the second generation and 90 percent never make it into a third generation. This is not to say that the businesses fail. Instead, the business eventually leaves family ownership and passes into other hands through a private sale, merger, acquisition, or public offering.

Due to the large number of family-owned businesses and the important role they play in the economy, there has been a tremendous amount of interest in them in the last few years as a special segment of the business world. Numerous studies and surveys have been done to identify the characteristics of these businesses in an attempt to better understand their nature and to improve the odds of keeping a family-owned business in the family. The most recent major survey completed at the time of the writing of this book is the *Arthur Andersen/MassMutual American Family Business Survey '97*. This survey is a comprehensive and statistically valid study that analyzes family-owned business planning, growth, and succession issues in detail. The Arthur Andersen Center for Family Business and MassMutual—The Blue Chip Company conducted the survey, with assistance provided by the Loyola University Chicago Family Business Center and the Family Enterprise Center at Kennesaw State University. Significant findings that you may find relevant to your business are as follows:

- Nine out of 10 heads of family-owned businesses believe that the business will still be controlled within their family five years into the future.

- About 40% of the family-owned businesses expect to change leadership within the next five years and more than 50% expect a change within the next 10 years.

- A surprising 10% of family-owned businesses are headed simultaneously by two or more CEOs. This is generally unheard of in the private business sector.

- Only about 5% of the current family-owned businesses are headed by a woman but 25% of the businesses surveyed say that the next CEO may well be a female.

- Approximately 75% of family-owned business CEOs have put in place some form of estate planning.

- Only 30% of family-owned businesses have a written strategic business plan to refer to for the future.

- Only 20% of the family-owned business leaders report having more than 80% of their net worth tied up in the business.

- The median annual revenues of the businesses participating in the survey are $9 million which seems to indicate that many family-owned businesses are not typical small "Mom and Pop" enterprises but frequently are much larger and more sophisticated organizations.

Whatever your status as a family-owned business, large or small, you will most likely want to consider the many issues involved in transitioning your business to a family successor. Chapter 8, "Resources for Preparing Your Business for Sale," contains information on how to contact the Arthur Andersen Center for Family Business, MassMutual, and other related professional organizations for further information.

One of the biggest overall mistakes that controlling owners in a family business make when it comes time for a transition is that they do not put the same time and effort in planning and structuring the business sale as they would if it was an "arms-length" transaction. Many of the same issues apply, such as pricing, terms of the sale, passing of control, timing, and security. These are the same issues that must be dealt with in the sale of the business to an outsider. Consequently, the same level of attention to these issues is required. This includes preparing the business for sale, good faith negotiations, and a spirit of give-and-take for all involved. This leads me to my next recommended strategic move:

Strategic Move #30:

"Transfer ownership in your business to a family member with much the same business considerations you would use in a sale to a stranger."

There are many more issues that work against a successful business continuing as a family-owned business from one generation to the next, than if the business were being sold to an outsider. These issues can be grouped into three significant categories:

- Personal Issues.

- Strategic Issues.

- Financial Issues.

Any one of these issues, if not properly addressed, can impede or even stop the successful transition of the business across the generation gap. I will talk about each of these issues now, and then I will discuss developing a Succession Plan to deal with each of the issues to enable a successful business transition within your family. Keep in mind that these issues are in addition to all of the recommendations I have already made in this book about preparing your business for sale.

Personal Issues

Giving Up Control

One of the most significant problems facing a succession within a family-owned business is the reluctance of the present owner to give up control of the company. This is especially acute if you, as the current owner, are the founder of the business and a transition to a second-generation ownership is being attempted. The root cause of this problem may be the very reason the business is successful; you most likely have put your heart and soul into starting and growing the business. The company has become an integral part of your life, and in many cases defines who you are in your personal and public life. This may be no less true if you are attempting to sell the business to an anonymous buyer, but somehow owners have a much harder time relinquishing control to Junior than they do to a one-time competitor, for example. I think this has to do with a carryover of the authority figure role that you have had to maintain for so many years with your offspring. The role is so ingrained that your psyche cannot conceive of relinquishing it and this sets up a tremendous potential roadblock to a successful transition.

Facing the Inevitable

Another problem that you may have as the business owner is your unwillingness to face the inevitability of your death or incapacitation. As a self-sufficient entrepreneur who has been fighting successfully to develop a strong business for so long, it's hard to imagine or anticipate a time when you cannot do this any longer. Let's face it. We all will physically and mentally decline sooner or later. It's far better to plan for that inevitability now while you are healthy and the business is running well than when you are too sick or tired to even care. You should be happy if you have children who can and want to take over the business! Solving the problems of succession in a family-owned business can be overcome and is almost always worth the extra effort it takes.

Capability of Your Children

In some cases, your children may not be capable of or interested in running your business. In the vast majority of instances, this is a problem that can be overcome by proper planning and careful nurturing and education/training of your business successor. What you need to understand is whether your child actually is not capable, whether your expectations are too high, or whether your intimidation factor is too strong. If there is a lack of interest on the part of your child, you must do everything you can to understand the nature of it. Is it a true lack of interest or a self-protection response that is triggered by a need for independent action that you may not have allowed?

Multiple Children and Leadership

Sometimes, your hoped-for successors may clearly be capable and interested in taking over the business, but there is more than one child, and only one leadership position in the company. Many business owners have struggled with this very issue and it has been known to trigger extremely divisive reactions within a family, including estrangement, life-long bitterness, and even intra-family rivalry and violence. Clearly, this is an issue that must be addressed carefully and effectively if it affects your particular situation.

Although there are a surprising number of family-owned businesses headed by two or more co-CEOs (as discovered by the Arthur Andersen—MassMutual Study), I cannot help but believe that this is not a good idea for a company in the long run. The study does not identify the special problems that go with having multiple people in charge of a business but intuitively I think that this could ultimately lead to serious management problems. It may be far better for your business if you make the sometimes tough decision for a single leadership successor.

Other Heirs

Another issue that faces many business owners who desire to transition their company to continued family ownership is what to do about those family members who do not want to be involved in the family business, but want their "fair share" of the business value as an inheritance. Even if they are not now involved in the business, they may have been an active participant at some point in time. Maybe they worked in the business after school or on weekends. Maybe they feel that they have earned some right to a share in the business because of the life events they or you missed as a result of the intrusion of the business. Perhaps they would like to work in the business if given a chance, but feel that you have not given them a fair opportunity.

Whatever the reasons, for the sake of family harmony you should take into account the feelings and needs of all your children and other close family members (a brother, sister, or brother-in-law, etc.). They may feel they have a right to a piece of the business as you transition out of it.

Inadequate Funding

Certainly, one of the biggest problems is that many times in closely-held businesses that transition to a child, there is barely enough money to adequately fund Mom and Dad's well-earned retirement. There just is not enough money to provide sizable funds for the other children and close family members. Although I have listed this as a personal issue, it also obviously crosses over into being a financial issue as well. I will further discuss this problem later.

Resolving the Problems

All of these aforementioned issues are well documented and have been extensively studied. Many of the personal issues and problems in a family-owned business are not much different than those within a purely family context. Negative factors, such as poor communication, a struggle for independence, high expectations, unresolved conflicts, and jealousy, can all play a role in the business environment, as well as at home in the family setting. The problems are exacerbated in the family-owned business by the fact that business and family issues are constantly intertwined. Sometimes it's very difficult to tell where business relationships end and family relationships begin. On the other hand, very positive factors are at play as well, such as trust, loyalty, understanding, and, of course, love. The key is to harness the positive attributes of family life and apply them to the business setting. But you also need to find a way to keep the two from interfering with the other.

It's no wonder that many business owners find succession planning for a family-owned business to be tougher than building and managing the company! Here are a few ideas and considerations for you to think about in resolving personal issues that may be affecting your family succession planning:

- One solution for dealing with the questionable capability and desire on the part of your children, or the problem of multiple children/family members who want control of your business, is to clearly define the replacement criteria for your role in the company and interview your successor candidate(s) for the position(s). Conduct the interviews much the same way as you would with a stranger. In fact, you may even want to advertise the position(s) and interview candidates from outside of your family for a realistic comparison of capabilities for the position(s). Even though you may really want your child to run the business as President and CEO, perhaps they are not ready yet. It may be wiser to hire an interim company head to help bring your successor along if you find you cannot do it yourself. You can still transfer ownership in the company to your child, while keeping strategic management control for yourself and day-to-day management for a hired professional.

- Sometimes you may find that your hoped-for successor is unwilling to work hard enough to learn the positions within your company that they must become familiar with before you can even consider transferring a modicum of control. The reasons for this can be complex, including laziness and/or an inability to appreciate the opportunity that they have. They may also be arrogant and feel that they are somehow better than the other employees in the company and should not have to learn their jobs. One possible solution for this is to require your child to go to work in another company to learn what the demands of a real job in an impersonal company is all about. If they are successful, this experience may give them a sense of independence and personal accomplishment that will accelerate their maturation process and allow them to return to your business ready and able to take over the mantle of leadership. Of course, there is always the old tried and true method of starting Junior out in the mailroom and requiring him/her to work their way up the corporate ladder to prove their mettle, as well as to learn the business.

- To minimize any internal family conflicts about who will be the one to run the business when you pass on the control, you should designate your successor as early in the process as possible and communicate this clearly to everyone in the family. To ease the inevitable jealousy that will occur among the other family members, be sure to explain why you have selected your particular successor by stressing their strong points relative to the business. Do not point out any shortcomings of the family members not selected. Additionally, you should stress that although your successor is being selected to replace you as the leader in the business, all family members will share in the ownership through stock ownership and/or a partnership interest. Carefully explain why this will be good for everyone involved in the long run.

- There are also times when the business owner may find that all of the possible successors are very capable of running the business. If this is your situation, you may want to carefully carve out important roles for each of the individuals. But you must still designate an overall leader. There are not many privately-held companies that can be successfully run by committee, especially if the committee is comprised of siblings! Your challenge will be to pick the best leader for your company and not necessarily the best salesperson, or best financial manager, etc. These other roles are important, but don't confuse narrow individual capability, however excellent, with an ability for general management capabilities and leadership.

- A good way of getting off the hook personally in a particularly troublesome succession process, where there is more than one possible successor and a competition for the leadership position, is to hire an outside arbitrator. The arbitrator may be able to take a fresh look at the situation and possibly offer solutions and/or compromises that you could not otherwise see (the "forest for the trees" syndrome). Even if the arbitrator does not come up with anything much different that what you tentatively decided in the first place, the whole concept of using an outside expert to recommend a course of action may be used to placate the unhappy family members. You can honestly say that it's the outside expert's idea, not yours.

- Most business owners find that the best way to transition control of the business to a family successor is through a gradual phase-in/phase-out process. This can be as short as a year, but more usually it will take place over several years. This will give you the opportunity to demonstrate every aspect of the leadership role and to observe, teach, and nurture your successor so that you may start your retirement with the confidence that your company is in good hands.

- As you begin the succession planning process, be sure to differentiate in your mind the concepts of management/leadership of your business and the very different concept of ownership. Even in transitioning the business to a family member, you should keep the distinction between management succession and ownership by your ultimate heirs. This will be important in resolving problems that arise in all areas, whether personal, strategic, or financial. For example, you can name many individuals as heirs to a portion of the corporate stock, but you most likely will want to select only one heir as your management/leadership successor in the company. Of course, you will also want your successor to ultimately have control over a majority of the corporate stock in order to maintain their role as your successor after your passing. But 51% is a majority; the other 49% of the company can be used in many other ways. You can pass a portion of ownership on to other heirs (spouse, children, etc.) in order to resolve potential inheritance tax issues, or to address various other strategic concerns.

- Never forget that you, as the founder and/or current leader of the business, have all the control and therefore the primary responsibility to make a successful transition. If you really want the transition to occur, and you are willing to be reasonable, flexible, and forward thinking, your family business can most likely be successfully transitioned.

- I have included an extensive listing of resources in Chapter 8 for you to look into if you want help with any aspect of succession planning, including your interpersonal family relationships. The good news is there are many commercial and public resources to help you keep your family-owned business in the family. In fact, this entire field of family-owned business succession planning and assistance is fast becoming an entire industry in its own right.

Strategic Issues

Often there is not a clear vision for the company that can be articulated and passed to the succeeding generation. Frequently, the business owner/founder has been so busy growing the business and reacting to opportunities and disappointments instinctively that it will be difficult for a successor to continue in the same successful direction. Whether the business is to be sold through an open market transaction or transitioned to a family member, this inability to articulate a long-term vision for the company could severely hurt the business. As it has been said, "You will never get there if you do not know where you are going." If you do not have a clearly written and well-thought-out strategic plan for your company, then it's imperative that you prepare one as part of the succession planning process. As discovered by the Arthur Andersen—MassMutual study referenced earlier, only about 30% of family-owned businesses have a written strategic plan.

Strategic Move #31:

"Develop a written strategic plan to address the long-term business issues of your company."

Other problems crop up if the business itself is undergoing a redefinition of its role in the marketplace at the time of transfer. Clearly this is not an opportune time for the sale of the business under any conditions, but it may be necessary due to a sudden illness of the current owner or a sustained economic downturn that is not expected to improve any time soon. Do not forget that the best time to sell a business, including transitioning it to a successor within your family, is when sales and profits are high and the economic outlook for your company and the industry in general is good. Also, you should not be under personal pressures, such as poor health, mental burn-out, an overwhelming desire to retire immediately, divorce, or any other of the curve balls that life can throw at you. Accordingly, you must plan the business sale/succession carefully and be ready to leave your ownership position somewhat earlier or later than perhaps you would like in order to be able to leave at an opportune time. Too many business owners hang on to ownership much too long and allow their businesses to decline through inattention. Then, without any planning to speak of, they try to transition the business to their children who are ill-prepared for the responsibility.

Sometimes the vision for the company of the family member you are grooming for succession is at extreme odds with your strategic plan. Perhaps your company has been very successful building residential homes for many years and as you begin the transition of the business to your child, you discover they want to stop building homes altogether and just concentrate on land development. Sure, there may be less headaches and problems, but the risks are greater and this is not what the company has been all about. This may present a serious dilemma to you: How do you relinquish control when the strategic vision of your successor is so much at odds with yours? Perhaps the only solution to this situation is compromise or capitulation on someone's part. I know of one company owner who set up a completely separate (but wholly owned) new business division in the company to let the planned successor try their hand at the desired new company direction for several years. My understanding is that this worked out well in satisfying both Dad as well as his daughter that the new business focus was not only viable but even proved to be more profitable.

One of the most critical strategic issues in succession planning is the issue of timing. In succession planning for a family-owned business, timing may be even more critical if you have a particular successor who may not be ready when you are. In a sale outside of the family, there may be many buyers who fit or closely approximate your particular timetable and you may even find it expedient to adjust the price and other conditions of the sale to fit your desired time frame. In a transition to a family member, you may be faced with the prospect of waiting years for your successor to reach the necessary education, experience, and maturity level to take over the business. For example, in my own case, I would like to pass on my business consulting and publishing enterprise to my only son who was born when I was 44 years old. Assuming a minimum need of a business education with an MBA and several years of real life experience, I cannot expect my son to be ready to take over from me until I'm 74! To my way of thinking, I have a timing problem.

Of course, timing problems can work the opposite way as well (and this is the situation in most cases). The potential successor to the business is ready, willing, and able to take over the company, but you have no desire to step down for many years to come. In most family situations, the parent is only in their 50s when the children are in their late 20s or early 30s. Many offspring by this age are anxious to take on the responsibility of the business. A well-thought-out and properly communicated business succession plan can help this situation immensely. A plan showing gradual but steadily increasing responsibility in the business for your successor, with a target timeline for your complete phase-out, will ease this situation. Such a plan can be written to satisfy everyone involved.

Do not overlook the option of *not* transferring ownership and control of your business to your heirs. This may sound somehow un-American, but there are times when the impediments to successful family succession cannot be overcome. You and your family may be better off if you sell the business outright, invest the proceeds wisely for your retirement years, gift what you can to your children and/or grandchildren, and leave the balance to be distributed to your heirs under a good tax-minimizing estate plan.

Financial Issues

Financial issues are probably the single biggest problem in the successful transition of a business within the family. The founder or present family owners need to take cash out of the business for their retirement purposes as their well-deserved reward for the years of risk-taking and hard work. Many times in first-generation ownership, the business is successful and the owners are living a very nice life as a result, but their child has no significant money to buy them out. The business cannot continue to support Mom and Dad in the retirement they envision as well as pay Junior an income to run the business. Although the business may have a good capital position, money is needed to continue to fund the operating expenses of the company and for continued growth and expansion of the business. We all know that a stagnant, undercapitalized business is not good for long-run success. Unfortunately, many businesses are in this dilemma. A majority of family business owners report that they have significantly more than half of their net worth invested in a nonliquid form in their business with no good way to get it out without selling or otherwise hurting the business.

Just like selling a company in the open marketplace, this situation requires a well-founded valuation of the business. In fact, it is probably more important, because in a sale to an outside buyer, a fair-market value for the company at that point in time will be arrived at through the give-and-take of negotiations. In the transition of a privately-held, family-owned business from owner to successor, there will probably be little or no real negotiations. The parent has all the knowledge and control, whereas the child is much less experienced, has little or no control, and generally has no leverage for negotiations. It will be up to you to ensure that you transfer ownership to your successor at a buyout price and terms of payment that do not hobble the company and demean your child. Of course, you need to ensure an adequate compensation for yourself while at the same time transitioning a company that can continue to grow and prosper without you. Adequate capital is the engine of growth in most businesses. The extent that capital can be funded from cash flow may well determine the ultimate long-run success of the company. In fact, there will be a strong incentive for a company that enjoys good profitability to try to minimize the overall value of the business for estate and other tax-minimization purposes. There are several different ways that the IRS will allow you to lower potential taxes but, in general, the IRS requires that the transfer of ownership within a family be a bona fide business transaction valued at a "fair-market price" in accordance with IRS Revenue Ruling 59-60. Any tax adjustments are based on an offset to the fair-market price for the business. I will discuss more about these tax issues later in the section titled "Developing an Estate Plan."

Strategic Move #32:

"Develop a valuation for your family-owned business transition using tax minimization criteria as your primary concern."

Exacerbating the financial picture can be the problem of fairly dividing the business income and ownership among the participating family members. I touched on the personal issues arising out of many family members feeling that they are stakeholders in the business who believe that they deserve their fair share. You may find it difficult to fund your income needs and compensate each succeeding family member for their share of ownership, their labor, and their management of the business. A distinction between compensation for services and transfer of ownership should be arrived at which is fair and balanced. Those family members who do not materially contribute to the operation of the business may have to settle for equity which may only be of tangible value to them at some later date. To paraphrase an old saw: Do not try to be so fair to all concerned that you end up cutting the baby in half. You will obviously end up without a baby!

Throw into this melee the need for estate planning which must take inheritance taxes into consideration and the transition of the business to your family members may not appear to be viable. You absolutely must develop a succession plan in the same way you would prepare your business for sale. Is that not what a transfer to a family member really is? It's a sale of your business to other than a stranger, but all of the same concerns and problems, plus quite a few more, come into play.

Developing a Succession Plan

Now that I have covered many of the issues that affect the successful transition of a family-owned business to another family member, let's look at the key elements that should be addressed in developing a succession plan. A good succession plan is really a set of several different subordinate plans all tied together into an articulate whole. The key elements of a succession plan should include:

- A Strategic Transition Plan.

- An Estate Plan.

- A Financial Transition Plan.

Developing a Strategic Transition Plan

A strategic transition plan should be closely linked with the overall strategic business plan of the company. The strategic business plan by its very nature should include such elements as product/service development, sales and profit goals, market share projections, etc. The *strategic transition plan* should tie into these elements by providing a timetable for disengagement of the founder, or current family member/owner. It should clearly lay out the involvement (or not) of the transitioning owner in each of the strategic elements. Perhaps the founder will relinquish all duties at first except for involvement in new product development, or simply continue as the primary interface with the company's most important customers.

Strategic Move #33:

"Develop a detailed, written Strategic Transition Plan to smooth the succession process in your family-owned business."

To make the transition phase of the succession plan truly effective, several factors should be addressed, decided upon, and then put into practice. A good Strategic Transition Plan will include:

- A process for identifying a motivated successor.

- Identification of the management team.

- Roles and responsibilities of corporate advisors.

- The new organizational structure.

- The role of the Board of Directors.

- The post-retirement role for the current owner.

The process of identifying a motivated successor for the family-owned business should be done as formally as if you were going to hire someone to replace you. Write a detailed position description and list all of the capabilities and attributes a successful successor should have. Interview each of the family member candidates for the position and make a selection on overall merit. If there is only a single child (or more than one), but none possess the capabilities you envision, ask yourself if education/training can be provided. Can the position be split to bring in an outsider with the talents your son or daughter lacks?

Based on the capabilities of the successor you select to head your company, you should identify a supportive and compatible management team to augment the transition. Perhaps you will need to hire an additional management level person to temporarily fill a void in your successor's experience and background. You should be careful to clearly identify the team members' job descriptions relative to your successor so that lead authority and responsibility is not undermined.

You may want to expand the *roles and responsibilities of your existing corporate advisors.* Perhaps your attorney could play a more active role in monitoring the contracts section or your accountant could be prevailed upon for more financial oversight. An increased effort on their part may or may not be needed, but either way you will want to clarify their roles relative to your successor's strengths and weaknesses.

Depending upon the decisions you make about a revamped management team, your continued involvement with the company and new roles and responsibilities for your corporate advisors, you may need to establish a *new organizational structure.* Having a well-defined, clearly articulated corporate structure that identifies duties, responsibilities, and lines of authority will be crucial to the company's ongoing success. A solidly defined corporate organizational structure should strictly minimize any behind-the-scenes intrigues and honest misunderstandings of "who's in charge."

Another effective, but unobtrusive way to maintain a steadying influence on your company during transition within the family, is to *expand the authority and control of the Board of Directors.* It will be best to appoint members to the Board who are respected business individuals but are clearly outside of the family. This will entail additional cost to the company, because as a "working" Board (rather than as a public relations or figurehead Board) the members must be compensated appropriately for their time.

Lastly, your Strategic Transition Plan must clearly define your continuing duties, responsibilities, and authority in the company after succession, i.e., *the post-retirement role of the current owner.* Nothing will hurt your business more than confusion among your employees, customers, and suppliers as to "who's in charge." Many business owners develop a phase-in/phase-out plan spreading the transition over a period of time, rather than making an abrupt change. Whichever course you follow, write it down, let every appropriate person know of the plan, and then follow it.

Developing an Estate Plan

Without proper estate planning, the inheritance taxes due upon your death could dramatically deplete your business capital to the point that requires a forced sale or liquidation of your company. With proper estate planning, you can avoid this potential disaster for your business and your family.

The objective of estate planning is actually very simple: to get the built-up capital in your business out and directed to where you want it to go. Generally speaking, to protect your business, you should get as much of your personal capital out of it as possible and transferred to your heirs before your death in order to minimize and even avoid estate taxes.

Strategic Move #34:

"Establish a professionally developed estate plan to minimize the inheritance taxes on the transition of your family-owned business."

There are basically two ways to get your wealth out of your business: Arrange a buyout between yourself and your heirs or make a gift arrangement. If you are very wealthy and do not require the funds that your interest in the business will generate, you may want to arrange transfer of ownership through a gifting process. But if you are like most business owners, you will need to arrange a buyout of your interest to provide you with the necessary living funds for your retirement years.

You need to seek the advice and guidance of experienced family business estate planning professionals to help you through the morass of legal possibilities. Although outright tax avoidance is probably not possible, tax minimization will most likely make the expense of the professional advice well worth it. The following brief descriptions of various estate planning strategies relative to family-owned businesses are provided to give you a sense of what is possible. Use them as a starting point for discussions with a competent professional.

- In transferring interest in a family business to the next generation, the Grantor Retained Annuity Trust (GRAT) and Grantor Retained Unitrust (GRUT), which I discussed earlier in Chapter 4, "Financial and Tax Consequences of Selling Your Business," offer the ability to reduce potential estate taxes. Both a GRAT and GRUT are irrevocable trusts in which the remainder interest is ultimately transferred to the younger generation family member who you have determined to be your business successor. In order to qualify for favorable estate tax treatment, you, as the grantor, must retain an income interest that meets certain specific criteria:

  - With a GRAT, the primary requirement is that you retain a right to receive a fixed annual annuity from the trust which does not vary according to which assets are in the trust.

  - With a GRUT, the owner retains the right to receive an amount each year which is a fixed percentage of the fair-market value of the trust property (your business).

- Estate tax minimization can also be accomplished in a number of other ways, including installment sales to family members, and preferred stock recapitalization if the older generation shareholder retains a cumulative dividend at a fair market rate.

Other business sale/estate planning techniques that you may want to explore include:

- Family Partnerships.

- Family Limited Partnerships.

- Private Annuities.

- Trusts.

  - Charitable Lead Trusts.

  - Charitable Remainder Trusts.

Family Partnership

A *Family Partnership* is generally nothing much more than a standard partnership in which you and other family members avoid double taxation problems by co-owning real estate and business assets. The portion of the partnership that is co-owned by your family members usually has restrictions on the transfer of ownership. In addition, there is reduced or no management authority which has the effect of lessening the value of that portion of the business. Consequently, you are able to transfer assets to your children at a discount or reduced value, thereby sheltering some of the asset value in your business from estate taxes. Basically, a family partnership is a business arrangement set up principally for tax purposes without the added advantages of a family limited partnership.

Family Limited Partnership

Strategic Move #35:

"Strongly consider forming a Family Limited Partnership; a very favorable way of transitioning ownership in a family-owned business."

A *Family Limited Partnership* (FLP) is created to hold real estate and/or family business assets. It is established in much the same way that a traditional limited partnership is formed. A partnership agreement is put in place with a general partner (usually yourself or your spouse) and limited partners (usually your children or your spouse). The limited partners are intended to be the recipients of complete control after your (the general partner's) demise. When the FLP is formed, the business assets including real estate and corporate stock are donated to the partnership. Because of your general partner status, you maintain complete control over the business including decisions on the disposition of earned income—whether they are reinvested in the business, taken as a distribution to yourself, or distributed to limited partners. The limited partners receive their interests in the FLP as gifts from you. Due to the fact that the limited partners have no control over the assets in the FLP, they are able to receive their portions at a discounted value. These discounts can range from 25% to 60%, depending on the type of assets. This process allows the limited partners to receive more of the business assets (which are sheltered from estate taxes) upon your death than if the assets were inherited and normal estate taxes paid.

Several key things must be done correctly in setting up an FLP to avoid problems with the IRS, which may see the partnership as only (or primarily) an estate tax dodge. The business assets must be properly valued; a partnership agreement must be formally created and filed with the IRS; the FLP must be operated with separate records, bank accounts, etc.; and the discounts applied to the assets for transfer to the limited partners must be independently appraised as to their value. Additionally, your children need to be treated as bone fide limited partners and not receive distributions from the partnership that are disproportionate to their share in the FLP.

As with all other estate planning tools for small-business ownership transfer, you must seek competent legal and accounting advice to ensure that you do things correctly. Advisors can also tell you if your approach properly fits your particular situation.

Private Annuity

A *Private Annuity* is also a good way of transferring ownership in a business from you to your children when the principal issue at hand is money. If you are willing to give up control of the business and your child(ren) is (are) willing and able to take over the running of the company but lack the funds to buy you out, then this may be a good approach. The basic premise of an annuity is much different than that of life insurance, a concept with which most people are familiar. An annuity establishes a contract which has the purpose of liquidating something that has been created to its recipient. Life insurance, on the other hand, is intended to create an estate for a beneficiary. Life insurance is used primarily to protect against loss of income for survivors of those who die prematurely. Annuities protect against the loss of income of those who live longer than their actuarial lives. Private annuities, then, are a contract between the successors to the business and their parents (usually) which stipulates that, in return for transferring ownership of the business to the next (or later) generation, the business owner will receive income from the business for as long as they live.

Strategic Move #36:

"Consider using a private annuity to transfer ownership in a family-owned business when your continued income is a primary issue."

Basically, this is how you would approach setting up a private annuity:

- Determine a conservative value for the business based on sound valuation principles. It's probably best to hire a professional appraiser who has a good track record with the IRS for this process. You will want the business value to be as close to reality as possible or else you may get into difficulty with the IRS. For example, a lower valuation than the fair market value will initially minimize the tax exposure. However, this may cause the IRS to eventually determine that a gift occurred. The result may be that they assess even higher taxes in the form of both gift and estate taxes.

- Once you have an acceptable fair-market valuation of the business, you will need to execute a sales agreement for the corporate stock and/or assets of the business which embodies a payment schedule (annuity) to be paid to you for the remainder of your life. The annuity amount (which can be paid monthly, quarterly, or yearly) is determined by dividing the valuation of the business by your life expectancy based on insurance industry actuarial tables.

- Set up life insurance policies on your successors to protect yourself against loss of income if they predecease you. The business operations, and therefore your income, could be threatened if this occurs. The insurance costs will most likely be substantially less for your much younger children than a policy would be on yourself.

A private annuity will provide income to you for as long as you and/or your spouse live. This makes this form of business sale unique in that the actual amount paid for the business will be determined by how long you live and not by a predetermined fixed amount. This is sometimes an excellent way to convey ownership in your business to your children if they are capable of and want to run the company. You receive lifetime income and your child(ren) get(s) control of the business at an amount they can afford. This is true since the payments will come from the cash flow of the business, and because you passed ownership of the business to your heirs before your passing. In addition, you will have reduced the estate taxes payable, perhaps significantly.

Trusts

And now a few words about *trusts* and their relationship to succession planning for family-owned businesses. Trusts are legal entities that are created for the purposes of transferring and managing property/assets. The person who creates the trust (referred to as the settlor) is not required to give up control over the property transferred to the trust (if revocable), nor do they have to give up the income and/or benefits resulting from it. What you can and cannot do with the trust will depend on the form of the trust that is used, and what you are trying to do with it.

To set up a trust for the transfer of your business, the corporate stock is transferred from you (the settlor) to another person or persons (the trustees) with an agreement that the recipient will hold the stock or use it in some specific way as directed by you. Whoever benefits from the corporate stock (such as receiving income) is known as the beneficiary. The trust does not last forever. When it ends, either at a particular time or upon a given event (such as the death of the beneficiary), those who then receive ownership of the stock are referred to as remaindermen. One of the keys to the usefulness of trusts is that the settlor, beneficiary, and remainderman do not have to be separate individuals. For example, you can set up a trust naming yourself as beneficiary if you want to have someone else (like your children) manage the assets in the trust.

There are many types of trusts, determined by when they are established and by what rights you keep as the settlor. You can have a revocable trust, which means that you can choose to dissolve the trust whenever you want. Or you can have an irrevocable trust, which only ends upon the occasion of a specific event such as the death of the beneficiary. In general, for the most favorable tax treatment, a trust must be irrevocable.

A trust can be an extremely useful tool in estate and financial planning relative to the transfer of the ownership of your family-owned business to another family member. However, setting up trusts properly can be legally and financially complicated, as well as very specific to your particular situation. Any discussion other than the general information in this overview is beyond the scope of this book.

Charitable Lead Trusts

Charitable Lead Trusts are usually established if you have a large estate consisting primarily of corporate stock in a family-owned business. Suppose you determine that the value of your company is such that the estimated estate tax (as much as 55% of the value of the corporation's stock, payable in as short a time after your death as nine months), could cause your company to be liquidated. Your calculations show that you do not have enough cash on hand, life insurance, or other assets readily convertible to cash to pay the estate tax, and the cost of adding the necessary life insurance is financially prohibitive. Although there are various other alternatives open to you such as selling the stock to an ESOP or establishing a charitable remainder trust, these may not fit with your desire to keep the ownership of the business within your family. A possibility to consider is to set up a charitable lead trust.

One way to set up a charitable lead trust (for illustration purposes) is to transfer all of the corporate stock in your business to your spouse with the stipulation that 60% of the current value is to be paid out in annual payments over a set period of time (say 20 years) to a charitable foundation. What's left would then be turned over to your children to hold in trust for your grandchildren.

At first glance, this may not seem to make sense, but let's do some math to see how this might come out. First, let's assume the value of your company's stock is $5,000,000 and growing at the rate of 10% per year. Then let's assume that the IRS-established discount rate for periodic charitable donations is 7% and the top tax rate for your heirs would be 55% (allowing for inheritance tax exclusions). The math is as follows:

Value of your corporate stock today	$5,000,000
Less charitable deduction for discounted present value of $463,000 for 20 years at 7% discount rate	$3,000,000
Taxable portion of the estate	$2,000,000
Estimated Tax Rate	55%
	$1,100,000

Versus

Estimated tax without a charitable lead trust: $5,000,000 x 55% = $2,750,000

As can be seen from the above figures, the estimated tax owed is substantially less with the charitable lead trust than without it. The amount of life insurance necessary to cover the approximately $1,100,000 of potential tax liability may be affordable whereas the insurance to cover the $2,750,000 is not. This then takes care of the estate taxes due. The $463,000 can be contributed in the form of stock to the charitable foundation, and thus not pressure the cash flow of the business. The increase in value of the company's stock (estimated at 10% per year) and the savings in estate taxes will more than make up for the charitable contribution of the stock at today's prices. Because your children are the trustees of the lead trust that you formed, they will be able to vote the company stock during the 20-year charitable trust period, giving them effective control of the company as you intended. In fact, they will have all of the practical benefits of owning the stock as if you had left it to them. Also, by actually leaving the stock to your grandchildren (in trust), another tax benefit occurs in that they may be able to further benefit by virtue of a "generation-skipping transfer" of assets.

Charitable Remainder Trusts

A *Charitable Remainder Trust* (CRT) is a tax planning tool that will enable you to substitute contributions to charitable organizations for the payment of estate taxes. There are several major benefits to a CRT:

- An ability to control the distribution of your "inheritance taxes" in the way you see fit.

- An ability to avoid capital gains taxes due on transfer of assets to the CRT.

- A greater flexibility in choosing and timing your income stream from your assets.

- An ability to realize substantial income tax and estate tax deductions.

Essentially, the CRT gives you the option of paying inheritance taxes to the government or making tax-deductible donations to charities in which you may have a personal interest. The CRT may also be used to aid the transition of family-owned businesses to your heirs. This simple example will clarify how this works in general:

> A business owner in a closely-held, private company donates a large percentage of his stock to a charitable organization within a public foundation. The public foundation then arranges to sell the stock to the second-generation members of the family business; the three children of the business owner/founder (and donor). A 15-year buy-back of the stock is arranged with the proceeds being used by the charitable organization for the charitable purposes desired by the donor. At the end of the 15 years, the stock ownership will entirely revert to the family. In addition, the donor will have realized his philanthropic goals, substantial tax savings will have resulted due to the "donation," and a tax-smart transfer of stock to the children will have been accomplished.

Obviously, there are many details left out of this simple example. But my objective in discussing this trust and the other estate planning tools I mentioned is to make you aware of some very sophisticated financial mechanisms available to help you keep the family business in the family. Before you decide that transitioning your business to Junior is not in the cards because of taxes or other money issues, talk to a professional financial planner. You may be amazed at what can be arranged which leads us to the next strategic move.

Strategic Move #37:

"Develop a Financial Transition Plan for your family-owned business to extract your wealth before succession."

Developing a Financial Transition Plan

The family business is very often the major, or even entire, portion of your net worth. Accordingly, you will probably need to extract enough wealth from your business upon turning it over to a family successor to allow you to live in the style you desire and deserve as a reward for your many years of effort. But there are potentially many other significant demands on the company's capital in addition to your financial security. For example:

- The business will need to retain enough operating capital, not only for day-to-day operations, but to continue the growth and vitality of the company.

- If there are additional family members who will not take an active role in the business, but who you want to compensate for their fair share of your estate, you will have to allow capital planning to provide for this.

- You may have personal notes and debts that cannot or should not be assigned to a family-owned business successor and which must be retired.

One eventuality that many people find uncomfortable to consider is their own death before an orderly transition of the business can take place. Many problems will undoubtedly turn up for your heirs at this time. With regard to the business, the biggest issue may be the inability to pay the inheritance taxes that will be assessed. Although recent U.S. tax legislation passed in 1997 will ease the estate tax burden on all business owners, it will definitely not eliminate it. Your heirs may find themselves owing such significant sums of inheritance taxes to both the state and federal government that the only way to pay the taxes due is to liquidate the business.

An additional financial problem presents itself if there is a nonfamily member owner/partner in the parent's business that must be bought out at the time of the parent's death. Frequently, partners have written arrangements usually called buy/sell agreements that spell out the rights of the partners and/or their heirs relative to buying out the other. These come into play in the event of the death of one of the principals. Most often, this involves the transfer of a relatively large amount of money over a short period of time. The surviving heir may discover that, because the business value has grown substantially since the buy/sell agreement was originated, they do not have access to the cash necessary to buy out the surviving partner. Accordingly, they must sell their interest to the partner or liquidate the business.

There are several ways to fund the purchase of an ownership interest by a successor:

- Life insurance.

- Personal savings.

- Installment purchase.

- Traditional bank financing.

- Public or private stock offering.

Life Insurance

In the previous section on estate planning, I suggested some approaches that the business owner and family members could take to ease the burden of transition of ownership in the business. Another option that can be used instead of, or with, these previously discussed approaches is the use of *life insurance*. The child of the business owner can purchase a life insurance policy on the life of their parent with the proceeds used to purchase the partnership interest or corporate shares of a nonfamily shareholder. The cost of the insurance premiums is not a tax-deductible expense for the child. But, since the business owner never owned the policy on themselves, the proceeds are not included in the decedent's estate and the money is tax free. The funds can then be used to pay the inheritance taxes and/or buy out the partner or remaining principal shareholder(s).

The main problem with using life insurance in this way is the premium cost to the child. If the amount of the policy is very high (typically in the tens of thousands or even hundreds of thousands of dollars) and the business owner is elderly and/or has a poor medical history, the cost may be prohibitive. Additionally, this is typically "lost money" to the family until the business owner dies. By that time, the premiums may well have exceeded the proceeds of the policy. Unfortunately, no one can predict the timing of the need for the life insurance, making the decision unique to your personal situation. Factors such as ability to independently raise funds some other way, aversion or acceptance of risk, age and health of the insured, ability of the child to afford the premiums, and a host of others will all play a role in deciding if you should use life insurance as part of your succession plan. One way to reduce the cost of life insurance intended to pay estate taxes is to use a type of policy known as the "second to die" policy. This form of life insurance is much less expensive than a policy on a single individual. In this case the policy does not pay off until the second named party, usually the spouse, also dies. By properly using estate planning techniques, the estate tax can be deferred until after the succeeding spouse passes away and, at that time, the life insurance proceeds become available for paying estate taxes.

One way some business owners have been able to have the business pay the premiums on their life insurance is to proportionately increase the pay of their child to cover the cost of the premiums. The child then uses the increased compensation to pay the life insurance premiums. The business is in effect paying the premiums. The child working in the business is not adversely affected financially, although they will be liable for the increased personal income taxes. This may not be completely acceptable to the IRS and you will want to thoroughly investigate this option with a tax professional before pursuing it. Life insurance by your heirs on yourself as the business owner only facilitates the financial requirements of the transfer if you die, which I'm sure you have no intention of doing.

Personal Savings

Using *personal savings* as capital in the transition of the family-owned business from you to your child is generally not a viable consideration. In most cases, your child will be relatively young and not yet have had the opportunity to accumulate any disposable wealth that could be used towards the purchase of your business. In some cases, the opposite may be true, especially in later-generation, family-owned business transfers. Perhaps your parent or grandparent founded the business and your child is the beneficiary of an inherited trust or other form of money from them. In these cases, personal savings may in fact be used to assist in the buyout of your ownership position as part of the transfer process.

Installment Purchase

An *installment purchase* of your ownership position by your successor will be the most likely way that ownership is transferred when you need to receive funds. This process combined with gifting is one of the most common ways that privately-held, family-owned, profitable businesses are transferred to family successors which do not use family limited partnership or private annuity arrangements. Installment sales must be structured to allow sufficient funds to flow to you, but must also be affordable to the business.

Bank Financing

Using *traditional bank financing* to fund a business buyout by your heirs and successors is a viable possibility if the company has the cash flow to support the debt repayment. Depending upon your relationship with your bank, their loan policies, their level of risk acceptance, and the stability and profitability of your company, you may be able to pave the way for a buyout of your interest in your company by your successor. If you need a large amount of capital at the time of succession for such possibilities as retirement of personal debt, purchase of a retirement home, a cruise around the world, or you just want to make sure that you get a solid amount out of your company no matter what the future, then bank financing should be one of the options considered. You may find that a bank's natural conservatism, high aversion to risk, requirement for significant collateral, and a relatively high interest rate for the borrowed funds may not make this a good option. However, there are circumstances where this may work for you, especially in conjunction with some of the other ways I have mentioned in which the bank financing is only a part of the total purchase package.

Corporate Stock Sale

A *public or private stock offering* is another option for raising capital to buy out a significant portion of your ownership in the business. If you are able to attain your cash requirements through a public or private stock sale for up to 49% of the ownership in the company, you may be able to gift or otherwise transfer ownership in the remaining 51% to your successor and still maintain the business as predominantly family-owned. Although most businesses are not large enough or do not meet other requirements for a formal initial public offering (IPO), you may be able to use the small corporate offering registration (SCOR) or other method for a private placement sale of your company's stock. However, a private stock sale has various limitations that restrict its potential. Factors such as the amount of money you want to raise, the number of potential new shareholders involved, and the type of corporation will determine the ease and cost of pursuing either of these options. Please refer back to the discussion of IPO's in Chapter 1, "Why You Need to Prepare Your Business for Sale," for more details on this subject.

Another alternative to the issue of public and private placement of stock is operating the corporation as a sub-chapter S. A sub-chapter S corporation may have up to 70 shareholders with little or none of the restrictions for a more formal public offering or a direct private placement. You may be able to sell a portion of your shares (up to 49% to enable you to retain control) in your sub-chapter S company to friends, relatives, and business associates in order to raise the capital necessary for you to transition the ownership of the remaining portion of the company (at least 51%) to your successor.

Notwithstanding the pros and cons of public and private stock offerings as a way for your company to raise funds for the purpose of funding a buyout of your stock to keep the business in the family, it will probably be an uphill battle to attract investors other than family and friends. Most stock offerings are "advertised" as a way of increasing the capital for a company. The capital is then used to expand product lines, acquire another company, or in some way materially improve the future potential of the company to expand and make more money. If the only reason for your company's sale of stock outside of the family is to fund your buyout, you may not find many investors. Why should someone invest money in a company to aid and abet the departure of its founder who is probably the key reason for its success? It would be a better idea for you to pursue either of these approaches in the context of a long-range plan that is tied primarily to company growth. This plan should include you at the helm for a few years, with the remainder of cash available for a buyout of your shares at a later date.

These issues should all be addressed as part of your financial transition plan which you should develop with the assistance of a competent professional advisor. It may be possible that your goals cannot be met without an outright sale of the family business to an outside entity. But you may be able to use one of the methods of sale discussed in Chapter 1 to accomplish all of your objectives. For example, an IPO or ESOP may be a very viable route to take that leaves your family successor in control of the business. Or you may want to arrange a formal sale as if your successor were a private outside buyer, but make arrangements for capital infusion through a banking or venture capital deal.

All of these elements taken together constitute a succession plan that lays the foundation for a successful transition of ownership from one family generation to the next. These issues have all become so complex and interrelated that succession planning has become a specialty practice for many accountants and attorneys who specialize in financial and estate planning. Many business oriented universities have also established various family-owned business succession planning centers of one kind or another around the country. For those of you wanting further information on this subject, I've included a listing of many of these University Centers in Chapter 8. Most of them publish detailed information regarding succession planning, conduct public seminars, and some offer personal consulting for business owners.

Succession planning is a highly complex issue in which you will need to involve a transition planning team consisting of an attorney, accountant, insurance professional, financial and estate planner, and other competent professionals such as an independent business valuation expert. Please note that your current company attorney and accountant may not have the full expertise needed in this evolving field of succession planning. For your information, I've provided the names and addresses of some organizations that specialize in this field in Chapter 8. Inclusion of their names does not constitute an endorsement on my part. My readers are cautioned to check out any resource thoroughly before engaging them to assist in your business's succession planning. Although the process may seem expensive and time-consuming, it's essential to the successful transition of your business to the next generation.

Succession Plan Checklist

The following checklist is provided for you to follow if you decide that you may want to pursue transferring your business ownership to a family successor. This is intended to be a broad guideline because the details, as well as the timing, will be very specific to your own personal situation.

❏ Make the decision that it's time to begin considering an exit process from your business.

❏ Begin implementing the advice and recommendations I have offered relative to preparing your business for sale.

❏ Verify that there is a potential family member/heir that could possibly succeed you. Carefully consider their capability, desire, maturity, etc.

❏ Decide if you want to pursue a family-owned business succession rather than accomplish a sale to an outside party.

❏ Establish a rough timetable for the overall succession process to take place within. Consider the need for a phase-in/phase-out process.

❏ Discuss your preliminary decision with your spouse, uninvolved close family members, and your closest professional advisors.

❏ Make a preliminary decision about what you will do with your life after the transition is complete.

❏ Confidentially discuss your preliminary plans with the person you have identified as your most likely successor to determine interest on their part.

❏ Have a professional begin the valuation of your business. You may want to use the valuation methods I have detailed in this book to provide you with an approximation, but for the purposes of tax minimization be sure to take a very conservative approach.

❏ Make a rough estimate of your income needs and desires as well as any lump sum financial requirements that you may have.

❏ Assemble a team of advisors to help you prepare and document a strategic transition plan.

❏ Update your personal estate plan to reflect your decision to transition the ownership of your company.

❑ Prepare a preliminary financial transition plan to cover some of the issues that require finding the necessary buyout capital.

❑ Communicate your decision about your succession plans to other family members, especially those who may feel that they are "stakeholders" in your business.

❑ Consolidate your decisions, goals, updated estate and financial plans, and other related information into an overall written succession plan. Include a specific timeline and communicate the plan to your spouse, successors, heirs, professional advisors, and other necessary, need-to-know parties.

❑ Begin implementation of your succession plan with allowance for contingencies which will inevitably occur. There may be many tasks to accomplish which require a long lead-time, such as:

> ❑ Training/grooming of your successor.
>
> ❑ Hiring outside management expertise.
>
> ❑ Setting up a working Board of Directors.
>
> ❑ Establishing trusts, wills, etc.
>
> ❑ Finding financing for your buyout.

In Summary

The subject of succession planning for the family-owned business can be complicated by the many financial, tax, and personal issues that will arise. The foregoing discussion has provided you with an overview of what you will need to consider if you plan to "sell" your business through a transition to a close family member. The extent of the subject matter is so broad as to require an entire book in itself. You will also need to hire competent professionals to lead you successfully through the morass of details. Even if you have decided to follow this path of transition for your company, you should still implement many of the recommendations made earlier in this book for maximizing the value of your company. If your objective is not to maximize the provable cash flow of your business (given inheritance and estate planning issues), you will still want to turn over a well-run and optimally operating company to your successors. Many of the recommendations in this book will help you to accomplish this. In the next chapter, I will provide you with some guidelines and ideas for assembling an effective professional team of advisors and representatives to assist you in accomplishing your business objectives.

6

Choosing Professional Advisors and Representatives

- *Selecting an Attorney*
- *Selecting an Accountant*
- *Selecting a Financial and Estate Planner*
- *Selecting a Professional Sales Representative*
- *Obtaining an Independent Business Valuation*
- *Involving Your Commercial Banker*

Introduction

Choosing professional advisors and sales representation for the sale of your business will be one of your most critical decisions as you prepare your business for sale. Good attorneys and CPAs are expensive, and professional business brokers generally charge a significant commission as well as up-front fees based on the entire value of your business sale. Only you can judge if and how much advice and representation you want and need in the sale of your company. I strongly advise that no matter how small your business, if you are going to sell it to anyone, you must obtain at least basic legal and accounting advice before and during the sale proceedings. A misstep during this process could not only wipe out all of the value that you have built up in your business over the years, but could even open you up personally to liability claims by the purchaser at some later time. For example, one case with which I am familiar involved a lawsuit brought by the purchaser of a manufacturing business against the seller more than two years after the closing. The lawsuit alleged misrepresentation of inventory value, inefficient manufacturing processes, and deception with regard to potential future sales of the products. The legal proceedings spanned several years and included many depositions (including depositions from the brokers involved), a lengthy bench trial, and even an appeal to the state's appellate court! The suit was eventually decided completely in the favor of the seller but not before he had spent tens of thousands of dollars in legal fees and experienced significant levels of stress and anxiety. What was amazing to me is that the dollar compensation sought by the lawsuit was many times more than what the buyer had actually paid for the business! In retrospect, it's clear that if the purchase and sale documentation had been worded more precisely as to what exactly was being sold and its condition at the time of sale, the lawsuit most likely would never have been filed.

So for many reasons, you should seek competent legal, financial, and accounting advice as you prepare your business for sale and as you proceed through the sale process. You will have to use your own judgment as to the level of professional advice purchased and the potential downside of a bad decision in the selling procedure. Also, as the business owner, you are generally not the right person to represent your business for sale. You usually are too emotionally involved to take a truly independent view of what you need to do to create a strong buying interest in your company. You also are most likely not familiar with the marketing process whereby independent agents are able to find and prequalify good potential buyers for operating businesses. You should seriously consider hiring a reputable business broker or investment banker to represent your interests in marketing your business and in negotiating the sale. The next strategic move you should make in preparing your business for sale is an extremely important one.

Strategic Move #38:

"Choose your professional representatives and advisors for your business sale team very carefully; they can make or break the deal!"

The following discussion provides you with guidance in the selection of professionals to work with you in preparing, marketing, negotiating, and selling your business.

Selecting an Attorney

Selecting the right attorney to represent your legal interests as you begin the process of selling your business is essential. Unfortunately, it's sometimes difficult to find a properly qualified attorney for a business sale because they are not licensed by specialty. Lawyers are lawyers are lawyers. Once they pass the bar exam in their state, they can practice any and all kinds of law. In actual practice, most attorneys specialize in a particular field of law and "advertise" their services accordingly. Legal specialists work in such areas as patent law, criminal law, civil law, divorce, real estate, estate planning, etc. Clearly, you need to find an attorney who specializes in corporate/business law. You will most likely be better off with one who further specializes in the purchase and sale of businesses and/or corporate mergers and acquisitions. Depending on your area of the country, this may be a challenge. In larger urban areas, these specialized attorneys are in abundance. You will most likely be able to find a high-quality lawyer to meet your particular needs and financial capabilities just by perusing the appropriate yellow pages of a telephone directory. If you are in a less densely populated area with only moderate business activity, you may find your selection options limited. It may be well worth your while in this case to expand your area of search to find the best qualified attorney for your requirements. I have listed some legal resources in Chapter 8, "Resources for Preparing Your Business for Sale," that you may want to consider if properly qualified legal representation is not otherwise readily available to you.

A note of caution in selecting an attorney to represent you in the sale of your business: There are some attorneys who may tend to get in the way of a business transaction because they define their role as a negotiator for you and attempt to get the "best deal" in your interests. A problem arises when the buyer's attorney also plays a similar role. If you do not recognize this situation, you may have two attorneys fighting to get the best deal for their clients. Generally, both parties to the purchase and sale of a business cannot get the *best* deal, and the way most business transactions of this nature are completed successfully is by both sides working towards a "fair deal." My advice in selecting an attorney to represent you in the sale of your business is to ensure that you hire someone who will carry out your objectives in a manner compatible with your own financial and personal goals.

Strategic Move #39:

"Be very wary of the deal-killing lawyer who may think that they have your best interests at heart."

Keep in mind that even if you or some well-meaning attorney is able to make a lopsided deal in your favor, you are still likely to be holding the financing for the sale of the business. Obviously, you have a vested interest in the business succeeding. If the business fails and you have to retake possession of it as the collateral to the sale, you will most likely be taking possession of a failed enterprise that no longer has any value because the business has been run into the ground in trying to meet the onerous payment requirements negotiated by you or your attorney. The best deal all around is the fair deal. You must leave enough on the table to allow the purchaser to run the business in a fiscally sound manner, pay themselves a market-rate salary if they manage the business, and also to make a reasonable return on their invested capital, even during the business payoff years.

Your attorney may not have these same concerns. It may sound cynical to say this, but the lawyer gets paid either way—whether the business sells or not and whether you receive your payout or not. Make it clear to your attorney right up-front that you are in charge of negotiations, that you want a fair deal and not necessarily the best deal, and that the big picture objective is to sell the business and get paid for it and not to get hung up over relatively minor points. Listen to all of the advice your attorney will offer, but retain firm control of the negotiation process and the ultimate sale of your business.

The timing of when to bring in an attorney to work with you on your business sale is important. Some business sellers feel comfortable in not involving an attorney until a binder, offer to purchase, or letter of intent has been signed. They then use the attorney strictly to prepare all the legal documentation necessary to convey the business to the purchaser. Other business owners involve the attorney very early in the process as a means of helping to prepare their business for sale. Some of these early tasks usually involve:

- Recommending the legal business structure of the sale (corporate stock or asset sale).

- Ensuring that the business can be conveyed using the structure anticipated. Such issues as stock options, preferred stock, pension funds, etc. must all be addressed and resolved, if applicable.

- Clearing up or otherwise addressing any legal encumbrances such as liens, unpaid taxes in arrears, outstanding lawsuits or judgments, etc.

- Identifying and obtaining any needed consents to the sale from partners, shareholders, spouses, etc.

If you have not involved your attorney throughout the business sale preparation process up to the receipt of a Letter of Intent, now is the time to bring them into the picture. Some of the things that your attorney should do for you at this stage of the process include:

- Assisting you and your broker with negotiations. (You may not wish them to be directly involved with this activity, but they should definitely be used as an "off-line" advisor.)

- Preparing the purchase and sale agreement.

- Investigating the legal and financial qualifications of the prospective purchaser.

- Preparing the business transfer legal documents (such as stock certificates, corporate resolutions, bill of sale, collateral agreements, compliance with state bulk sales laws, etc.).

- Assisting with the actual closing and acting as your fiduciary agent in receiving and disbursing funds.

Probably the two most important things an attorney should do for you are:

- Ensure the wording in the purchase and sale agreement clearly and definitively describes what is being sold and under what conditions.

- Ensure that you are well-protected by a collateral arrangement if the business sale involves you holding a promissory note.

In addition to all the legal boilerplate and seemingly endless recitals and provisions in a standard purchase and sale agreement, make sure that your attorney clearly identifies in plain language exactly what is being sold. For example, in the transfer of inventory, describe the number of items, their current condition, cost basis, age, and any other identifying characteristics. Many post-business-sale points of contention focus on nonsalable inventory that a seller has managed to unload onto an unsuspecting buyer. The same is true of equipment essential to the operation of the business. If you know of any deficiencies, such as aged equipment for which replacement parts are not available, disclose this during negotiations and have your attorney include this issue in the purchase and sale agreement.

Many business sellers are pressured to take only business assets as collateral when they finance part of the purchase price of their business by accepting a promissory note. The buyer will argue that if the business is as good as represented, there should be no problem with you accepting the business itself as security for the funds they will pay you over time. While this is most likely true if you have fairly structured the business sale, it does not protect you against an unscrupulous or incompetent buyer. There have been many business sale transactions that have resulted in the seller never receiving their full payments. Either the buyer has milked the business for as much cash as they could extract or otherwise ran the business into the ground due to unwise operations. If the only collateral you have is in the business assets, by the time you take the business back there may be nothing left of value. A good attorney should be able to negotiate a collateral agreement that includes the buyer's personal assets. They will afford you much better protection in the event of a default.

The real issue here is whether you want to sleep well every night after the business sale. A good attorney should be able to structure the business sale so that the business stays sold and you receive your well-deserved money without worry or problems. Scrimping on the cost of an attorney in this process may later cost you many times more.

Selecting an Accountant

Selecting the right accountant, preferably a certified public accountant (CPA), to provide you with advice regarding your financial interests and tax obligations as you begin the process of selling your business is just as essential as picking the right attorney. In some ways, perhaps, the CPA may be even more important as they will help you to prepare your business for sale for the most money. In addition, they will help you make wise financial decisions about properly structuring the sale to minimize income tax consequences. Incorrectly structuring the financial portion of the sale of your business could have detrimental side effects with respect to the actual funds that you receive from the sale of your business.

As described in Chapter 2, "What Is Your Business Really Worth?," the primary way a buyer will look at your business is as a cash-generating entity or money conduit to themselves. Therefore, the financial health and track record of your business will be subjected to close scrutiny, making it necessary for you to provide information in a format acceptable to financially-oriented entities. This financial format is essentially a language unto itself as demonstrated in something called Generally Accepted Accounting Principles (GAAP). Fortunately, a CPA or other qualified accountant will be able to help you put your records in GAAP format if they are not already in that form. Additionally, you may want your CPA to prepare a special midyear interim financial report if you are between fiscal years. Also, some buyers will require audited financial reports which only a qualified CPA can prepare.

The issues and concerns with selecting the right CPA to work with you are very similar to those I have previously discussed regarding the selection of an attorney. The CPAs are also not licensed according to a particular specialty, but many of them do specialize in certain areas. The principal difference between selecting an attorney and a CPA for your business sale is that you will most likely be better off with two CPAs involved with your sale—the one you now use for your general financial accounting and the one you will find who specializes in business purchases and sales. If you use a large CPA firm you may be able to obtain this specialized accountancy within one organization. Otherwise, you will have to find a specialist compatible with both yourself and your business's general CPA. The reason you want to keep your general CPA involved is for the history and background of your company that they can bring to the process. All the depreciation schedules, tax loss carry-forward issues, prepaid taxes, payroll issues, pension fund payments, etc., are well-known by your current CPA. These records must be accessible to help structure the actual sale of the business. In most cases, your business CPA is also your personal CPA and will therefore be in the best position to advise you on such important issues as the impact of personal income tax. You will find that the financial consequences of the sale of your company are woven together from both business and personal considerations.

I observed a recent situation in which a buyer and seller decided to "go it alone" in the sale of a small-business. It clearly illustrates the need for a CPA's advice. The business itself was basically a small physical-fitness-related company that sold annual memberships in the form of dues payments as well as related physical fitness items. The corporation was operated as a sub-chapter S with a fiscal year from January 1 to December 31, and the seller was the sole shareholder. The business space was leased on a long-term basis with very favorable terms by the corporation. The buyer and seller agreed on the selling price for the business (about $150,000) as a corporate stock sale. The primarily reason for a corporate stock sale was to not disturb the real estate lease which stayed with the corporation independent of the officers or shareholders in the company. The buyer agreed to let the seller take all of the cash out of the business and the seller agreed to settle all of the business accounts payable. The transfer was done as an all-cash deal and an attorney was used only to document the agreement, comply with the state's bulk sales law, and transfer the corporate stock ownership to the new owner. The services of an accountant were not used. The sale was consummated on March 31.

A year or so later, when the new business owner went to an accountant for help in preparing the company's income tax return, it was discovered that $100,000 of the cash taken out of the business by the seller was for prepaid annual dues. The seller had dutifully reported a first quarter prorated $25,000 of income on his personal income tax return through the business sale date of March 31. The corporation, and therefore the new owner was liable for the income taxes on the other $75,000 (about $30,000 in taxes for this particular case), but the cash that generated that tax liability had been taken out of the business on March 31 by the seller! The seller had since retired and was living on a modest invest-ment and social security income.

Although the seller apparently did not mean to defraud the buyer, he con-tended that a deal was a deal and he could not afford to pay the $30,000 any-way. The IRS wanted their $30,000 and because the new owner was the S-cor-poration's sole shareholder, he was liable for the tax payment. Consequently, the buyer sued the seller and a legal mess was underway.

Even though this anecdote relates primarily to the ineptitude of the buyer in not using an accountant to provide advice in the transaction, the seller is now suffering also. He will spend several of his retirement years defending himself in a civil trial. Remember, the best deal is a fair deal and you need solid pro-fessional advice to assist you in avoiding legal and financial pitfalls.

Strategic Move #40:

"Selecting the right accountant to properly structure your business sale is crucial to maximizing the value you receive and avoid-ing later problems."

You should use an accountant to:

- Prepare audited financial statements if they are requested by a poten-tial buyer.

- Prepare interim financial statements if the sale negotiations are taking place mid-fiscal year.

- Prepare pro forma financial projections for the future business operat-ing year(s) to help substantiate an asking price for your business.

- Examine the proposed financial transaction to ensure all corporate/ partnership/sole proprietorship tax issues are properly addressed and adjusted, as of the closing date of the sale.

- Develop strategies to minimize your personal income tax exposure and shift as much personal taxable income into capital gains rather than ordinary income.

Although they are relatively rare, there are some CPAs who are also licensed attorneys (or vice versa) specializing in business purchase and sale transactions as well as mergers and acquisitions. These professionals would appear to be the best of all worlds for the serious business seller. Although their fees are relatively high, they may be less expensive in the long run. Of course, the size of your business sale must warrant such high-priced talent. You will need to balance the estimated costs of their services against the expected proceeds from your business sale.

Selecting a Financial and Estate Planner

If you do not have a financial and estate plan and feel that you should have one after reading the pertinent sections in Chapter 4, "Financial and Tax Consequences of Selling Your Business," and Chapter 5, "Succession Planning for the Family-Owned Business," here are some guidelines for finding and selecting a good estate planner. This is another professional area where you are well advised to not "do it yourself." You also probably do not want to rely on your everyday attorney and accountant for this very specialized guidance. Many of the professionals normally associated with an ongoing business are either general practitioners or business specialists who may not be up to date in the latest issues affecting financial and estate planning. Here are some things to think about as you consider selecting these professionals:

- Look for someone with at least five to 10 years of recent experience in creating financial and estate plans specifically for small-business owners.

- Verify that they have high-level professional credentials related specifically to financial and estate planning. The field of financial planning has a large number of professional affiliations and designations. A few of them include:

  — Certified Financial Planner (CFP), conferred by the International Association for Financial Planning (IAFP).

  — Chartered Financial Consultant (ChFC), also conferred by the IAFP.

  — Registered Financial Planner (RFP), awarded by the Registered Financial Planners Institute.

- Before you interview potential financial and estate planners, become as knowledgeable as you can about what the process entails so that you can communicate your broad goals and objectives to them.

- Do a preliminary assessment of the extent of your estate to arrive at a broad estimate of value (personal assets – your liabilities = your estate).

- Ask for and follow up on at least three references of businesspersons similar to yourself. The type of company does not have to be exactly the same, but the situation should be closely related.

- Consider hiring a financial and estate planner that has a close professional relationship with an insurance resource. Most likely, life insurance will become a component of your estate plan.

Selecting a Professional Sales Representative

I believe that the use of a professional sales representative in the sale of your business is as essential as a good attorney and a CPA. Some very large complicated transactions will require the services of a mergers and acquisitions specialist or an investment banker rather than a business broker. For the vast majority of business sales, however, a good business broker will play an important role in the successful sale of your business.

Strategic Move #41:

"Use a broker to represent you in your business sale. Going it alone could be very hazardous to your wealth."

There are no hard and fast rules about whether you should use the services of a business broker, mergers and acquisitions specialist, or investment banker. Many potential business sellers are confused as to which professional they should use to assist them in selling their company. I wish I could provide you with a hard and fast rule, but I cannot. The key criteria for you to consider is which of these professionals understands your business and industry the best. Then you must interview them to get the best fit between their capabilities and your needs. A guide as to which type of professional you should hire is based on the projected dollar amount of the sale. This usually indicates the complexity of the deal—the higher the selling price, the more complex the deal (in general), and the more sophisticated representation you will need. I offer the following overlapping criteria as a general guide for you:

Estimated Business Sale Price	Professional Representative
Up to $10 million	Business Broker
$5 million to $50 million	Mergers and Acquisitions Specialist
$20 million and up	Investment Banker

Many firms advertise themselves as providing services in two or even three of the above professional representative categories. In fact, most large firms have individuals that can cover the full gamut of business sales. Your particular business situation will be assigned to an individual in the brokerage firm who best fits your needs.

If you expect to sell your business for under $1 million though, your best bet is a good reputable business broker serving your region of the country. Roughly 70% of all business sales will fit this category.

Selecting a Business Broker or M&A Specialist

Selling your business will probably be one of the four or five most important events in your life. You owe it to yourself and all you have worked for to get the best possible assistance with this complex transaction. How do you ensure that you get the right person and firm to represent you and your business for sale? Well, as a start, before you list your business for sale with a broker, you should ask them the following probing questions:

Number of Businesses Sold

How Many Businesses Have You Successfully Brokered In The Past Year? This is a very important question to ask, but you have to carefully evaluate the answer. What you want to find out is how active the broker is in marketing and closing the sale of businesses. Because some business transactions involve very large dollar amounts and are quite complicated, a good business broker may only handle two or three actual closings per year. On the other hand, if the broker is primarily representing small "Mom and Pop" operations that sell in the $100,000 range, then you should expect that the broker will handle about 10 to 15 closings annually. Many general business brokers will in fact have a range of closings from $25,000 up to an occasional $500,000 (plus) sale. In general, business brokers who close deals in the $1 million to $10 million range are considered "middle-market" brokers. Those who operate in the rarefied air of the $10 million (plus) range are generally referred to as mergers and acquisitions specialists because most deals in these upper price ranges involve the sale of a business to another company. What you are trying to learn with this first question is not only how active the business broker is, but how successful. Although there are no reliable statistics by which you can compare business brokers, you should look for a success ratio of about one to five, or better. This means that a broker sells one business out of every five businesses listed. The trouble with this statistic is that it does not take into consideration the brokers who accept many marginal listings to "have them on the shelf," yet still manage to sell a good number overall. It also does not consider the multi-broker office or co-listings which can skew a broker's apparent performance one way or another. The best that you can do with this question is to satisfy yourself that the broker is apparently actively taking listings and routinely closing deals.

Types of Businesses Sold

What Types Of Businesses Have You Successfully Represented For Sale? It's very important that the business broker you retain to represent your business for sale is somewhat familiar with the type of business you are in. Realistically, it is not absolutely necessary that a broker has actually sold a business exactly like yours, but you should look for someone who is at least familiar with your industry. You will find it much easier to explain your business operations to the broker and they, in turn, will be much more able to represent your business in its best light. If the business broker is familiar with your specific type of business or its industry, they will know the business jargon, sales trends, projected growth rates, and other information important to communicating with you and knowledgeable prospective buyers. Nevertheless, you may want to select a business broker who concentrates in your particular type of business. I have listed some examples of specialties here, so you will have an idea of the range of specialization that you will find.

• Restaurants	• Country Stores
• Franchise Resales	• Marinas
• Manufacturing	• Bed & Breakfast Inns
• Relocatable Businesses	• Hotels and Motels
• Vending Routes	• Self-Storage Facilities
• Professional Practices	• Farming-Related

Range of Business Values

What Is The Range Of Business Values That You Have Successfully Brokered? This question is similar to the first one except that the answer tells which portion of the general business market the broker is most active in. If you expect your business to sell for a million-plus dollars, then the broker who has never made a deal over $150,000 would probably not be right for you. On the other hand, you may not want to hire the multimillion dollar mergers and acquisitions specialist to represent your one-location retail store that you expect to sell for about $100,000. It could be that your situation would not get the attention that it deserves from the broker because of its relatively small size. Due to the complexity of most business sales, even small ones, it's usually better if you retain a business broker who is working towards the high end of their range than one who is working towards the lower end. You most likely would not suffer from a lack of expertise and you almost certainly will gain a much more interested broker. Do not forget that most business brokers work on a contingency fee basis with their fee dependent not only on a successful sale, but on the size of the sale. A broker may work extra hard to close a deal at the higher end of their normal range because the incentive is greater.

Advertising Methods

What Advertising Methods Do You Use For Finding A Buyer For My Business? Advertising methods are important to the successful sale of a business, but not crucial. Many experienced business brokers have a substantial backlog of potential prequalified buyers that they can present your business to without ever having to expose your business to the general marketplace. Additionally, most business brokers have extensive business community contacts that they can use to discreetly seek a potential buyer without having to advertise. However, many businesses must be marketed in a broader venue, and it's in your best interest to learn what advertising methods the broker intends to use for your business. Many professional business brokers will present you with a marketing plan for your business and seek your input about ways to enhance their proposed approach. Some of the advertising methods a business broker might use are:

- Newspaper classified ads.

- Magazine classified ads.

- Broker agency newsletters to other brokers, as well as potential buyers.

- Classified ads in national periodicals specifically selling businesses.

- Marketing on the Internet.

This last item is becoming extremely important. It's always been a tremendous challenge for buyers, sellers, and brokers of small businesses to efficiently find each other. Many would-be business buyers are willing to relocate to anywhere in the country for the right business. Many businesses themselves are not geographic specific and can be relocated to the buyer's area. Business brokers have many times found themselves in the position of having a motivated and financially capable buyer wanting to buy a particular type of business, but they have been unable to locate the right situation. Similarly, business brokers sometimes find themselves with a high-quality business for sale but have difficulty finding the right buyer for the business within their immediate geographic area.

At any given point in time there are approximately 850,000 small- to medium-sized businesses for sale in the United States. Concurrently, many brokers estimate that they have at least five qualified buyers for every business they have for sale. This means that there are approximately 4,000,000 buyers spread across the country from Maine to Hawaii right now looking for a business to buy! The logistics of matching the right business with the right buyer has, until now, been overwhelming when you consider these numbers. The traditional method of print media advertising is cumbersome, not especially effective, very expensive, and extremely inefficient. These problems are all quickly coming to an end through the use of the Internet and the World Wide Web by business brokers, mergers and acquisitions specialists, and even investment bankers.

As a business seller, you should closely question the business broker about how they intend to use the Internet to find a qualified buyer for your business. Does the broker have their own Web page? Do they know the best sites to discreetly advertise your business for sale? Any good marketing plan for the sale of your business should include an Internet strategy, or you may not be getting the best exposure for your planned business sale.

Valuation Method

What Valuation Method Will You Use In Helping Me To Establish A Selling Price For My Business? If you are going to rely on the business broker to assist you in establishing a value for your business, you will want to find out what business valuation method they intend to use. If your business is currently a profitable operating company with at least three years of history, then the capitalization or present value methods are most likely the best approaches to setting a realistic asking price, if your most likely buyer is financially motivated. Although many business brokers have developed "rules of thumb" for arriving at a ballpark estimation for the value of a business, you should never allow your asking price to be based on such a crude estimate. You may want to ask the business broker to estimate the value of your business using both the capitalization approach and their particular favored valuation approach to see if there is a significant value difference in your favor. Either way, the broker will need to rely heavily on you to provide specific details about the financial operation of your business before they use any valuation method.

You may want to seriously consider having a separate, independent business valuation done by a CPA, a certified business broker, or other qualified appraiser. You will have to pay separately for this, and fees can typically range anywhere from $500 to $5,000 (and even higher), depending on the complexity of your business. The advantage to you is that you can have the most confidence in the appraisal because the appraiser has no vested interest in skewing the value one way or another. You will also have a written copy of the valuation and its uses for your broker to use with prospective buyers. If you rely on your listing broker to do a valuation, you most likely will not receive a copy of the appraisal itself. Business brokers working on a contingency basis are reluctant to release their valuation analysis to a seller because some sellers have been known to use business brokers to receive a "free" business valuation. However, you may want to ask the business broker what their policy is in this regard. Refer back to Chapter 2 of this book for a more extensive discussion of the business valuation topic.

Confidentiality of the Business Sale

What Steps Do You Take To Ensure The Confidentiality Of My Business Being For Sale? Many business owners are very wary of letting it be known to anyone that their business is for sale. There are many good reasons for this and the ability to maintain the confidentiality of the planned business sale is an important capability of the business broker.

However, one of the hardest things to do when selling an operating business is to maintain the confidentiality of the sale. Although no reputable broker can ever guarantee complete confidentiality, there are many steps they can take to maximize the chances that your business sale will remain discreet. The two most important actions are:

- Using discretion in the details that are included in any advertising for your business.

- Requiring legally binding documentation signed by potential buyers which requires them to not disclose any of the details they learn about your business (or even the fact that it's for sale).

Most professional business brokers will use some form of confidentiality agreement with potential buyers. Eventually, however, the business broker is going to have to actually show the physical assets and premises of the business. In an effort to maintain confidentiality, the business broker should:

- Be willing to show the premises after normal business hours.

- Be willing to pose as an insurance agent or some other professional having a legitimate, benign interest in touring the business during normal hours.

Safeguarding Financial Information

How Will You Safeguard My Business Financial Information From Inappropriate Use? To facilitate the process of selling your business and to allow the business broker to present your business in its best light, you will need to provide sensitive financial information about your business. Every business owner naturally has a concern about safeguarding that information from competitors and others with no legitimate need to know. A good business broker will require that a potential buyer sign a nondisclosure agreement of some kind before any sensitive information is released.

Additionally, the business broker should have a security arrangement within their office where only the listing broker controls the access to the seller's detailed financial information. No one other than the listing broker should have access to the seller's business financial information without the express consent of the listing broker. Furthermore, a business broker should be able to articulate this security policy to a seller. In some cases, sellers may want to restrict access to their financial statements to only themselves or their accountants. This is less efficient than letting the business broker handle things, but it will add a measure of security to your financial information. You should ask the business broker what their policy is about this.

Education and Training

What Is Your Education And Training Background? A business broker's educational and training background is not always a good indicator of a successful brokering endeavor. Brokers come from many walks of life and hugely divergent backgrounds. In general, a broker's track record in selling businesses is much more indicative of their potential than their education and training. However, you may be able to get a feel for the broker's sophistication and sense of your business based on their education and training. Typically, a broker with an engineering background will be more successful with technology- or manufacturing-based companies. A broker with a Bachelor of Arts degree may be more sensitive to the nuances of a publishing company, graphic arts studio, bookstore, etc. A business broker with an MBA or a CPA may have a better understanding of business fundamentals than someone without a formal business education. The most important aspect of this question is to find out specifically what business education and/or training they have had. It's also important to determine if the broker is keeping up with the latest knowledge and approaches in the field by finding out what professional training they have taken and what designations or certifications they have earned, and when. Various professional organizations offer rigorous certification programs for business brokers. For example, the International Business Brokers Association (IBBA) will designate an individual as a Certified Business Intermediary (CBI) upon completion of specified courses and testing.

Client References

What References From Satisfied Buyers And Sellers Can You Provide To Me? All experienced brokers usually have a portfolio of testimonials, thank you letters, and names of satisfied clients that they will provide to a serious prospective client. Most often these references will be from the sellers, the business broker's most usual client. Some brokers have also represented buyers or have received positive comments from satisfied buyers on the other side of the transaction. These are all important for you to check out in order to judge the degree of satisfaction by the broker's other clients.

Additionally, you should ask for references from attorneys, accountants, and bankers that the broker has recently worked with in closing business deals. Most likely, the broker will not have any written testimonials from them. However, you should be able to obtain several names of professionals who may be familiar to you from whom you can receive an unbiased opinion as to the broker's expertise in facilitating the sale of a business. These references may be of more significance to you than the testimonials of past clients. The broker most likely will only provide you with satisfied clients as references. By talking with the attorneys and CPAs involved in the broker's more recent closings, you may be able to get a broader perspective of the business broker's capabilities.

If you are dealing with an investment banker, they keep a record of their successful transactions in a written form which are referred to as "tombstones." Some business brokers and mergers and acquisitions specialists may also refer to their completed deals as tombstone listings. Be sure to ask for a copy of them for your review and consideration.

Finding Qualified Buyers

What Steps Will You Take To Ensure That You Introduce My Business To Qualified Buyers Only? A qualified buyer is someone who is ready and able to buy a business such as the one being offered for sale. I have deliberately left out the second word from the real estate phrase that most of us know: ready, *willing,* and able. In the first exposure of a business for sale to a potential buyer, you certainly cannot expect them to be willing to buy, but your broker should have a way to qualify a buyer as ready and able, or you will all be wasting a lot of time.

A ready and able buyer, i.e., a qualified buyer is:

- Someone who is honestly looking for a business to purchase.

- Someone who has the motivation and personal commitment to purchase a business.

- Someone who has the financial resources (or access to them) to consummate the purchase.

- Someone who has the "right" motivations (e.g., you don't want sensitive business information being given to one of your business competitors!).

A professional business broker should know how to sort through the many nonqualified buyers to get to the few who actually do have the means and motivation to buy your business. The good news is that once the unqualified potential buyers have been culled, a high percentage of qualified buyers eventually do buy a business.

Many business brokers use a questionnaire, sometimes referred to as a Buyer's Financial Qualification Statement, to qualify a buyer. It's usually not very easy to get this from a prospective buyer in such an early stage of the sale process, but a good business broker will know how. If it's determined that the buyer is not financially qualified to buy your business, a great deal of wasted time on everyone's part will be avoided. One strategy that the broker can use in asking the potential buyer to fill out the statement is to say that it's for a reciprocal exchange of sensitive financial information between business parties. The seller provides the business's IRS tax returns and other financial data to the buyer, and the buyer provides pertinent personal financial data about themselves to the seller.

Licensing

Are You A Licensed Real Estate Broker? This question is important to the business seller for several reasons.

- You want to find out if the business broker splits their time between selling real estate and businesses, or if they concentrate on selling businesses only. Usually you will receive much better service and results if the business broker concentrates on selling businesses only.

- Many businesses involve some sort of real estate to be transferred as part of the business. In all 50 states, a real estate license is required to represent real estate for sale. In addition to actual land and buildings, real estate laws also cover a lease for the rented premises. You want to make sure that the business broker either is a licensed real estate agent, or works with a real estate agent, if your business sale will involve the transfer of any real estate, including assignments of leases.

- In several states, it's required by law that business brokers be licensed as real estate agents whether the sale of the business involves real estate or not. These states (as of 1997) are:

Alaska	Illinois	Oregon
Arizona	Iowa	South Dakota
California	Louisiana	Utah
District of Columbia	Michigan	Washington
Florida	Minnesota	Wisconsin
Hawaii	Nebraska	Wyoming
Idaho	Nevada	

It should be noted that Illinois also requires that a business broker doing business in the state be registered with the Illinois Security Department.

I want to make one last point concerning this issue of needing a real estate sales license in connection with a business sale. If the real estate is owned by a corporation and the business broker is selling the shares in the corporation, then a real estate license is generally not required because, technically, it's the corporate stock that is being sold and not the real estate. If this is an issue in the sale of your business, you could check with your secretary of state to learn the specific laws in your locale. In general, though, this is the business broker's concern and not yours.

Fee Structure

What Are Your Fees For Representing My Business For Sale? Many business brokers have a standard fee that they charge which is usually 10 percent of the total value of a business sale up to some set value. After reaching this value, the percentage declines on some scale. Frequently, the total value includes all tangible and intangible assets, including the cash, accounts receivable, and inventory if these are conveyed as part of the business transaction. Please refer back to Chapter 4 for a more detailed discussion of the brokerage fee structure.

You should also keep in mind that there is no standard fee structure in the industry. Any quoted fees are open to negotiation between yourself and the business broker. Not only is it possible to negotiate a different fee structure, but you may want to exclude certain assets, such as accounts receivable and cash, from the application of the fee.

I have been asked many times why business brokerage fees seem so exorbitant. At first glance, a 10% fee to procure a buyer for your business and facilitate negotiations may seem very high, and it usually is relative to the amount of actual time applied to a successful sale. The problem is that business brokers, M&A specialists, and investment bankers typically work on a contingency basis. That means many business sales do not actually close, and thus no commission is received. There are many reasons for this, but the final result is that you essentially compensate the brokers for the sales that they did not close. In general, brokers work very hard and, on average, earn a reasonable living consistent with their education and the service they provide. Most successful business sellers feel that the fee earned by those representing their business for sale is well earned.

Other negotiating points you may want to address are the payment terms of the fee. Most business brokers want to receive their entire fee at the closing, but payout terms may be negotiated to lower the up-front cash requirements for the buyer and therefore improve the ability for you to sell your business.

In some cases, a broker will require that an up-front fee be paid to represent your business for sale. The amount paid will usually be deducted from the sales commission at the time of sale. If no closing takes place, the fee is not refundable. Many of the more successful and highly qualified brokers are requiring this arrangement as a way of smoothing out the vagaries of the contingency fee process. It can be argued that you will receive more competent professional representation with this fee arrangement. If you do pay an up-front fee as an advance against a future commission, you should insist on a written appraisal of your business valuation as a quid pro quo. In the event your business does not sell, you will at least have the written valuation to use in any future sales attempts.

Listing Agreements

What Type of Listing Agreement Do You Want To Enter, And How Long Will It Take To Sell My Business? There are basically three types of listing agreements or "authorizations to sell" that you can enter.

The "open agency listing" gives the broker the right to sell the business, but without any specified performance requirements for either the seller or the broker. You still have the right to sell the business yourself and also to enter into other open listing agreements with other brokers. The broker, in turn, does not have any obligation to use their best (or any) effort in marketing your business. In general, open listings are the least desirable to the broker. Most will avoid them if possible because they will be competing against too many other brokers, including possibly you.

The "exclusive agency listing" gives the broker the exclusive right to sell your business as an agency (brokerage firm). You retain the right to sell your business personally, but cannot give a listing to any other agency during the term of the agreement. The broker is required to exert their full and best efforts to market your business.

The "exclusive right to sell listing" is the most desirable situation from the broker's point of view and, in my opinion, the best arrangement for you as well. Most businesses that are sold are done so under exclusive right to sell agreements. This listing gives the broker the sole and exclusive right to sell your business. The advantage to the broker with this listing is that they will feel much more secure in investing their time, effort, and advertising money in promoting the sale of the business without fear that you or anyone else will cut them out by finding another buyer. The advantage to you is that you will receive the best efforts and service from a protected, and therefore, highly motivated business broker working to earn a commission.

Another point to consider on the subject of listing agreements is the length of time that the agreement is valid. It's unreasonable to expect to sell a business in much less than six months. Twelve months is a better estimate, given the complicated nature of the transaction. Consequently, a listing agreement should be for no less than six months. Realistically, a year is a more reasonable term for both parties. If you are nervous about committing to one broker for that length of time, then insist on putting an escape clause in the agreement that lets you opt out after six months if the broker has not used a reasonable effort (in your opinion) to sell your business.

Seller Financing

Do You Think I Will Need To Finance The Business Sale? No matter whether you like the idea or not, you as the business seller will most likely have to take a promissory note ("hold paper") to complete the sale of your business, if the selling price is under a million dollars. I know most sellers just want to sell their business and be done with it, but it usually does not work like that. Unless your business is extremely profitable, very well established, has a strong, consistent, and loyal customer base in a growing market, most banks and other lending institutions will loan only a relatively small portion of the business value to a buyer, if anything at all. This is especially true if a significant portion of the business value is in "goodwill." In fact, many lending institutions will not loan more than 70% of the fair-market value of the tangible assets alone, and will not loan any portion of the goodwill at all. So, unless the buyer has the entire amount of the purchase price in cash, you might want to think about how much, and under what conditions, you will take back a promissory note against the sale of your business.

You should ask the broker what percentage of their business sales include seller financing and if they have alternate sources of financing that they can make available to qualified buyers. Some brokers have good contacts for sources of capital from SBA participating banks or venture capital funds. Additionally, many of the larger brokerage firms and M&A specialists require that prospective buyers prequalify themselves with evidence of cash available and/or letters of credit before businesses are introduced to them.

Information Requirements

What Information Do You Need From Me About My Business? To properly represent your business for sale for the best value to the widest array of qualified potential buyers, the business broker will need as much information about your business as you can reasonably provide. At a minimum, the broker should ask for:

- Financial Statements (Income and Expense Statements and Balance Sheets for the last three fiscal years).

- Interim Financial Statement (this fiscal year).

- IRS Tax Returns (last three years).

- Lease or Rental Agreement (including renewal options).

- Franchise Agreement (if applicable).

- List of furniture, fixtures, equipment, including estimated or appraised "fair-market value."

- Licensing, Distributorship, Manufacturing Agreements, etc.

- List of current contracts, including face amount, completion date, and percentage completed.

- Copies of patents, trade names, trademarks, or copyrights.

- Customer Lists.

This listing is a subset of all of the information that I recommend in Chapter 7, "Putting It All Together: Preparing an Exit Plan," that you prepare as part of "The Book" which will become a selling prospectus for your business.

Selecting an Investment Banker

Many business sales will not require the involvement of an investment banker, especially if the estimated sale price is under $10 million and the likely purchaser is a private party. In general, the value of investment bankers is in their ability to find strategic buyers and to structure very complex deals involving LBOs or IPOs where corporate stock and cash are the medium of exchange. Usually, investment banker fees are contingent upon the successful sale of the business. They are based on the Lehman formula for "smaller" deals and approximately 1% of the total selling price for very large deals. What constitutes small and large and thus the exact fee is totally negotiable. There is no governing board of investment bankers that establish rates, so they will basically try to get whatever the traffic will bear. Many investment banking firms, however, have similar, non-negotiable fee structures. Most of you will not require the services of an investment banker but for those of you who want to investigate this resource further, I have provided a listing of some investment bankers in Chapter 8.

Some advantages of using investment bankers are their adeptness at establishing a reasonable valuation for your company and their knowledge about potential buyers for your business. They are also skilled negotiators, and most will prepare much of the information needed by buyers into a formal professional sales package which they generally refer to as "The Book."

When considering which investment banker to use, you should carefully consider their "tombstones." Tombstones are synopses of each major deal in which the investment banker has been involved. They will be happy to provide you with a list upon request. You should look for an investment banker that appears to have done deals like yours: similar business, industry, valuation, etc.

Obtaining an Independent Business Valuation

Strategic Move #42:

"Consider an independent business valuation as a sanity check against everyone else's opinion."

You may want to hire an independent firm to provide a business valuation for you rather than rely exclusively on yourself, your accountant, your business broker, mergers and acquisitions specialist, or investment banker. Although this may not be necessary, some business owners feel more comfortable having an outside third party with no vested interest in the outcome of the transaction providing an opinion as to the selling price of their business. Some arguments for and against this are:

- A broker/representative is usually working on a contingent fee basis which implies they will try to get the most for your business. This is not always the case. You may be pressured to take less for your business than its true value by a broker who considers "a percentage of something is better than a percentage of nothing."

- Because each business and each buyer is unique, it is very difficult if not impossible to put a definitive price on a business. The best you can hope for is a ballpark estimate that will start negotiations with a potential buyer. If you have selected a reputable broker/representative that understands your company and the industry it's in, then you will most likely receive a reasonable valuation estimate that you can use as a starting point for the business sale process.

- An independent business valuation can be quite expensive if the valuation firm performs it with no prospect of a large commission as a result of the sale of your business.

If you decide that you want or need an independent business valuation, there are primarily two professional designations which are meaningful when selecting an appraiser. One is the ASA, which signifies membership in the American Society of Appraisers, and the other is the Certified Business Appraiser (CBA) designation awarded by the Institute of Business Appraisers. Both organizations provide extensive training, testing, and professional certification for their members.

Of course, if you are planning to sell your business within your family or to your employees through an ESOP process, you will need to obtain an independent appraisal of its value. In fact, the requirements for a business valuation appraisal are quite stringent under the ESOP rules. In these cases, you will not need the services of a business broker or investment banker to find a buyer for your company. I have listed some resources for business valuations and appraisals in Chapter 8, including how to contact the American Society of Appraisers and the Institute of Business Appraisers.

Involving Your Commercial Banker in the Sale

Strategic Move #43:

"Involve your commercial banker in your business sale from the very beginning of the process."

If you have a good and long-standing business relationship with a commercial banker, it's an excellent idea to involve your banker early in your plans to sell your business for the following reasons:

- The buyer will need to establish credit sources for business operations and other banking services, and the continuation of the current arrangements will be one less problem for a new owner.

- The buyer may need to obtain some bank financing for the purchase of your business. Who is more likely to loan the necessary funds than the bank that knows your business the best?

- Your banker may be able to play an extremely important independent advisory role during negotiations.

- Your banker may also be able to refer you to prospective buyers that they are aware of within your community.

You should approach your banker early in the process and ask them to participate on your team. Most bankers will be happy to help you for at least two sound business reasons:

- They will want their bank to continue as the source of banking services to your business under a new owner.

- They will want to help you to manage and invest your money that you realize from the sale of your business. Most commercial banks have a Trust Department that you may find to be a valuable source of money management and investment services.

However, you should keep in mind that most commercial bankers will not have the expertise or inclination to become actively involved in the actual negotiation and sale process. Their principal value will be in providing financing support for the buyer, whether for purchasing the business or by providing loans of operating and/or expansion capital.

In Summary

Now that you understand the roles of the potential members of your team, it's time to talk about how to pull together everything that I have discussed in this book and create a practical approach to selling your business. In the next chapter, I will present a process for preparing an exit plan for you from your business.

7

Putting It All Together: Preparing an Exit Plan

- *Preparing an Exit Plan*
- *Composing Your Company Overview, Financial History, and Forecasts*
- *Assembling "The Book"*
- *Accelerating the Sale Preparation Process*
- *Marketing, Negotiating, and Selling*
- *Managing Your Sale Proceeds*

Preparing an Exit Plan

This chapter will show you how to pull together everything that has been covered in this book in the creation of an exit plan for you from your business and the preparation of a business sale prospectus. I highly recommend that you thoroughly document your exit plan so that you can use it as a road map as you progress through the process of preparing and selling your business. I know that writing things down takes time but it will help you to think through all of the issues that you need to carefully consider as you prepare your business for sale. Additionally, several parts of your exit plan must be put in writing anyway as part of the business selling process. Some of these items are:

- Advisor Agreements.

- Product and/or Service Descriptions.

- Company Overview.

- Financial History and Forecasts.

- Key-Person Employment Contracts.

- Legal Documentation.

In fact, it will be to your advantage to combine the company overview, financial history and forecasts, product/service descriptions, and key-person employment contracts as well as other pertinent information into a sales document for your business that is sometimes referred to as "The Book" by investment bankers. This is essentially a detailed prospectus, or selling document, that many business brokers as well as investment bankers have found to be extremely useful in presenting key information about a business to prospective buyers. Even though you may not use an investment banker in your business sale, it will be smart to have "The Book" prepared for whomever represents your interests with potential buyers. This is true even if you sell your business yourself. "The Book" will be the key document that you use to present your business to potential buyers. They, in turn, will use it as they conduct their due diligence of your company. Having the information gathered ahead of time will not only smooth the selling process, but it will reinforce the notion of professionalism and sound management practices of your business, both of which are extremely important to convey.

As you prepare your information, both for your own use and that of a possible buyer, keep in mind that many potential business sales fall through because of a lack of honesty, candor, and disclosure on the part of the seller. Any legitimate buyer will be accomplishing a thorough due diligence process, and any warts or wrinkles in your business will most likely be discovered during this examination. If the buyer finds a significant undisclosed problem with your company, it may irreparably damage the good business relationship that will be needed to consummate the sale. A buyer will naturally wonder whether there are any other hidden problems that they have not been able to find. Even if you successfully hid a significant defect during the due diligence process, intentionally or not, it will most likely come to light after the business sale. Then you will have opened yourself up to possible litigation. Full disclosure to a prospective buyer during the due diligence process is by far the best policy. A high standard of ethics is essential to the successful sale of an operating business.

Strategic Move #44:

"Develop your business sale information with the highest degree of ethics and full disclosure of pertinent facts to ensure an orderly and successful sale."

I strongly recommend that business owners personally develop as much of their exit plan as possible. You most likely know your business better than anyone, and consequently you will be able to address the various issues with a greater understanding and in more detail than anyone you could delegate the task to. You should put as much personal attention into preparing a lucrative and worry-free exit strategy as you once put into building your company. This is the end-game of your business life for many of you and it's no time to relax and rest on your laurels. Summon the energy and fortitude to continue to push through to the end—the successful sale of your business.

As you progress through the process of preparing your business for sale, you should use your exit plan as a checklist for things that need to be done. It will also be important in helping you to stay focused on the reason you have decided to sell your business. Most business owners by their very nature are good salespersons. But, in the marketing of their business, they sometimes forget what motivated them to begin the sales process in the first place. What then happens is that they oversell themselves on what a great opportunity their business presents and they begin to waver regarding their decision to sell. This may cause you to lose sight of your real objective which is to sell the business, to cash-out and take your chips off of the table. In most cases, your original decision to sell was arrived at thoughtfully and with very good reasons. Being able to refer back to an exit plan where you have documented those reasons will help you to stay focused on your objective.

Strategic Move #45:

"Prepare a written exit plan from your business as far in advance as possible and well before you actually put it on the market."

There are many business consultants and advisors who advocate that business owners should prepare a long-range exit plan at the same time as they *start their business!* They feel that this will help to keep the owner focused not only on developing the business, but also on maximizing its eventual selling price. In fact, if you start a business with venture capital financing, your backers will require that you show them in a written exit plan how they can get their investment plus profit out of the business in a particular period of time. With venture capitalists this typically takes the form of a corporate stock sale through an IPO (see Chapter 1, "Why You Need to Prepare Your Business for Sale"). Of course, this is usually not how an average private business is sold. However, even if you are not using venture capital or other investment backing, I recommend that business owners have a written exit plan as far in advance of the actual sale of the business as possible for the following reasons:

- Many of the methods of sale for a business, as discussed in Chapter 1, take a substantial amount of planning and preparation. You will never get there if you do not know where you are going, and an exit plan will help you to establish your goals.

- An exit plan can constitute an excellent strategic planning tool for the small-business owner. It sets both short- and long-range business goals and helps to keep you focused on your objective. Even if you are not planning on selling your business for several years, you and your business will benefit by having an exit plan.

- In case of your unexpected death or incapacity, your heirs or assigns will know what you intended for the business and they will have a general road map to help them follow your wishes for the future of your business.

- The exit plan can provide a useful yardstick for you to evaluate where you are in your business and help you to make adjustments from time to time to stay on track toward your business sale objectives.

Exit Plan Key Points Checklist

Your exit plan will be a very personal, and certainly "company private," document that outlines and details your plans for disengaging yourself from your business. If you do not have a written exit plan (studies indicate that the vast majority of small-business owners do not), now is the time to develop one. A well-written exit plan will document the following points:

☐ *Your reason for wanting to sell your business.* Do not forget that all businesses will eventually be sold in one form or another; either by you to an outside party, as a transition to a successor family member, in the probate of your estate, or in some other sort of liquidation process. One way or another, your business will ultimately be sold. Carefully think about the reason you have for wanting to sell your business and document it as part of your exit plan.

❑ *Identification of the type of buyer that will be most likely to buy your business.* Before you begin the process of selling your business, you should make a preliminary assessment of the most likely type of buyer for your business because this will direct you in the steps you should take in preparing your business for sale. In Chapter 1, I described the various types of potential buyers:

- Financial Buyer (usually an entrepreneurial-minded individual).

- Strategic Buyer (usually another company in, or wanting to be in, your industry; and having strategic motives).

- Family Buyer (usually one or more of your children).

- Partner, Shareholder, or Employee Buyer.

- Industry Buyer (usually another company within your industry).

❑ *A preliminary decision as to the most likely method of sale.* Once you have identified the type of buyer most likely to purchase your business, you can now make a preliminary decision about the method of sale you want to pursue. Although you are not locking yourself into a particular method at this point, you should have some idea as to which one you intend to follow. You may want to refer back to Chapter 1 for a discussion of the various methods you could use to sell your business:

- Sale to a private party (Private sale).

- Sale/Transition to a family member (Succession planning).

- Sale to a partner or shareholder (Buy-Sell agreement).

- In-House Management Buyout (MBO).

- Sale to your employees (ESOP).

- Merger or Acquisition by another company (M&A).

- Corporate stock offering (IPO).

- Leveraged Buyout (LBO).

❑ *A time frame within which you hope to accomplish the sale of your business.* Depending on the type of buyer and the method of sale that you plan to pursue in the sale of your business, the time frame will vary widely. Your personal timetable may dictate the type of buyer and method of sale that you decide to attempt. For example, if you are in a rush to sell the business, then the ESOP or IPO route may not be practical to even consider.

❏ *The actions to take relative to your particular business and method of sale to enhance the sales value.* In Chapter 2, "What Is Your Business Really Worth?," I showed you how to determine a "ballpark" estimate of your business value and in Chapter 3, "Enhancing the Sales Value of Your Business," I provided many recommendations on how you can improve the potential selling price of your business. Depending on the type of buyer and method of sale that you have targeted, you should begin a selective implementation of these recommendations. For example, for a financial buyer in a private party sale, you will primarily want to maximize the provable profit-generating capability of your business. However, if you are planning to "sell" your business to a family member as part of a family-owned business succession process, you may not want to emphasize profitability due to the negative tax consequences. You will, however, want to tailor the business structure, implement estate planning techniques, and employ various other factors discussed in Chapter 5, "Succession Planning for the Family-Owned Business," to smooth the transition process.

❏ *Identification of your team of advisors and marketing representatives to implement the business sale.* You will now be ready to form a team to accomplish the sale of your business within the broad outline of your overall goals and objectives. Your targeted buyer and method of sale will guide you towards a selection of the right disciplines and expertise you will need both for your advisors and for your business marketing representative.

❏ *A determination of the price range for the sale of your business.* By this point, you have made many preliminary decisions about the type of buyer, the method of sale, and you have implemented many business operating improvements to enhance the value of your business. With your team of advisors and representatives, it's now time to establish final estimates of the value range for your business. You should have at least three valuation estimates for your business at this time:

• A liquidation value (to establish the absolute "floor" value for your business).

• A capitalization (CAP) value based on your last full fiscal year's reported earnings.

- A recalculated capitalization value based on the financial enhancements you have implemented and a reconstruction of your latest income and expense figures.

❏ *Identification of key persons that may require employment contracts.* Many good businesses are very dependent on the continued performance of at least a few important employees in the company. If this is true for your business, you should attempt to sign these key persons to some sort of contractual relationship so that you will be able to demonstrate employee continuity to a prospective buyer. This will be very difficult to accomplish while maintaining important confidentiality about your planned business sale. Consequently, you will most likely need to explain the reasons for the employment contracts to these key individuals. You should consider requiring a confidentiality agreement as part of their employment contract.

❏ *A plan to communicate your intentions to sell your business to selected important persons with a bona fide "need to know."* It is very important to explain to certain key individuals your decision to sell your business. The timing of this communication and who you tell will be very specific to your particular personal and business characteristics. Be sure to think this through carefully and balance the need for confidentiality against the need to maintain a close team of people you can rely on to help make the sale successful. People to consider confiding in include:

- Close family members.

- Key company managers.

- Other key employees.

- Important suppliers and customers.

❏ *Documentation of your company overview, financial history, and forecasts.* Most prospective buyers considering the purchase of your business will require this information as part of their due diligence process. It will be a very good selling point to have all of this information prepared and ready for transmittal to a prospective buyer, rather than to provide it in disconnected portions only in response to their request. The downside is that the preparation of this documentation can be time-consuming. Consequently, it should be begun as soon as you have firmly decided to offer your business for sale.

❏ *Assembly of "The Book" as a sales prospectus for your business.* Although investment bankers and business brokers usually offer their services in preparing their version of a sales package, you will be much further ahead if you prepare your own sales documentation for them to use. You may even be able to negotiate a lower sales commission or have any up-front fees waived if the broker does not need to prepare "The Book." The additional advantage of your preparation of this information is that you may be able to find trouble spots in your business picture that you can correct or explain before the information is actually provided to a prospective buyer.

❏ *A decision as to a preliminary structure for the sale of your business.* Although it is probably impossible to predict the ultimate structure of your business sale before you actually negotiate with the buyer, it's wise to at least outline what your optimal sale structure would be. You can then privately refer to this during the negotiation phase as a reference point for yourself and your advisors to keep your business objectives in mind. For example, some of the conditions that you may want to include as the basis for a sale structure are:

- A corporate stock or asset sale.

- An all-cash sale or owner financing (and to what extent).

- An earn-out agreement

- Conditions of a noncompete agreement

- Your continued involvement after the sale or a clean break.

- The real estate being part of the sale or handled as a separate item.

- How accounts receivable are to be transferred (if at all).

❏ *A process for marketing, negotiating, and selling your business.* You should decide on a plan of action with your advisors and marketing representatives about how your business is to be marketed, how negotiations are to be conducted, and the actual sales or closing process that you want to see followed. This is also the point where you may want to decide on how not to market your business. I know of one business owner who refused to allow their broker to approach a particular competitor (a long-standing arch rival). This particular business owner would rather liquidate his business than to sell it to "the enemy."

❏ *And lastly, your exit plan should include how you will receive the payment for your business, what you will do with it, and how you will disengage from the business.* These are key points that should be considered well in advance of the business sale. If you plan properly, you will avoid what many times turns out to be the very stressful circumstances of having to suddenly deal with a large amount of cash. Equally problematic is the issue of making a graceful exit from your company and a smooth transition into the next phase of your life.

I will now cover each of these points in greater detail in order to provide you with more food for thought as you begin putting your own exit plan together and just as importantly, preparing your business for sale. The process of writing things down necessarily requires the writer to select a sequence in which items appear. I have tried to logically order the major events that will happen as you prepare and eventually sell your business. In actuality, you may find that you accomplish one or more of these items before another, and you may even skip one or another entirely. This is, of course, totally up to you. I recommend that you read this chapter in its entirety to get an understanding of the entire process, and then modify the steps and approaches to fit your particular needs and way of looking at things. As a lead-in to the next section, I offer strategic move #46.

Strategic Move #46:

"Establish a logical and convincing reason for wanting to sell your business, both for a buyer and for yourself."

Make the Decision to Sell

Establish a well-thought-out reason for selling your business, both for your own purposes and also to satisfy a buyer. One of the first and most important questions a buyer will ask is, "Why does the owner want to sell?" The buyer is naturally going to be anxious about many things concerning the purchase of your business and they will need a good answer to this question. Conversely, if you have not carefully thought through the reasons that you want to sell your business, you may very well have second thoughts as you get closer to the sale. If you are not 100% committed to actually selling your business, you should not even begin the process. In addition to wasting everyone's time, you may open yourself up to potential financial liability regarding misrepresentations with the business broker and any potential buyers who invest time and effort in good faith negotiations and due diligence efforts. There is no "right" or "wrong" reason for wanting to sell a business, but some reasons resonate better with potential buyers than others. Some of the "better" reasons are:

- *Retirement:* You are elderly, or otherwise getting on in years, and have owned the business for a significant length of time so that you honestly wish to retire and enjoy the financial rewards of a successful, profitable business. You may even be relatively young, but have built a successful business enterprise that allows little time for you to otherwise enjoy life. You want to get out of the race while you are still relatively young.

- *Poor Health:* You are experiencing significant health problems that are adversely impacting your ability to run your business effectively. You may also have a spouse or other close loved one who is experiencing medical problems that require your full-time attention.

- *Death or Incapacity:* You are the surviving spouse or heir of a successful business owner who has recently passed away or become permanently incapacitated. You have no interest and/or capability in running the business and wish to sell it as an ongoing entity rather than as a liquidation.

- *Unsolicited Offer:* You have recently received an unexpected offer by another company or individual to purchase your business at a price and terms that are attractive to you. You will still need to demonstrate the value in your business to the prospective purchaser during the due diligence process.

- *Business Plan Objective:* It may have been part of your original business plan to sell your business at a key point to realize some targeted financial objective. Many new companies, with and without venture capital, are launched primarily to establish themselves in a newly emerging market (e.g., the Internet, Web TV, bio-technology, etc.) and then to sell themselves off either through an IPO or via a merger or acquisition.

Some other reasons that may be just as valid as those listed above, but which may not be perceived as well by potential buyers are:

- *Divorce:* While the breakup of a marriage can indeed be a good reason to force the sale of a business, many buyers will question why, if the business is so good, the couple cannot keep ownership themselves under some arrangement. Logically, a profitable business may be the "cash cow" that supports the lifestyle of both individuals. Therefore, many believe that some accommodation could be reached so that a sale is not necessary to satisfy the aggrieved spouse. Unfortunately, many divorce proceedings do not operate under the rules of logic and the only solution may be a sale of the business.

- *Other Interests:* This is frequently perceived by a potential buyer as a poor excuse to sell a lucrative business. If the owner really is bored with the business and wants to do other things, why not hire a manager for the existing company and pursue the new initiative concurrently? If this is really your reason for wanting to sell, I suggest that you carefully document this for the buyer's information and address why you do not want to stay in your current business.

- *Stress and/or Burn-out:* Although this may be your real reason for wanting to sell, I wonder how many buyers will want to buy a business that caused this condition with you.

- *Relocation:* If you have to relocate for personal health or spousal career reasons, you should consider whether the business could also be relocated. Also, buyers may be wary of a supposedly profitable business that you are willing to give up because your spouse has had their job transferred to another part of the country.

Whatever your reason for wanting to sell your business, be sure to write down your reasoning as part of your exit plan. Although you will primarily use this aspect of the plan as a reminder to yourself and as information for your family and close advisors as to why you want to sell your business, you should also include it as part of the information you include in "The Book."

The next step in the business selling process is to identify the most likely potential buyers for your company. Just as you pay careful attention to identifying your customer base for your product or service, you will need to make a preliminary judgment as to the type of buyer for your business. Doing so will enable you to tailor your sales approach and implement other related considerations.

Strategic Move #47:

"Target the type of buyer most likely to purchase your business and customize your marketing efforts accordingly."

Identify the Most Likely Buyers

Who do you believe is the most likely potential buyer for your business? It's important for you to make a preliminary judgment about this because the answer will guide your efforts in selecting a method of sale, the makeup of your team of advisors, your selection of marketing representatives, the steps you take to enhance your business value, and the types of information you include in "The Book." Please understand that just because you are identifying a particular type of buyer and a method of sale, this does not lock you into that sales approach exclusively. What it does is give you a firm basis to begin the important process of preparing your business for sale and bases the process on logical criteria. Some assumptions must be made early to begin the process. If a different type of buyer emerges later, you can easily switch your focus at that time. For now, you should choose your most likely type of buyer and begin preparing your business for sale on that premise.

The five general types of potential buyers discussed in Chapter 1 are:

- The financial buyer who will most likely be an individual or partnership primarily interested in the financial return on their investment, based on your past and projected future company earnings.

- The strategic buyer who will most likely be another company looking to acquire your company for business reasons other than the basic financial bottom-line of business.

- The family buyer to whom you wish to transition ownership for the purposes of keeping the business as family-owned, and to minimize the income taxes associated with the transfer.

- The partner, existing shareholder, or employee buyer who already knows your business well and will be primarily interested in striking a fair and affordable deal.

- The industry buyer who will most likely be another company looking to acquire your company assets for their liquidation value.

Once you have made a preliminary decision about the most likely buyer for your business, you should determine your most likely method of sale.

Strategic Move #48:

"Maximize your business sale possibilities by focusing on the most likely method of sale."

Identify the Most Likely Method of Sale

You need to make a preliminary decision as to the most likely method of selling your business based on the type of buyer you envision. Earlier, I discussed the methods of selling your business. They included:

- A sale to a private party, individual, or partnership, likely to be unknown to you at the time of offering your business for sale (Private Sale).

- A sale or transition to a family member (Succession Planning).

- A sale to an existing partner or minority (or equal) shareholder (Buy-Sell Agreement).

- A Management Buyout (MBO), where the buyers of the business will be your in-house management team.

- An Employee Stock Ownership Plan (ESOP), where the buyers will be your employees.

- A Merger or Acquisition (M&A), where your company will be bought by or merged with another company.

- An Initial Public Stock Offering (IPO), where the buyers are generally anonymous investors who purchase your company's stock in the hopes of future gain through dividends and/or stock price appreciation.

- A Leveraged Buyout (LBO) where your company is bought by an outside entity using borrowed funds with the corporate assets used as collateral.

The following Table depicts the most likely method of sale relative to your most likely potential buyer.

Table 7-A

Method of Sale Versus Type of Buyer

Type of Buyer	Method of Sale							
	Priv. Sale	Succ. Plan	Buy/Sell Agreement	MBO	ESOP	M&A	IPO	LBO
Financial	X						X	
Strategic	X					X		X
Family		X						
Partner/Employee/ Shareholder	X		X	X	X			
Industry	X					X		

The vast majority of business sales will occur in the following buyer/method combinations and in this order of frequency:

1) Financial buyer—private sale.

2) Family buyer—succession planning process.

3) Strategic buyer—merger and/or acquisition.

The predominant theme of the following discussions will focus primarily on buyer/methods 1) and 3) above. The reader is referred to Chapter 5 for the special issues relating to successfully transitioning a family-owned business to a family member successor. The key difference between the recommendations in this chapter and Chapter 3 and the special considerations discussed in Chapter 5 for a family-owned business is the desire on the part of the business owner to minimize the provable operating profit. By taking this course, the buyer can minimize potential estate taxes and actual gift and income taxes associated with the transfer of ownership. While tax minimization is also a concern when you are selling your business to a private buyer, the total valuation of the business is by far the principal concern. Even if the marginal tax rate on your business sale is 40% (40 cents on the dollar), you will still net an additional 60 cents for every dollar increase in valuation. Most business sellers will take that deal every time.

If your particular buyer/method of sale is most likely one of the other combinations, you should still follow the recommendations in this book. In addition, you will want to pay particular attention to selecting your team of advisors and representatives so that they have specific experience with your specialized method of sale. For example, if you are anticipating an ESOP sale to your employees or an IPO to the general public, then you will want to be sure to select an attorney and a CPA who have specific experience with this type of sale.

Another consideration, which is not nearly as critical as properly selecting your advisors, is the amount and type of information you need to prepare as part of "The Book." If you are planning a sale to your in-house management team through an MBO process, then such information as the company overview and financial forecasts may not be required since the prospective buyers will have intimate insider knowledge of your company. On the other hand, if you want to try an IPO (even a simplified IPO under the private placement rules), the quantity and detail of information that you need to prepare about your company will likely be substantially greater than what I would recommend for a traditional arms-length sale to a strategic or financial buyer.

You are now ready to make a reasonable estimate of the time it will take to complete the sale of your business. Now that you understand the most likely type of buyer and the probable method of sale (together with other considerations), you will be able to plan an appropriate time frame for exiting your business.

Establish the Time Frame for the Selling Process

It's very important that you establish a reasonable timetable for yourself to fully accomplish the sale of your business. If you set too short a time frame, you will inevitably become discouraged when the business is not yet sold. This may cause you to make poor judgments in trying to speed up the sale process. On the other hand, if you set too long a time frame, you may not create the sense of action needed to adequately prepare your business for sale at maximum value. Additionally, if the sale process is too strung out, your professional advisor fees will rise and your broker may lose the high degree of enthusiasm needed to consummate a successful business sale. In your time frame, you will need to allow for the preparation of your business for sale, the courtship process (finding a buyer), the actual sale (closing), and a payout or earn-out period for all funds due to you.

Strategic Move #49:

"Determine a realistic time frame to adequately prepare and sell your business."

There are many factors that will affect the selling process time frame, including:

- How well your business is prepared for sale.

- The method of sale you choose.

- How anxious you are to sell.

- Economic market conditions.

- Whether you elect to finance the purchase and under what terms and conditions.

To help you in your planning relative to a selling timetable, I have provided the following typical estimates of time frames. The amount of time may be different for you since you control some of the aspects of selling your company. Most business sales take longer than the owner anticipates because "things happen." These are things you may not be able to anticipate and that you have little or no control over. I can almost guarantee that no matter how well you have arranged your business sale, something unexpected will arise to delay the closing process. Here are the estimates for the time frames:

- Preparing your business for sale will take anywhere from one to two years if done properly, and as I recommend in this book. Of course, you can skip the preparation process and simply reconstruct your income and expense statements and prepare an optimistic pro forma in the hope that you can "sell" the reconstructed earnings to a buyer. In this case, you may be able to sell your business in as few as six months.

- The courtship process involves letting potential buyers know your company is for sale, finding a financially qualified and motivated buyer, and negotiating the terms and conditions of the sale. Some business sellers have done this in approximately six months and others can take up to two years, or even more.

- The actual closing of the sale may seem straightforward, but it's best to allow three months for the lawyers to do their thing, the buyer to get their funds and financing in place, and all permits, approvals, etc. to be obtained.

- If you have elected a payout or earn-out, then the sale is not yet completed until you have received your funds in full. Seller financing generally ranges from three to seven years, although longer term payouts are not unheard of.

So, the time frames for selling your business will range from about six months with no seller financing and no preparation up to eight to 10 years with full planning and preparation, "normal" sales processes, and seller financing. That is quite a range of time, and most business sales tend towards the intermediate to longer time frames than the shorter ones.

These time frames really begin to work against you if your age and/or health are a factor. Do not box yourself into a corner by waiting too long to start the process. If you are desperate to sell for compelling reasons, you most likely will not receive anything close to the true value of your business. On the other hand, if you have properly prepared your business for sale and have a well-defined exit plan with the time to implement it, you will most likely get the highest value for your company. In addition, you will be able to negotiate a favorable buyout on your terms.

There are some other considerations that could affect the time frame for the sale of your business. If you think one or more of these issues may apply to your business sale, you will want to have your professional advisors take the appropriate action to address them as early in your sale process as possible:

- Some companies have collective bargaining agreements with their employees that may have to be adjudicated before the completion of a sale.

- Some companies may have outstanding tax liens or pending litigation that must be cleared (or court approval obtained) before a sale can take place.

- Some companies have stockholder or partnership agreements, or some other form of equity ownership arrangement, that requires approval before a sale of the company can take place.

Take Action to Enhance the Sales Value of Your Business

Strategic Move #50:

"Optimize the opportunity to sell your business by increasing profits and reducing risks before you offer it for sale."

Chapter 3 provided a detailed discussion of many of the things that you can do to enhance the sales value of your business. Although beauty is truly in the eyes of the beholder, the odds are that a potential buyer will be inclined to value your business in direct proportion to the levels of verifiable net cash flow that they believe will accrue to them as a result of purchasing your company. On a secondary level, there are nonfinancial matters which will further add value in the buyer's mind. These will help to reduce the level of risk felt by the buyer purchasing your business. The level of risk has been shown to be inversely proportional to the amount that a person will pay for an investment. The lesser the risk, the more they will pay.

Consequently, you should begin an aggressive campaign to increase sales, reduce expenses, and enhance your management and operating procedures in order to maximize the selling price of your business. The following is a checklist from which you can pick and choose so that you can tailor your own approach to enhancing your business value. Details for implementation of each of these items are contained throughout this book, but are primarily covered in Chapter 3.

Business Value Enhancement Checklist

❑ Examine your key financial operating ratios and, if necessary, develop and implement a plan of action to bring them in line with your industry norms.

❑ Develop a preliminary business valuation to use as a benchmark against which to compare your later selling price valuation range.

❑ Evaluate all leased and financed assets for possible conversion to owned assets.

❑ Evaluate all ongoing service and material contracts and agreements for possible competition or renegotiation.

❑ Examine your physical plant to identify possibilities for reduced cost and/or increased revenues.

❑ Evaluate every employee's position for elimination or conversion to less expensive contracted services.

❑ Evaluate all office equipment and computer software for efficiency, productivity, and cost-effectiveness.

❑ Evaluate all production-related equipment with the objective of reducing maintenance and repair costs, operator training costs, energy costs, downtime costs, and thus create a potential for increased productivity.

❑ Examine your practices regarding unreported cash sales and implement a plan to begin bringing them into your revenue stream.

❑ Examine your need for luxury automobiles and eliminate those that are not absolutely needed to maintain your business sales.

❑ Examine the need for all other "nice-to-have" luxury items being paid for by the company such as boats, aircraft, ski lodges, sports skyboxes, etc.

❑ Evaluate the continuing need for family members on the company payroll.

❑ Examine all miscellaneous expenses to ensure that no personal benefit items are being paid for by the company.

❑ Examine all of your travel and entertainment expenses to ensure that they are absolutely necessary to maintain the company's customary level of sales.

❑ Examine any personally owned assets that are leased back to the company for possible reduction in lease costs to a fair-market level.

❑ Examine all product lines and services for acceptable contributions to profitability.

❑ Evaluate the possibility of hiring outside consultants to advise you on increasing company profitability.

❑ Ensure the business's inventory is current and appropriately valued to maximize your last year's profitability.

❏ Ensure that all company leases, mortgages, agreements and contracts are fully assignable to a new owner.

❏ Evaluate the desirability of having your financial statements professionally audited by a CPA to establish a solid financial baseline.

❏ Have interim financial statements prepared if you are beginning the business sale process in the middle of your fiscal year.

❏ Collect or write-off all aging accounts receivable.

❏ Settle all outstanding lawsuits, tax liens, disputes, union grievances, and other similar corporate baggage.

❏ Resolve all partnership and shareholder disputes.

❏ Take action to ensure the continuity of corporate management and key employees.

❏ Revitalize your Board of Directors to ensure that they are an asset to your company.

❏ Ensure that the company's product/service liability insurance coverage is up-to-date.

❏ Ensure that all of the company's sales and marketing literature is current.

❏ Ensure that your company has an up-to-date Operations and Procedures Manual and a Human Resources Manual.

❏ Consider doing the following miscellaneous things to help to establish a positive outward appearance for your business:

   ❏ Ensure all business signage is up-to-date, in good repair, and clearly visible.

   ❏ Consider asking your employees to wear uniforms to help convey a sense of teamwork on the part of your workforce.

   ❏ Ensure that all of the areas of your business premises are neat and orderly.

   ❏ Ensure that your company has a well-stocked supply room.

   ❏ Ensure that all of your company awards, plaques, citations, business affiliations, etc. are prominently displayed.

   ❏ Ensure that all employees are busy and courteous when prospective buyers visit your business facilities.

❏ Consider involving the local and/or state economic development officials in the business sale process if you determine they may be useful to you.

❏ Ensure that there is ample customer and employee parking.

❏ Ensure that the business's public and private grounds are maintained in good condition during the entire time of the selling process.

Before leaving this section on things you can do to enhance the sales value of your business, I want you to consider some additional things you should do if you lease your business premises rather than own them.

Strategic Move #51:

"Lock in a long-term lease for your rented business premises before you offer the business for sale."

Special Considerations for Business Real Estate Leases

If you rent your business premises and the company is dependent on the location, you need to obtain the most favorable terms for as long as possible (using renewal options) before the landlord has any inkling that you are planning to sell your business. Nothing can kill a deal faster than a greedy landlord (except maybe a misguided lawyer). There are many businesses that rely on their location for the bulk of their business. Retail stores, walk-in service companies, and restaurants are just a few of the businesses that are usually very dependent on their physical location. Even if you are not 100% tied to your location, it's usually a major expense and inconvenience to move. The landlord usually realizes this and when a sale of a business is in the offing, they frequently see this as a good time to increase the rent. Even if you try to keep things secret from the landlord, eventually they will have to become part of the transaction. Additionally, the potential business buyer will probably want to lock in a longer-term lease arrangement than you have left in your existing lease. This will necessitate negotiations with the landlord.

Consequently, as soon as you begin thinking about putting your business up for sale, you should approach your landlord with a proposal to extend your lease with as many priced options as you can get. You may even hint about the possibility of relocating to a better location, larger space, or more modern facility. Your bargaining position will be the strongest at this point because the landlord will most likely not want to run the risk of losing you as a tenant. After a landlord learns that you intend to sell the business, the advantage shifts because you need a stable business location to attract a good buyer and the landlord will realize this. This will give the landlord the upper hand in negotiations and may drive the rent payments up so much that it adversely affects the selling price of your business.

You also want to make sure that your lease is assignable. This is another "must." Otherwise, the lease is good for only as long as you are the tenant. Upon a business sale, the lease will be extinguished. The uncertainty that this will put into negotiations for the purchase of your business could kill the sale. If you don't already have a "right to assignment" clause in your lease, you should add one during your negotiation to extend the period of the lease. Here is a sample clause that you and your attorney can tailor to fit your needs:

> "Lessee may not assign this lease in whole or in part, or may not sublet all or any part of the leased premises, without the prior written consent of the lessor, which shall not be unreasonably withheld. If this lease is assigned, or if the leased premises or any part thereof be sublet or occupied by anybody other than the lessee, lessor may collect rent from the assignee, sublessee or occupant, and apply the net amount collected to the rent herein reserved, but no such assignment, subletting, occupancy or collection shall be deemed a waiver of this covenant or the acceptance of the assignee, sublessee or occupant as a lessee or as a release of lessee from the further performance by lessee of the covenants contained herein. Lessor shall not unreasonably withhold consent specifically to subleasing and assignment. Lessee may not sublet if it is in default of any of the terms and conditions of this lease."

While we are on the subject of leases, you will want also to make sure that your lease allows you to sublet portions of your premises. As discussed in Chapter 3, it may make excellent economic sense to convert some of your unused facility space to an income-producing sublet arrangement. The wording in the clause above will also allow you to sublet your space.

There may be other things particular to your unique business that you can do to improve your profitability or enhance the "look" of the company. I recommend that you add them to the list of ideas that I have provided here and begin implementing them as soon as practical within your business selling process.

You should now consider assembling your team of professionals to help you actually sell your business. In the next section, I provide you with some things to think about as you proceed with this next facet of preparing your business for sale.

Strategic Move #52:

"Select a team of professional advisors and marketing representatives dedicated to selling your business."

Select and Assemble Your Team of Advisors and Representatives

By this point in time, you have made a firm decision to sell your business, and you have taken the necessary action to enhance your business income by maximizing the revenues and minimizing the expenses. You also have a rough idea as to the time frame in which you want to sell, you have identified the potential buyers most likely to buy your business, and you have selected a method of sale. Now it's time to select and assemble the team of professional advisors and marketing representatives that you will need to accomplish the sale of your business.

In all likelihood, you have already consulted one or more of your potential team members relative to the possible sale of your business. You may have worked with your business accountant to establish a "benchmark" valuation for your company. You may already have contacted your attorney about any potential legal impediments to selling your business. Now you need to carefully consider whether these are the right individuals to help you in the actual business sale. If they are not, then you need to find professional advisors who have specific experience in this specialized field of business. I have included in Chapter 8. "Resources for Preparing Your Business for Sale," a listing of potential professional resources that you may want to consider about your specific type of business sale transaction.

Professional Advisors

Your first step is to determine which advisors you actually need (and can afford). For example, if your company accountant is fully competent in preparing a professional business valuation, you may not need to hire an independent business appraiser. You may also be completely comfortable with your usual company/personal attorney and do not feel the need to hire a specialist in the field. Only you can decide the best mix of advisors for your team as you prepare your business for sale. However, this is not an area in which you should try to save money. If you are absolutely sure that you want to sell your business and are committed to doing the many things necessary to successfully accomplish the sale, you will need professional advice and services. Please refer back to Chapter 6, "Choosing Professional Advisors and Sales Representatives," for a detailed discussion regarding the selection of professional advisors.

Once you are comfortable that you have carefully identified the players for your advisory team, I recommend that you prepare draft agreements and task assignments for each of them. You should include the following considerations in these agreements:

- Description of services to be provided.

- Fees, payments, and commissions to be paid.

- Time frame of the agreement.

- Requirement for confidentiality.

- Provision for changes to the agreement.

Of course, some of these considerations will have to be discussed and negotiated with your advisors, especially remuneration issues. It's better if you have an outline of an agreement and some idea of what you want before you even discuss hiring them.

Marketing Representatives

In addition to professional advisors, you will most likely need to select a marketing representative for your business. Depending on the type of business you have and its expected selling price (and, therefore, the potential complexity of the transaction), you will select either a business broker, mergers and acquisitions specialist, or investment banker. For simplicity, I will refer to these business marketing representatives in the following text collectively as "brokers." Although some business owners "go it alone," I do not recommend it. However, there are some circumstances where you may want to avoid the expenses of a broker. For example, if you feel that the most likely buyer for your company is a competitor or someone in a similar business, and you do not mind personally approaching them, then you may not need the services of a broker. However, a good broker will do much more for you than locate a qualified potential buyer for your business. A professional broker will act as the "middle man" during negotiations, help to resolve deal-killing issues, act as a conduit for information between the buyer and yourself, and assist in arranging the many details of the actual closing process. Most business sellers find a broker's services indispensable during the sale process and well worth the fee.

Even though I have chosen to make a distinction between professional advisors and brokers, an experienced broker will often be an excellent advisor for you as well. They tend to have much more actual negotiation experience than an attorney and/or accountant and will usually be able to suggest creative ways to structure business sales that can mean the difference between success and failure. Please refer back to Chapter 6 for further discussion of this issue and guidelines for selecting the type of broker suited to your particular transaction.

Forming the Team

Your next step, after you have prepared your draft advisor agreements and draft marketing representative listing agreement and after you have discussed them with each person individually, is to assemble your advisors together with you in a group. Before any agreements are finalized, you especially want to discuss the description of services that each are expected to provide. You also want to identify any overlap or find any gaps in what needs to be done. At this meeting, it will be a good time to lay out the general ground rules you want them to follow. For example:

- Reiterate to them that you are the decision maker and they are the advisors.

- Tell them that you sincerely want to sell your business and you want that goal fixed firmly in everyone's mind. The advisors are there to help you sell the business within the range of price and conditions you have determined and they must be problem solvers not problem creators.

- Let the advisors know that they are not hired to help you get the best deal necessarily, but rather a fair deal for everyone involved. Always remember that a fair deal for everyone is most likely the best deal for you.

- Tell them that you want everyone to work together in your best interests and not at cross purposes to each other. Any difficulties with each other or unforeseen issues that may arise during the sale process are to be brought to your attention immediately.

It's now time to determine the selling price range for your business and the conditions of sale that you want to impose. You will want to involve certain members of the team that you have just assembled either to lead this task or to work with you in the process. Many marketing representatives, whether business brokers, M&A specialists, or investment bankers, will want to participate very closely with you in this valuation process. You may want to rely heavily on their recent real-world experience as you arrive at a selling price range.

Strategic Move #53:

"Establish a reasonable and flexible price range for your business, including conditions of sale, that will encourage negotiations."

Determine the Price Range and Your Conditions of Sale

Notice that the title of this section includes the words "price range." This is because there is no foolproof way to establish an absolutely definitive selling price for your company. In Chapter 2, I discussed the different methods of pricing a going business, but I also cautioned you that your company is really worth only what someone is willing to pay for it at a given point in time. While this is absolutely true, you will still need to come up with a liquidation value, an asking price, a selling price range, and your conditions of sale.

- The liquidation value will be used to establish the absolute floor that you will accept as the price for your business.

- The asking price and your conditions of sale will be used to attract and qualify potential buyers.

- The selling price range will encompass the potential high and low points of the expected value of your business within which you expect to negotiate.

It's also important to understand that the selling price of your business and the conditions of sale are so interrelated that they must be considered together in the actual sale of your business. The following example illustrates this point:

A business seller offers his business as a corporate stock sale at an asking price of $1,000,000. For simplicity's sake, let's say that all current assets exactly equal all liabilities and so no adjustments need to be made to the selling price. The buyer will receive all of the corporate stock for $1,000,000. This includes all of the company assets: inventory, real estate, equipment, goodwill, etc. The seller wants an all-cash deal. The buyer offers $700,000 cash for the corporate stock and a guaranteed consulting contract with the seller for $110,000 per year for three years. The total cash to the seller is $1,030,000, but the purchase price of the stock in the company is $700,000. The extra $30,000 represents additional compensation to the seller for the time value over three years of the $300,000 consulting contract which is in effect a deferred payment of the original asking price.

When a business value is estimated, it usually represents the total cash compensation that a seller expects to receive for the business. Any deviations will inevitably require negotiations. This is because deviations will not only affect the time value of future payments, but also the income tax treatment (capital gains versus ordinary income) of the actual flow of net cash to the seller. In the above example, the seller will likely end up paying more in income taxes because the $330,000 will be taxed at ordinary income tax rates (nominally 31% for federal taxes) versus capital gains tax rates of 20%.

The actual tax implications to you will be very specific to your personal financial situation, the cost basis in your company, depreciation recapture requirements, issues involving tax-loss carry-forward, and a host of other issues. You will need to consider all of these factors in evaluating the price and structure of the sale of your business. This is one of the many reasons that you need to have a very capable tax accountant as part of your advisory team.

Pricing

The very first step you will have taken in setting a selling price for your business was to establish a "benchmark" value based on your reported net earnings before you took any action to enhance the value of your business. If you followed the recommendations in this book, you will have established a "benchmark" value one or two years ago. You will then have implemented the appropriate recommendations to enhance the value of your business. You would have done this by increasing the provable bottom-line profits and by also taking other suggested actions to lessen the perceived risk in the business. Now you are ready to establish an asking price and negotiation range for your business.

The first thing you should do at this point is to follow the guidelines in Chapter 2 to determine an asset based valuation (*liquidation value*) for your business as of this point in time. Be sure to include not only the fair-market value of your assets (net of your liabilities), but also to deduct the legal and administrative costs associated with liquidation. This value should establish the absolute floor value of your company. It's a worst case situation which reflects the least amount of money that you can expect to receive for the sale of your company.

Of course, this is not the objective of selling your business, but it will help you during negotiations if you understand the total "component part" value of your business versus what you are asking for the company as a going concern.

Once you have a liquidation value established, you should now calculate an asking price for your business based on one of the "going concern" valuation methods discussed in Chapter 2 if you are expecting to sell to other than a strategic buyer (refer back to my earlier discussion about not setting an asking price at all for a possible sale to a strategic buyer). I recommend using the capitalization of current net earnings valuation (CAP) which is based on your business's reconstructed income and expenses for the past full operating year. Use a realistic capitalization rate based on the criteria that best suits your company. Be sure to fully document your reconstructed earnings in detail, as shown in Table 2-D. If you have followed the recommendations in Chapter 3 about maximizing the provable bottom-line profit of your business, there may not be many reconstructed expense items. Once you have arrived at a valuation using this method, increase this amount by 10% and this will establish a good asking price for your business. The 10% premium will allow for some downward negotiation room if necessary while still allowing you to arrive at a selling price close to the valuation you have calculated. As a "sanity check," compare your liquidation value and your asking price to ensure that you are not setting a selling price for less than you can liquidate the business. As strange as this may seem to you, the liquidation value sometimes exceeds the going concern value even in a profitable business. Usually this is due to a very high real estate value that has evolved over time.

Now that you have established an asking price for your business with which you are comfortable, you need to establish a negotiation range for you and your advisors to work within. This is not particularly critical because, in reality, the conditions of the sale to be negotiated between you and the buyer will drive the actual selling value of the business. However, you do want to have a range to work within and I suggest setting a price range that is plus or minus 10% of your calculated value. The math looks like this:

Calculated Business Value (CBV)	= $1,000,000	(using the CAP approach with reconstructed earnings)
Business Asking Price	= $1,100,000	(10% increase over CBV)
Negotiation Price Range	= $ 900,000 to $1,100,000	(lower end is 10% less than CBV)

You should now consider your conditions of sale that you want to impose in conjunction with the selling price.

Conditions of Sale

The actual conditions of the sale of your business will depend a great deal on the negotiation process that you enter into with a prospective buyer. At this point in time, you may want to establish certain conditions that you would like to see as part of the business sale and which can be used to screen and pre-qualify potential buyers. Some conditions of sale that you may want to consider establishing are:

- A corporate stock or asset sale.

- All-cash sale (or cash equivalent such as corporate stock) or seller financing.

- Willingness to enter into a noncompete agreement.

- Terms and conditions of seller financing (amount, time period, interest rate, and security requirements).

- Willingness to accept an earn-out arrangement.

- Amount of cash down.

- Minimum personal net worth of the purchaser.

- Seller employment or consulting agreement.

- Nonfinancial considerations such as:

  — Maintaining a certain trade name or trademark (or not).

  — Retaining certain employees.

  — Continuing certain business policies or procedures.

  — Maintaining a particular image.

You may also want to establish some criteria about which potential buyers *may* not be approached. For example, some business owners wouldn't sell out to their long-time competitors for 100 times what their business is worth (at least that's what they say!). Other sellers do not want their company sold to a national chain or a particular person.

Establish Key-Person Employment Contracts

Almost every business has one or more key employees that would seriously and negatively impact the business if they left the company. You need to identify who these individuals are and negotiate an employment contract with them prior to offering your business for sale. Some employees, upon learning that you intend to sell your business, may become very apprehensive about their future with the company. This may affect their productivity and worse, may cause them to actually find positions elsewhere.

Strategic Move #54:

"Wrap up your key managers and key employees with employment contracts or other incentives before you offer your business for sale."

Before any of this happens, you should negotiate an employment contract with them that explicitly protects their jobs under a new owner and provides for substantial compensation to them if their jobs are eliminated within a certain time period of the sale of the business. Typical provisions for key employees are:

- Employment at their present salary (or with an increase) plus any perks for at least one year after the sale of the business.

- Compensation equal to at least six months of salary if they are discharged earlier.

- Continuation of insurance benefits for at least 12 months after employment termination.

Of course, you will want to customize your employee contracts (also known as "golden parachutes") according to your employee's particular circumstances and your own circumstances and concerns.

You will also want to be careful about the number and generosity of these contracts as they could negatively affect the sale of your business. On the one hand, if you lose a key employee or two during the sale process (which could take months or even years), the company's profits may sag so significantly as to adversely affect the selling price of the business. On the other hand, if you sell your business to another existing company, they may want to combine operations for greater efficiency and ultimately reduce staff as well as facilities. Consequently, having too many employees with expensive employment contracts could weaken the attractiveness of your company. You will need to balance the pros and cons of this for your particular situation. Whatever you do, do it before it becomes general knowledge that your company is for sale. If your key employees hear things "through the grapevine," the damage may be done before you ever get to offer them an employment contract. You should also disclose to them during the contract negotiation process that you are considering selling the business. It's important that they see the employment contract as a benefit to themselves and not feel tricked into some agreement by you.

As a last thought on this topic, I recommend that you require absolute confidentiality through a signed agreement from the employees to whom you offer a contract. They must agree not to discuss the terms of their contract with other employees, or even the fact that they have a contract. Otherwise, this may become a serious negative issue with the employees to whom you choose not to offer an employment contract.

Communicate Your Intention to Sell

Strategic Move #55:

"Do not keep your plan to sell your business such a secret that you exclude those that need to know"

There is another aspect of timing that is important to consider. You must decide when to tell your non-key employees, family, senior management, suppliers, and customers that you have decided to sell your business. There are many schools of thought on this but in general, you may want to adhere to the following timetable:

- Family: They should be told as soon as you begin *considering* the idea of selling. They may be able to provide personal advice and raise concerns that you may not otherwise think of.

- Senior Management and Key Employees: These people should be told very early in the process, right after you have discussed the issue with your family. You will need their support in the sale process. They can help to prepare the business for sale, assist in negotiations, and provide continuity in the company for a new owner.

- Non-Key Employees: They should be told of the business sale just before the actual closing takes place. You will want to allay any concerns they may have at that time, but do not disclose anything to them before you are reasonably certain that the actual sale is imminent.

- Customers: Ideally, customers will not be told of the sale of the business until after the closing has taken place. The sale process should be transparent to your customers and arranged so that they feel no effect from the change in ownership. Notable exceptions to this are large accounts and/or customers that you personally service. If there is a concern that these accounts may "jump ship" as a result of the sale, you should personally introduce the prospective new owner before the sale takes place. Assist in transitioning these key accounts as part of your responsibilities in the sale.

- Suppliers and Vendors: They will need to be informed of the pending business sale before the actual closing in accordance with specific requirements of the Bulk Sales Law pertinent to your state. Frequently, a minimum of 30 days notice is required to allow any supplier or vendor having a claim against your assets to come forward before the sale is completed.

Composing Your Company Overview, Financial History, and Forecasts

Strategic Move #56:

"Document the history and project the future of your business. Tell the story of your company and where you think it's headed."

No matter what business your company is in, whether it sells goods or services, you are most likely adept at preparing sales literature that motivates your customers to buy. You should apply that same sales and marketing skill to preparing a "sales package" about your business. You probably will not call it that, but that's what it will be. As a minimum, this sales material should consist of two separate documents each containing many separate pieces of information needed by a buyer to evaluate your company:

- Company Overview and Financial History.

- Financial Forecasts.

The Company Overview

The company overview is important because it will put into a concise, single package all of the information that defines what your company is and what it does to generate its sales and profits. Even if you publish an annual report for shareholders, it will not provide enough information for a buyer. It will most likely make a good addendum to the company overview, but will not be sufficient by itself. The contents of a good company overview are listed in the next section regarding assembly of "The Book." Each of the areas to be included in the company overview should be elaborated on in as much detail as reasonably possible. You may want to have two versions of the overview: one for the initial meeting with a potential buyer, and the second, more detailed version, for use with a serious qualified buyer who has executed a confidentiality agreement with you.

Financial History

The financial history is just what the name implies: the historical financial results of your company for at least the last three years. If the data demonstrates a strong growth pattern going back even further, than use that information as well. Most buyers will be satisfied with the previous three full fiscal years of company financial results, including income and expense and balance sheets. All of the data you present should be backed up with IRS income tax returns and audited financial statements for the years presented. The tax returns and/or audits should be included as appendices to the summary information. If you are offering your business for sale mid-fiscal year or later, but before a full current year's worth of financial information is available, you should have your accountant prepare an interim financial statement. This will show the current status of the company and help to eliminate any concerns with current business performance.

This is also the place where you should present a "reconstructed" or "recast" income and expense statement to show the hidden value in your business. Of course, if you have followed the advice I have presented in Chapter 3 over the last one or two years, reconstructing your income and expense statement will consist only of showing the excess depreciation and amortization charges as available cash flow!

Financial Forecasts

In almost every business sale, the purchaser is really buying expectations in addition to provable profits. What your business did this year, last year, and the years before are history that benefited you, not the buyer. Past performance may or may not make a good predictor of the future for your company. What will help you to sell your business is to accent the sizzle (the future) and not just try to sell the steak (the assets and current performance). The selling price of the business may still be based on your current financial picture, but every buyer wants the opportunity for growth and increased profits in the future. You will need to provide a view of the future for them by preparing financial forecasts based on optimistic but realistic assumptions. The buyer will, of course, take your forecasts with a grain of salt (and sometimes a whole bag full), but it's important for you to show a context for growth of your company that may not otherwise be apparent to the potential buyer. Things to take into consideration in the financial forecasts are:

- New product/service development.

- New markets to be entered.

- New technology to be exploited.

All of the above issues should be addressed in narrative form with any supporting documentation included such as:

- Market surveys.

- Test marketing results.

- Industry trade association projections.

- Independent study/survey results.

The key to wrapping up your financial forecasts will be in preparing a set of pro forma financial statements for the next one to three years. You will want to include your increased sales projections as well as your reconstructed expenses as part of the pro forma. A word of caution is in order here. Creating and providing a pro forma financial statement may instill certain financial expectations on the part of the buyer that could result in litigation against you if your projections are not met. Although pro forma statements definitely have their place in the financial world (certainly for considering the purchase of a new franchise or for applying for business financing), I recommend that you be very careful with your use of this document when representing your business for sale. Be sure to document all of your assumptions and include language that explains that the pro forma is a projection, not a promise.

Assembling "The Book"

Earlier in this chapter I introduced you to the investment banker term: "The Book." Now is the stage to assemble "The Book" for your use with prospective buyers of your company.

Strategic Move #57:

"Prepare 'The Book' as a sales prospectus for your company with as much attention to detail as if you were launching a new service or product line."

"The Book" should take the form of a single complete document, appropriately bound (3-ring binder or comb-binding is fine) and tabbed for easy reference by the reader. It's also advisable to prepare a table of contents. The following presents a sample table of contents as a checklist for "The Book" of a typical company.

"The Book" Table of Contents

The Company Overview

❏ Description of the Company's business

❏ Personal profile of the Company's owner/manager

❏ Reason for the desired sale of the Company

❏ The Company's products and/or services (include photographs if appropriate)

❏ The Company's primary business markets

❏ The Company's primary customers

❏ The Company's primary suppliers

❏ Major or primary customer testimonials

❏ Significant industry recognition (awards, citations, etc.)

❏ Listing of key-employee personnel (including short personal biographies) with organization chart

❏ The Company's owned assets (include photographs if appropriate)

❏ The Company's primary business locations (include maps)

❏ The Company's leased assets (include photographs if appropriate)

Marketing Information

- ❑ Sales catalogs, brochures, flyers
- ❑ Advertising examples
- ❑ Overview of Internet site
- ❑ Product specification sheets
- ❑ Marketing plans

Legal Information

- ❑ Corporate charter (if incorporated and a stock sale)
- ❑ Corporate by-laws (if incorporated and a stock sale)
- ❑ Corporate minutes (if incorporated and a stock sale)
- ❑ Partnership agreement (if a partnership)
- ❑ Subsidiary documentaion
- ❑ Joint-venture agreements
- ❑ Fictitious name filing
- ❑ Sales and use permits
- ❑ Copies of real estate deeds and/or leases
- ❑ Zoning approvals
- ❑ State and federal licenses (if applicable)
- ❑ Franchise agreement (if applicable)
- ❑ Pending litigation

Financial History

- ❑ Profit and loss statements for the previous three years
- ❑ Balance sheets for the previous three years
- ❑ Dividend payment history
- ❑ The Company's service contracts
  - ❑ Waste/rubbish removal contracts

- ❏ Janitorial and maintenance contracts
- ❏ Landscaping contracts
- ❏ Telephone answering service contracts
- ❏ Order fulfillment service contracts
- ❏ Telephone service contracts
- ❏ Security service contracts
- ❏ Uniform and laundry contracts
- ❏ Fuel service contracts (bulk oil, propane, etc.)
- ❏ Advertising and marketing contracts
- ❏ The Company's long-term liabilities
  - ❏ Real estate mortgages
  - ❏ Promissory notes (including officers' loans)
- ❏ IRS tax returns and/or audited financial statements
- ❏ Reconstructed earnings (income and expense statements)
- ❏ Industry trends

Financial and Business Forecasts

- ❏ Pro forma financial statements for the next three years
- ❏ Existing open contracts (with percentage-of-completion)
- ❏ Planned new products or services
- ❏ Potential new business markets and supporting documentation
- ❏ Emerging new technology to be exploited
- ❏ Key-personnel employment contracts
- ❏ Personal biographies of key personnel
- ❏ Synopsis of main contract provisions

Miscellaneous

- ❏ Insurance
    - ❏ Group hospitalization and medical
    - ❏ Malpractice
    - ❏ Errors and omissions
    - ❏ Worker's compensation
    - ❏ Car and vehicle
    - ❏ Life (key person and employees)
    - ❏ Health and disability
- ❏ Collective bargaining agreements
- ❏ Employee stock option plans
- ❏ Accumulated sick leave and vacation liabilities
- ❏ Severance pay agreements
- ❏ Pension plans
    - ❏ Simplified Employee Pension (SEP) plans
    - ❏ Keogh plans
    - ❏ 401(k) plans
    - ❏ Deferred benefit plans
- ❏ Corporate community involvement

General Provisions of Sale

- ❏ All-cash or minimum cash required
- ❏ Stock or asset sale
- ❏ Time frames expected
- ❏ Owner post-sale employment contract
- ❏ Buyer criteria (net worth, U.S. citizen, noncompetitor, etc.)

I want to stress a very important point relative to providing "The Book" to a prospective buyer. "The Book" will contain very sensitive and confidential information about your company and should be provided to a potential buyer only after a Letter of Intent, or Binder and Earnest Money Agreement, has been signed and a strict Confidentiality Agreement has been executed. A complete version of "The Book" is only for those very serious buyers who really intend to buy your business and are proceeding with the due diligence process prior to final negotiations and closing the sale. You may want to prepare a shortened, nonsensitive version of "The Book" to be used for newly identified prospective buyers as a way of introducing them to your company.

Accelerating the Sale Preparation Process

As you have most likely realized by now, the best way to properly prepare your business for sale requires a significant amount of lead time—one or two years. I understand that some of you will abruptly decide to sell your business and want it sold tomorrow and therefore will not have the time for long-term preparations. There are many reasons for this including:

- A sudden onset of a serious debilitating illness.

- A complete mental burn-out where you become unwilling to continue with the daily stress of running a business.

- A realization that your business is seriously declining and you no longer have the energy or enthusiasm to stop the slide.

- Just plain old procrastination in putting off the inevitable until the last minute.

In fact, most business owners of companies with under $1 million in annual sales do very little preparation at all. I believe that the sales price of their businesses suffers accordingly and needlessly. Whatever your reasons for putting off your decision to sell your business until you have little or no time for proper preparation, there are still many things you can do in the short-run to enhance the value of your company.

Essentially, you should still try to accomplish as many of the recommendations presented in this book as possible. The principal exceptions are that you should not take the cost-cutting actions that may lead to long-run profit increases. You will not have enough time to prove their effectiveness and you may make serious mistakes by rushing your actions.

If you determine that the type of buyer most likely to purchase your business is a strategic buyer, then very little financial preparation may need to be made.

Instead, you should develop "The Book" profiling your company with an emphasis on the aspect that you believe will be of most importance in attracting this type of buyer. For example, if you believe that a strategic buyer will be primarily interested in your customer base, then you should ensure that this component of your business records are well documented and easily accessible through an up-to-date computer database. Even though a strategic buyer will most likely not be interested in your financial picture, you should still do an income and expense statement reconstruction and a valuation based on the CAP approach. This will give you a good estimate of what a financial buyer may pay for your company and will be useful as a yardstick against which you can measure a strategic buyer's offer.

If you believe that the most likely buyer for your business is a financial buyer, as the great majority of buyers are, then an income and expense statement reconstruction is essential, along with a CAP valuation. If you believe that there are significant financial improvement steps that you could take if you had more time, you should prepare a three-year pro forma financial statement that includes all of the cost-saving and revenue-enhancing items that you would have implemented if you had enough time. These items must be carefully documented and thoroughly explained in the pro forma as to their prospective nature.

Be advised though, that financial buyers are generally very adverse to paying for future profits based on projected revenues and/or planned cost-cutting actions that have no guarantee of success. You may want to base your asking price for your business on your out-year pro forma projections and settle on a negotiated price that moves you as close as possible to that value. Again, it will be difficult to induce a financial buyer to pay for future profits that they will have to take the tough management action to realize.

No matter what type of buyer or method of sale you anticipate, in a short-run sale with little preparation time, you should accomplish all of the physical enhancements to the business described in Chapter 3 and provided as a checklist earlier in this chapter. The following additional checklist is provided as a guide for short-run initiatives that you can take to prepare your business for sale.

Accelerated Business Sale Preparation Checklist

❑ Identify the most likely type of buyer and method of sale. Some methods of sale necessarily take longer than others but each situation is so different that it's difficult to say which is the faster process. Clearly, if speed is of the essence, you will want to avoid the more complicated methods of sale such as an IPO, ESOP, MBO, or LBO.

☐ Reconstruct your most recent income and expense statement for your last full year of operations. (Note: If you are more than six months into your fiscal year, you should develop a projected income and expense statement upon which you base your valuation.)

☐ Calculate a liquidation value and a CAP value for your business based on your latest financial information. Use these results to establish baseline valuations for your business to aid you in establishing an asking price.

☐ Take immediate action to accomplish as many of the nonfinancial business value enhancement and risk reduction recommendations provided in this book as possible. These actions will help to support an upper-range asking price for your business.

☐ Review your business operations to identify revenue enhancement and cost reduction initiatives you would take if the time was available.

☐ If appropriate, develop a one- to three-year pro forma financial statement and calculate a new CAP value for your business based on your projections identified in the previous step. Use this new CAP value as the asking price for your business if you believe that your projections are realistic and can be "sold" to a prospective buyer.

☐ Prepare as much of "The Book" as possible within the time that you have to provide a strong sales prospectus for your company. Many business brokers will perform this service as part of their sales efforts and you may want to rely on them for this. However, you will still need to gather the necessary information together for it to be properly documented.

☐ Assemble a team to advise you in your business sale negotiations and hire a business broker or other appropriate professional to find prospective buyers for your business.

The process for preparing your business for sale with little or no preparation time is essentially the same as what you would do if you had a longer period. There are three key differences:

• You will not attempt to make cost-cutting or revenue-enhancing changes to your business because they will not show up in your financial statements within the time you need to sell the company. Instead, you will try to "sell" these financial improvements through the use of a pro forma statement during the negotiation process.

• All other enhancement efforts will necessarily be accelerated with the possibility that they will not be able to be implemented in enough time or with enough quality as to favorably affect the business sale price and process. In other words, do the best you can with the time you have.

- The accelerated preparation process should be continuous, if possible. Even after you list your business for sale and begin to deal with possible buyers, you should continue to make the changes and improvements appropriate to your company. It may take longer than you think to actually find a buyer for your business. By the time the right buyer comes along you may have implemented many of the improvements that you did not think you had the time to accomplish. This will most likely be reflected in the sale price for your company.

Whether you have taken one year to prepare or one month, you are now ready to sell your business. You will need to market, negotiate, and actually close the deal for your company which involves another host of considerations I will very briefly cover here. These issues are covered in more detail in one of my other books that you may wish to read, entitled "Strategies for Successfully Buying or Selling a Business." I have included ordering information for this book on the last page of this publication.

Strategic Move #58:

"Develop a negotiation game plan to follow for the sale of your business"

Marketing, Negotiating, and Selling

By this point, you have done everything logically possible to prepare your business for sale for the most money. But do not forget that value is still in the eye of the beholder and what's important to you may not be at all important to a buyer. That's why you will have to negotiate to sell your business. You, the buyer, and your respective teams of advisors will need to work together to creatively solve the inevitable differences in your positions. The actual sale and negotiation process are beyond the scope of this book which has shown you how to prepare your business for sale. However, here are a few considerations for you to think about after you have found a viable buyer and have embarked on the process of actually closing a deal:

- Negotiation processes are as different as the people involved.

- Some negotiations are simple and concluded in a matter of days, and some drag on for months.

- The amount of the business sale price frequently has no bearing on the length or complexity of negotiations.

- Successful negotiations involve give-and-take on the part of both parties. You cannot expect to win every point.

- Negotiate the most important things first; selling price, form of compensation, term of payout, etc. Leave the less important points for later.

- Always move ahead. If one point becomes a roadblock, put it off until later.

- Negotiate in a few long sessions rather than stretch things out with many short meetings.

- There are almost an infinite number of ways to structure a sale so that both the buyer and seller get what they each want.

The last part of your business sale preparations should include preparing for what you will do with the proceeds from the sale. In Chapter 1, I covered the things you should do to prepare yourself for exiting your business. You should also ensure that you have a plan for what you will do with the cash you are soon to receive. The next, and final section, addresses this concern.

Strategic Move #59:

"Plan how you will handle the proceeds from the sale of your business. Money is always easier to make than it is to keep."

Managing Your Sale Proceeds

Many business owners are very pleasantly surprised by how much money they will receive as a result of selling their business. After years of working to build the business and receiving very little compensation, the business evolves to a level of profitability where they can enjoy incomes in the six figures, but they still plow much of the profits back into the company. Frequently, a retiring business owner has relatively little cash savings and has never had to deal with significantly large sums of personal cash. Suddenly, business owners find themselves with funds in the six- or seven-figure range and all the responsibility of managing that much money. You should make it a part of your exit plan to decide in advance how you will approach investing your cash. I do not mean deciding now on specifically what investments you will make, but you should decide well before you receive any funds as to what you will actually do with them on at least a near-term basis. For example, you may want to consider investing in:

- Bank CDs (pay attention to $100,000 maximum FDIC guarantees).

- Money market funds.

- A short-term investment portfolio managed by professionals.

The one characteristic that seems to be dominant among business sellers is that they shift their investment approach from "risk-taking" to "risk-avoidance." This is not always easy for you to do because by the very nature of being a business owner and entrepreneur for all those years, you have necessarily faced risky decisions and ventures almost every day. Most successful business sellers realize that it may be time to protect what they have earned. Conservative investments (low risk mutual funds, government bonds and the like) thus become the norm. Depending upon your sophistication and the amount of money you have received, you may consider hiring both a financial planner and an investment manager.

- A financial planner should provide advice and guidance regarding tax planning, estate planning, wills, and trusts.

- An investment manager or advisor (depending on how involved you intend to become) should provide investment strategies consistent with your risk threshold.

No matter what your personal situation—retirement, bold new ventures, philanthropy, or some other endeavor, you should have some idea and plan on what you are going to do with the proceeds of the sale of your business well before you actually receive the funds.

In Summary

In this book I have presented you with many ideas, suggestions, and recommendations about how to prepare your business for sale. Unfortunately, the road is not an easy one. The process of preparing and actually selling your business involves a great deal of time, frustration, and more than a little money. However, the goal is well worth the effort. As a hard-working business owner you have earned the rewards of selling your successful business and moving on to the next phase of your life. I sincerely hope that I have helped make things easier and more profitable for you.

The next, and last, chapter in this book contains resources that you may want to contact for additional information or actual assistance in preparing and successfully selling your unique and special business.

I will leave you with one last strategic move that might be the most important of all.

Strategic Move #60:

"Maintain a strong sense of optimism and a keen sense of humor throughout your business preparation and sale process. You will surely need it!"

8

Resources for Preparing Your Business for Sale

- *Introduction*
- *Business Brokers*
- *Mergers and Acquisitions (M&A) Specialists*
- *Investment Banker Resources (Large Firms)*
- *Investment Banker Resources (Mid-Range Firms)*
- *Internet Sites for Buying or Selling a Business*
- *Employee Stock Ownership Program (ESOP)*
- *Financial and Estate Planning Professionals*
- *Succession Planning Organizations*
- *Business Valuation and Asset Appraisers*
- *Business Valuation Data and Information*
- *Initial Public Offering, SCOR, and DPO*

Introduction

Preparing your business for sale will require you to have access to certain information, or knowledge of professional resources, which is often difficult to find. Many business owners do not know where to even start looking for the information they will need. Or who to contact to locate a reputable professional who has specific experience with their type of business sale. I have devoted this entire chapter to providing you with many of the information sources and professional resources you are likely to require as you undertake the process of preparing your business for sale.

Please note that the resources provided herein are by no means complete nor are they endorsed or recommended by the author. They are provided for your use as a starting point for gathering information relative to preparing your business for sale. Every effort has been made to ensure that the address, telephone, e-mail and Internet site information are accurate, but due to the time-sensitive nature of this kind of data, not all information may be correct at the time of your reading.

Business Brokers

The vast majority of you will most likely benefit from the services of a reputable and well-qualified business broker. There are approximately 2,700 business brokerage firms doing business in the United States in 1998. Since it's not practical to list even a few of them here, I have instead provided information about some of the various business broker associations that exist. I recommend that you contact an association in your area and request a referral of a reputable firm that has experience with your type of business. However, the best way to find a good business broker will most likely be based on a referral and recommendation that you receive from a satisfied business seller who you know has recently sold their business.

New York Association of Business Brokers
111 Grant Avenue
Endicott, NY 13760
Phone: 607-754-5990
e-mail: hncohen@aol.com

New England Business Brokers Association
15 Walden Street
Concord, MA 01742
Phone: 508-287-5278
e-mail: sas5500@aol.com

Georgia Association of Business Brokers
5920 Roswell Road, Suite B-107
Atlanta, GA 30328
Phone: 770-491-3710

California Association of Business Brokers
1608 West Campbell Ave., Ste. 248
Campbell, CA 95008
Phone: 408-379-7748
http://www.cabb.org

Association of Midwest Business Brokers
121 Fairfield Way, Suite 100
Bloomingdale, IL 60108
Phone: 630-893-5500

Michigan Business Brokers Association
1568 Mt. Mercy
Grand Rapids, MI 49504
Phone: 616-945-5874
http://www.mbba.org

**International Business
Brokers Association**
11250 Roger Bacon Drive, Suite 8
Reston, VA 20190
Phone: 703-437-7464
e-mail: IBBAInc@aol.com
http://www.ibba.com

**Texas Assoc. of Business
Brokers**
P.O. Box 820398
Dallas, TX 75382-0398
Phone: 214-373-1560
e-mail: info@tabb.org
http://www.tabb.org

Mergers and Acquisitions (M&A) Specialists

Many business owners will benefit from the services of a mergers and acquisitions oriented firm that serves the $5 million plus business sale market. These professionals are especially useful to you if you expect the most likely buyer for your business will be a strategic buyer. There are many hundreds of firms that identify themselves as specializing in mergers and acquisitions, and it's not practical to list them all here. Instead, I have listed several organizations that you may contact for the name of a reputable M&A firm in your area.

The **International Business Brokers Association (IBBA)** promotes professional development within the business brokerage industry and sponsors the Certified Business Intermediary (CBI) designation program.

International Business Brokers Association
11250 Roger Bacon Drive, Suite B
Reston, VA 22090-5202
Phone: 703-437-4377

The **Association for Corporate Growth (ACG)** is an international nonprofit, professional development organization dedicated to all aspects of sound corporate growth. It has approximately 3,500 members from 2,000 companies in its 26 chapters throughout the United States and Canada.

Association for Corporate Growth
4350 DiPaolo Center, Suite C
Glenview, IL 60025
Phone: 800-699-1331
e-mail: acghq@aol.com

The **International Merger and Acquisition Professionals (IMAP)** is the product of a recent merger between the International Association of Merger and Acquisition Consultants (INTERMAC) and the Institute of Merger & Acquisition Professionals.

International Merger and Acquisition Professionals
60 Revere Drive, Suite 500
Northbrook, IL 60062
Phone: 708-480-9282
e-mail: imap@imap.com

The **Society for Competitive Intelligence Professionals (SCIP)** has a diverse membership of 3,800 professionals from companies and consulting firms around the globe.

Society for Competitive Intelligence Professionals
1700 Diagonal Road, Suite 520
Alexandria, VA 22314
Phone: 703-739-0696
e-mail: scip@dc.infi.net

The **M&A Source** is an association of M&A intermediaries specializing in middle market transactions. Its members include over 115 firms in the United States, Canada and Europe.

The M&A Source
11250 Roger Bacon Drive, Suite B
Reston, VA 22090
Phone: 703-437-4377

Investment Banker Resources (Large Firms)

Most of the readers of this book will not require the services of an investment banking firm which typically deals with very large business sale transactions in the $50 million plus range or for Initial Public Offerings. I have included a few resources here for those of you who may fit this very rare category.

Advest, Inc.
280 Trumbull Street
Hartford, CT 06103
Phone: 860-525-1421

Bear, Stearns & Co., Inc.
245 Park Avenue
New York, NY 10167
Phone: 212-272-2000

Citicorp Securities Inc.
399 Park Avenue
New York, NY 10043
Phone: 212-559-5224
http//www.citibank.com

The Geneva Companies
5 Park Plaza
Irvine, CA 92174
Phone: 800-854-4643

Goldman, Sachs & Co.
85 Broad Street
New York, NY 10004
Phone: 212-902-1000

Lehman Brothers
3 World Financial Center
New York, NY 10285
Phone: 212-526-7000

**Merrill Lynch Capital
   Markets**
World Financial Center, N. Twr.
New York, NY 10281-1327
Phone: 212-449-8521

Morgan Stanley & Co., Inc.
1251 Avenue of the Americas
New York, NY 10020
Phone: 212-703-4000

Salomon Brothers Inc.
7 World Trade Center
New York, NY 10048
Phone: 212-783-7000
http//www.sbi.com

**Smith Barney, Harris
   Upham & Co.**
1345 Avenue of the Americas
New York, NY 10105
Phone: 212-698-6730

Investment Banker Resources (Mid-Range Firms)

I expect that many of the readers of this book will not need the services of a mid-range investment banking firm to sell their business. These firms have special expertise in business sales that have a price range of about $20 million and up. For those of you who believe they fit this category for a business sale's price, I have included a geographically dispersed representative sample of the several hundred mid-range investment banking firms throughout the United States. These firms also offer expertise in Initial Public Offerings (IPO), Direct Public Offerings (DPO), and Small Corporate Offering Registrations (SCOR).

Alex, Brown & Sons
135 East Baltimore Street
Baltimore, MD 21202
Phone: 410-727-1700

Allen C. Ewing & Co.
1020 N. Orange Avenue, Ste. 300
Orlando, FL 32801
Phone: 407-423-2525
http://www.allenewing.com

Andover Capital, Inc.
31500 Northwestern Hwy.,
   Suite 120
Farmington Hills, MI 48334
Phone: 810-851-9200

Asset Services
530 Oak Court, Suite 155
Memphis, TN 38117
Phone: 901-684-1274
http://www.mergers.net

**Barber & Bronson
   Incorporated**
201 S. Biscayne Blvd., Ste. 2950
Miami, FL 33131
Phone: 305-536-8508

Barrington Associates
11755 Wilshire Boulevard
Los Angeles, CA 90025
Phone: 310-479-3500

**Berkshire Capital
Corporation**
399 Park Avenue, 28th Floor
New York, NY 10022
Phone: 212-207-1000

Bowles Hollowell Conner
227 West Trade, Suite 2400
Charlotte, NC 28202
Phone: 704-348-1000

Bubnack & Co.
7915 Terraza Disoma
Carlsbad, CA 92009
Phone: 760-634-4815

Capital Dynamics, Inc.
1920 Vindicator Dr., Suite 214
Colorado Springs, CO 80919
Phone: 719-598-4680

Capital Investment Partners
17 Glenwood Avenue
Raleigh, NC 27603
Phone: 919-831-1351

Crown Capital Corporation
540 Maryville Center Drive,
Suite 120
St. Louis, MO 63141
Phone: 314-576-1201

Dillon, Read & Co.
535 Madison Avenue
New York, NY 10022
Phone: 212-906-7301

Founders Capital Corp.
1632 N. Hudson Ave.
Chicago, IL 60614
Phone: 312-440-0811

The Geneva Companies
5 Park Plaza
Irvine, CA 92174
Phone: 800-854-4643

Goldsmith Capital Advisors
15332 Antioch Street, Suite 326
Pacific Palisades, CA 90272
Phone: 310-459-7520

Greene Holcomb & Lannin
90 South Seventh St., Ste. 5450
Minneapolis, MN 55402
Phone: 612-904-5700

Hempstead & Co., Inc.
807 Haddon Avenue
Haddonfield, NJ 08033
Phone: 609-795-6026

Jack Augsback & Assoc., Inc.
505 S.E. 1st Avenue
Boynton Beach, FL 33435
Phone: 561-735-4565
http://www.vfund.com

Larchmont Associates
120 Village Square, Suite 152
Orinda, CA 94563
Phone: 510-253-0777

**Merchant Banking
Strategies**
7817 Ivanhoe Avenue, Ste. 300
La Jolla, CA 92037
Phone: 619-454-3284

**National Lone Star
Corporation**
11032 Lakewood, Suite 101
El Paso, TX 79935
Phone: 915-591-2103

Needham & Co., Inc.
400 Park Avenue
New York, NY 10022
Phone: 212-371-8300

Niven Associates
3050 Post Oak Blvd, Ste. 590
Houston, TX 77056
Phone: 713-961-9661

Paramount Securities Corp.
225 W. Washington Street, Ste. 220
Chicago, IL 60606
Phone: 312-552-7800

Rhode Island Capital Partners
115 Brisas Circle
East Greenwich, RI 02818
Phone: 401-885-4357

Sigma Technology, Inc.
1045 Bullard Court
Raleigh, NC 27615
Phone: 919-850-0033

Slavitt Ellington Group
100 Oceangate, Suite 600
Long Beach, CA 90802
Phone: 562-495-7870
http://www.slavitellington.com

Stonemark Investment Bankers
4180 Montecito Avenue
Santa Rosa, CA 95404
Phone: 707-578-0556

The Atlantic Group
475 Hillside Avenue
Needham, MA 02194
Phone: 617-444-0400

The Hales Group
One Westbrook Corp. Center
Westchester, IL 60154
Phone: 708-409-0080

Throne & Company
49 North Main Street
Stewartstown, PA 10363
Phone: 717-993-3201

Veber Partners, LLC
4380 S.W. Macadam Ave., Ste. 250
Portland, OR 97201
Phone: 503-229-4400

Woodbridge Group, Inc.
264 Amity Road, Suite 106
Woodbridge, CT 06525 USA
Phone: 203-389-1599
http://www.woodbridgegrp.com

Internet Sites for Buying or Selling a Business

It's always been a challenge for buyers, sellers, and brokers of small- to medium-sized businesses to find each other and close a deal. Also, many would-be business buyers are willing to relocate to anywhere in the country for the right business. A substantial number of businesses themselves are not geographic specific and can be relocated to a buyer's area. The Internet is an ideal medium for enabling buyers, sellers, and brokers to quickly and easily find the right situation to match their needs. There are several very good Internet sites dedicated to this process of matching buyers and sellers of operating businesses. I have listed a few of the best ones here, but you may also want to use one of the several search engines such as Yahoo or InfoSeek to locate other ones that may have evolved since the writing of this book.

http://www.bizbuysell.com is an excellent Internet site that lists over 5,000 businesses for sale and has over 200 member business brokers. There are many special features including posting a free "business sought" advertisement for buyers as well as free listings for sellers.

http://www.bizquest.com is another excellent site for buyers or sellers of businesses with over 3,000 listings at any one time. There are several features and resources to assist the buyer or seller to make the right match.

http://www.mergernetwork.com is a very professional site geared to the mid-market mergers and acquisitions-minded user. The site offers a number of excellent fee-based services as well as free searchable databases of businesses for sale.

http://business-broker.com is The Business Broker Web which is a resource for entrepreneurs and business brokers to list businesses for sale in the U.S. and Canada.

http://www.mergernetwork.com is a fee-based site for the purchase or sale of middle market companies. Listings are free but there is a modest charge to search the listings. Additional features include discussion groups and related news headlines.

http://www.bizguide.com is the Mid-Atlantic Business Opportunities Guide which features existing businesses for sale in DE, DC, MD, PA, VA, and WV. In addition, a quarterly printed guide is available from the publisher at 1920 Narrows Lane, Silver Springs, MD 20906. The telephone is 301-924-5805.

http://www.nbe.com is the National Business Exchange web site which carries over 5,000 businesses for sale in its database. A monthly newspaper style publication is also available which is updated with 2,500 new listings in each issue. Sample issues are available from the National Business Exchange at 1125 Lindero Canyon Rd. #A8, Westlake Village, CA 91362. The telephone is 818-879-9319.

Employee Stock Ownership Program (ESOP)

The **National Center for Employee Ownership (NCEO)** is a private, non-profit membership and information organization. Supported by its members and services, the NCEO serves as the leading source of information on employee stock ownership plans (ESOPs), employee stock options, and other forms of employee ownership.

National Center for Employee Ownership
1201 Martin Luther King Jr. Way, 2nd Floor
Oakland, CA 94162
Phone: 510-272-9461 Fax: 510-272-9510
e-mail: nceo@nceo.org   http://www.nceo.org

The **National Association of Stock Plan Professionals (NASPP)** is a national organization dedicated to providing its members with information relating to stock plan design and administration.

National Association of Stock Plan Professionals
P.O. Box 21639
Concord, CA 94521-0639
Phone: 510-685-5402 Fax: 510-685-5402
e-mail: info@naspp.com http://www.naspp.com

Financial and Estate Planning Professionals

There are many professional organizations that provide information to the public and also provide professional certification for their members. These organizations will be able to provide you with the names of qualified professional practitioners (planners, accountants, and attorneys) in your geographic area and suitable to your particular needs.

The **American College of Trust and Estate Counsel** maintains a list of 2,700 member attorneys with at least 10 years experience in trusts and estates.

American College of Trust and Estate Counsel
3415 S. Sepulveda Blvd., Suite 330
Los Angeles, CA 90034
Phone: 800-862-4272 Fax: 310-572-7280
e-mail: info@actec.org http://www.actec.org

The **Institute of Certified Financial Planners** maintains a national referral service to match potential clients with professional members of the Institute.

Institute of Certified Financial Planners
3801 E. Florida Avenue, Suite 708
Denver, CO 80210
Phone: 303-759-4900 Fax: 303-759-0749
e-mail: info@icfp.org http://www.icfp.org

The **International Association for Financial Planning** is an international membership association dedicated to the financial planning process to help people make informed financial decisions.

International Association for Financial Planning
5775 Glenridge Drive, NE, Suite B-300
Atlanta, GA 30328
Phone: 800-945-4237 Fax: 404-845-3600
e-mail: info@iafp.org http://www.iafp.org

The **American Bar Association** has approximately 370,000 members and provides information and training primarily for attorneys but is a good source of references for lawyers to assist you with the sale of your business.

American Bar Association
750 N. Lake Shore Drive
Chicago, IL 60611
Phone: 312-988-5000
e-mail: info@abanet.org   http://www.abanet.org

The **American Institute of Certified Public Accountants** has more than 330,000 members and is the premier national professional association for CPAs in the United States.

American Institute of Certified Public Accountants
1211 Avenue of the Americas
New York, NY 10036-8775
Phone: 212-596-6200 Fax: 212-596-6213
e-mail: info@aicpa.org   http://www.aicpa.org

The **Small Business Accountants of America** is an organization that maintains an extensive database of accountants and attorneys listed by specialty and geographic area.

Small Business Accountants of America
6 East 45th Street, Suite 1602
New York, NY 10017
Phone: 212-972-5270 Fax: 212-972-5336
e-mail: info@sbaa.com   http://www.sbaa.com

The **National Association of Financial and Estate Planning (NAFEP)** is a private association created for the purpose of developing financial, estate, and business planning tools. Members of NAFEP are professionals and experts in a variety of legal, estate, financial, and business disciplines. Certified members are designated as Certified Estate Advisors (CEA) and/or Certified Estate and Financial Consultants (CEFC).

National Association of Financial and Estate Planning
525 East 4500 South F-100
Salt Lake City, UT 84107
Phone: 801-266-9900 Fax: 801-266-1019
e-mail: nafep@nafep.com   http://www.nafep.com

The **Registered Financial Planners Institute** provides the professional designation of Registered Financial Planner (RFP) to their members who have completed a prescribed course of study and who conform to a strict code of ethics.

Registered Financial Planners Institute
2001 Cooper Foster Park Road
Amherst, OH 44001
Phone: 440-282-7176
e-mail: info@rfpi.com   http://www.rfpi.com

The **Financial Planning Network** provides a listing of over 40,000 financial planning professionals who are listed by specialized services, location, and name.

Financial Planning Network
2124 Broadway, Suite 315
New York, NY 10023
Phone: 1-800-274-0059 Fax: 888-678-1877
e-mail: staff@pnetwork.com   http://www.pnetwork.com

Succession Planning Organizations

Since March 1995, **NetMarquee** has been working actively with a growing number of universities to disseminate research as well as information about their family business programs and entrepreneurship centers. They cover a wide range of business fields and disciplines, including succession and estate planning, business valuation techniques, legal, marketing and strategic planning. They also provide a continuing forum for discussion and debate on good business and management practices.

NetMarquee, Inc.
687 Highland Avenue
Needham, MA 02194
Phone: 617-433-5890 Fax: 617-449-2128
e-mail: info@netmarquee.com   http://www.nmq.com

Arthur Andersen Center for Family Business is a national firm which has dozens of Centers for Family Business throughout the U.S. in most major cities.

Mr. Ross W. Nager
Arthur Andersen LLP Center for Family Business
711 Louisiana Street
Houston, TX 77002-2786
Phone: 713-237-2724
http://www.arthurandersen.com/bus-info/cfb/CFBCENTR.htm

The **Baylor University Institute for Family Business** was established in 1987 to provide a forum for the development and dissemination of information relevant to the continuity and health of the family business. The Institute is committed to helping family businesses survive to the second and third generations and beyond.

Dr. Nancy Upton
Ben Williams Professor of Entrepreneurship
Baylor University
Post Office Box 98011
Waco, TX 76798
Phone: 817-755-2265

The **Loyola University Chicago Family Business Center** is an internationally recognized pioneer and leader in family business program development and research, serving as a resource to family businesses in the Chicago region and throughout the nation.

Loyola University Chicago
Family Business Center
820 North Michigan Avenue
Chicago, IL 60611
Phone: 312-915-6490 Fax: 312-915-6495
http://www.luc.edu/depts/fbc

Bryant College Institute for Family Enterprise was founded to assist family-owned firms in meeting the unique managerial challenges associated with operating and sustaining a successful family enterprise.

Institute for Family Enterprise
Bryant College Box A
1150 Douglas Pike
Smithfield, RI 02917-1284
Phone: 401-232-6477 Fax: 401-232-6945

The Family Business Institute, The Center for Entrepreneurship Canisius College's primary goal is to facilitate problem solving and foster business continuation of family and closely-held businesses in western New York.

Center for Entrepreneurship at Canisius College
2001 Main Street
Buffalo, NY 14208
Phone: 716-888-2615 Fax: 716-888-2895
e-mail: lograssm@gort.canisius.edu

Family Business Research Institute Bronfenbrenner Life Course Center at Cornell University was the first family business program to focus on the family side of issues in their field and takes the lead role in family business research. Their mission is to strengthen families and their businesses given their respective vital societal and economic roles, with primary emphasis on small- to medium-sized businesses.

Professor Ramona K.Z. Heck
J. Thomas Clark Professor of Entrepreneurship and Personal Enterprise
Director, Family Business Research Institute
103 MVR Hall
Cornell University
Ithaca, NY 14853-4401
Phone: 607-255-2591 Fax: 607-255-0799
e-mail: rkh2@cornell.edu

DePaul University Family Business Program offers consulting services to businesses in which both students and faculty work directly with family businesses. They have provided counseling and consultation services since 1972. Services are free of charge and the family business owners have their problems analyzed and a report containing proposed solutions is provided.

Dr. Harold P. Welsch
DePaul University
1 East Jackson Boulevard
Chicago, IL 60604
Phone: 312-362-8471 Fax: 312-362-6973
e-mail: hwelsch@wppost.depaul.edu\

Center for Family Business—Creighton University was created in 1993 for the purpose of generating, stimulating and disseminating information on family-owned businesses. The only one of its kind in the area, it is an independent, nonprofit professional organization operating under Creighton University's College of Business Administration. It focuses on owners and managers who lead the businesses, all family members involved in day-to-day operations, and professionals who serve family-owned businesses.

Joyce Bunger, Director
College of Business Administration
Creighton University
2500 California Plaza
Omaha, NE 68178
Phone: 402-280-5521 Fax: 402-280-2172
e-mail: jbunger@creighton.edu

Duke University North Carolina Family Business Forum provides resources dedicated to the growth and success of family businesses.

Duke University
North Carolina Family Business Forum
Hartman Center, Fuqua School of Business, Box 90120
Durham, NC 27708
Phone: 919-660-7742 Fax: 919-660-8033
e-mail: pcbl@mail.duke.edu

Fairleigh Dickinson University George Rothman Institute of Entrepreneurial Studies is dedicated to the study and promotion of entrepreneurship in our society. The Institute offers academic courses and they encourage research in entrepreneurship and family business.

Mary Suchcicki, Forum Administrator
Family Business Forum
The George Rothman Institute of Entrepreneurial Studies
Fairleigh Dickinson University
Madison, NJ 07940
Phone: 973-443-8880
e-mail: rothman@FDU.edu

The **Goering Center for Family and Private Business** was founded in 1987 at the University of Cincinnati's College of Business Administration. Their objective is to improve the success of private firms in business vitality and continuing over multiple generations via educational programs and related services. They address issues unique to family and privately-held businesses and sponsor research to extend knowledge in these areas of business.

Sidney L. Barton, Ph.D., Executive Director
The Goering Center
University of Cincinnati
606D Carl H. Linder Hall
Cincinnati, OH 45221-0177
Phone: 513-556-7185 Fax: 513-556-6044

McMurry University Family Business Center's programs are designed to assist the family business in day-to-day operations and succession. Major areas pertaining to family business are addressed by experts in law, accounting, finance, insurance, investments, and financial planning, banking and trusts, and human resource management.

James Myers
McMurray University
Family Business Center
Abilene, TX 79697
Phone: 915-691-6396

Northeastern University's Center for Family Business offers programs, articles, and academic courses dedicated to preservation and education of the family-owned business.

Paul Karofsky, Director
Northeastern University's Center for Family Business
Phone: 617-320-8015
e-mail: pkarofsky@lynx.neu.edu

Institute for Family Business, NOVA Southeastern University offers programs and services that foster growth, health, success, and continuation of family businesses.

Patricia M. Cole, Ph.D., Director
Institute for Family Business
Nova Southeastern University
3301 College Avenue
Fort Lauderdale, FL 33314
Phone: 954-424-5700 Fax: 954-424-5711

Oakland University Center for Family Business provides a forum for the development and dissemination of information relevant to the advancement and vitality of family businesses. Their goal is to encourage healthy family businesses by providing a variety of educational and informational services to family business owners and their advisors. They target established family businesses with sales revenues in excess of $5 million.

Robert T. Kleiman, Ph.D., Director
Center for Family Business
School of Business Administration
Oakland University
Rochester, MI 48309
Phone: 810-370-3509
e-mail: kleiman@argo.acs.oakland.edu

Jefferson Smurfit Center for Entrepreneurial Studies Family Business Program was established in 1994 to provide stimulating setting for family businesses to develop strategies for growth. Topics include relationships in a family firm, transfer of leadership and strategic planning.

Jeanne Rhodes
Saint Louis University
221 North Grand Blvd.
St. Louis, MO 63103
Phone: 314-977-3850 Fax: 314-977-3627
e-mail: rhodesja@sluvca.slu.edu

University of Massachusetts Family Business Center assists family businesses in recognizing their common problems and in finding solutions to the unique challenges confronting them. They offer members a series of educational, interactive, and entertaining forums led by experts in the field of family business consulting, advising members in relevant areas of the law, accounting, estate planning, and banking.

Ira Bryck, Director
Family Business Center
Division of Continuing Education
608 Goodell Building
University of Massachusetts, Box 33260
Amherst, MA 01003-3260
Phone: 413-545-1537 Fax: 413-545-3351
e-mail: bryck@admin.umass.edu

University of Connecticut School of Business Administration Family Business Program has established high quality programs to provide assistance to Connecticut family businesses, to explore their problems and create solutions. They provide education, professional advice, peer networks to facilitate positive and cooperative interaction among family members, managers, professional advisors, and university faculty on unique challenges that business owning families face.

Family Business Program
School of Business Administration
University of Connecticut
368 Fairfield Road
Storrs, CT 06269-2041
Phone: 203-486-4483
e-mail: Richard Dino@sbaserv.sba.uconn.edu

University of Louisville Family Business Center was specifically designed to address the challenges and conflicts associated with family business. Participants learn techniques and methods designed to manage the stress-related issues of a family-owned business. Business and family issues often overlap and are examined while processes for managing them will be developed and employed.

Family Business Center
College of Business and Public Administration
University of Louisville
Louisville, KY 40292
Phone: 502-852-4792 Fax: 502-852-7557

University of Memphis Family Business Forum provides an educational environment for family enterprises to develop strategies to deal with unique personal, family or business challenges. Seminars are conducted by nationally recognized experts and provide opportunities for members to learn from dynamic presentations and interactive workshops.

Dr. Dennie Smith
The Family Business Forum
University of Memphis
Fogelman College of Business, Room 431
Memphis, TN 38152
Phone: 901-678-4799 Fax: 901-678-5433

University of San Diego Family Business Institute was founded in 1991 and is a member organization made up of owner/senior generation and successor/junior generation family members as well as nonfamily member managers from many of the largest and most successful family-owned and operated businesses in the San Diego area.

Dr. Scott Kunkel
School of Business Administration
University of San Diego
San Diego, CA 92110
Phone: 619-260-2376 Fax: 619-260-2961

University of Toledo for Family Business was created by and for northwest Ohio and southeast Michigan family businesses. It serves the needs of area family businesses and promotes greater incorporation of family business issues into curriculum and research.

Debbie Skutch
Director of the Center for Family Business
University of Toledo, College of Business
Toledo, OH 43606-3390
Phone: 419-530-4058 Fax: 419-530-8497

USC Family Business Program is a resource for families and their businesses and provides a sophisticated forum for information about management, growth, continuity, and strategy. It's a membership organization offering seminars and annual forums geared towards founders/owners, successors, professional managers and nonparticipating family members.

Steven Gal
USC Family Business Program
University of Southern California, Bridge Hall, Room 6
Los Angeles, CA 90089-1421
Phone: 213-740-0416 Fax: 213-740-2976
e-mail: 74774.1522@compuserve.com

The Partnership with Family Business, Weatherhead School of Management was established at Case Western Reserve University's George S. Dively Center for Management Development. This is an action-research based program for family-owned businesses. It provides business owners, their families and their company employees with a snapshot of their organization's culture and managerial practices, and the family's culture and practices.

The Partnership With Family Business
Weatherhead School of Management
George S. Dively Center for Management Development
Case Western Reserve University
10900 Euclid Avenue
Cleveland, OH 44106-7166
Phone: 216-368-2041 Fax: 216-368-4793

Business Valuation and Asset Appraisers

The **Institute of Business Appraisers (IBA)** was established in 1978 and is a pioneer in business appraisal education and certification. IBA is the original professional society devoted exclusively to the appraisal of closely-held businesses, and has a membership of over 2,900. The Institute provides members and the public with seminars, educational workshops, and member support services including market data, bibliographical research, as well as the wealth of experience amassed by the appraisers who have contributed their talents to IBA.

Institute of Business Appraisers
P.O. Box 1447
Boynton Beach, FL 33425
Phone: 561-732-3202 Fax: 561-732-4304
e-mail: iba@instbusapp.org

The **American Society of Appraisers (ASA)** is an organization consisting of hundreds of accredited appraisers throughout the country who provide professional business valuation as well as other appraisal services. Member appraisers have undergone specific training and education that is endorsed by the organization. All members are governed by the Principles of Appraisal Practice Code of Ethics. The ASA is divided into 16 geographic regions. You may contact the below listed Regional Governor in your specific area for a recommendation of an appraiser for your particular needs.

Region 1
Delaware, Pennsylvania,
Southern New Jersey
Richard A. Hause, ASA
Accredited Senior Appraiser
5 Clark Gap Court
Medford, NJ 08055
Phone: 215-561-5600
Fax: 215-557-7280
e-mail: ptshause@aol.com

Region 2
Connecticut, Maine,
Massachusetts, New Hampshire,
Rhode Island, Vermont
William H. King, ASA
P.O. Box 585
West Brookfield, MA 01585-0585
Phone: 508-867-2600
Fax: 508-867-2600
e-mail: whking1@juno.com

Region 3
Maryland, Virginia, D.C.,
N. Carolina, S. Carolina
John D. Wiley, ASA
Roanoke County Admin.
P.O. Box 298000
Roanoke, VA 24018-0798
Phone: 540-387-6073
Fax: 540-387-6112
e-mail: aglenn@www.co.
    roanoke.va.us

Region 4
Illinois, Indiana, Kentucky,
Eastern Wisconsin
Eugene G. Kaczkowski, ASA
American Appraisal Associates, Inc.
511 East Wisconsin Ave., Ste. 1900
Milwaukee, WI 53202
Phone: 414-319-4661
Fax: 414-225-1908
e-mail: kaczkowski@american-
    appraisal.com
http://www.american-
    appraisal.com

Region 5
Florida, Puerto Rico, U.S. Virgin
Islands, Caribbean Islands
Anthony A. Hodge, Sr., ASA
20811 NW Miami Place
Miami, FL 33169
Phone: 305-653-4701
Fax: 305-653-8055
e-mail: taxinfo@bcpa.enet

Region 6
Texas, east of time zone, Texas
Panhandle, Latin America,
Arkansas, Oklahoma
Leslie H. Miles, Jr., ASA
MB Valuation Services, Inc.
1111 Empire Central Place
Dallas, TX 75247-4305
Phone: 214-631-4707
Fax: 214-638-7576
e-mail: mbv@ix.netcom.com
http://www.mbval.com

Region 7
Iowa, Kansas, Missouri,
Minnesota, N. Dakota, Western
Wisconsin, Eastern S. Dakota,
Eastern Nebraska
Yale Kramer, ASA
Reiss Corporation
8033 University #A
Des Moines, IA 50325
Phone: 515-224-0104
Fax: 515-224-4536
e-mail: reiss@dwx.com

Region 8
Arizona, Colorado, Utah, New
Mexico, Wyoming, Western S.
Dakota, Western Nebraska,
Texas (west of time zone), Mexico
Larry D. Phillips, ASA
Larry Phillips & Assoc.
2430 Juan Tabo NE, Suite 275
Albuquerque, NM 87112
Phone: 505-299-7999
Fax: 505-299-7999
e-mail: phillips@gemologist-
    appraiser.com

Region 9
Southern half California,
Southern half Nevada
Noël Burndahl, ASA
11860 Goldring Road, Suite B
Arcadia, CA 91106
Phone: 626-301-9277
Fax: 626-301-9267
e-mail: nburndahl@loop.com

Region 10
Canada, Europe
Rene C. Mutsaerts
2373 West Hill Drive
West Vancouver, BC V7S 2Z2
Canada
Phone: 604-926-0218
Fax: 604-926-0218
e-mail: mutsaerts@intergate.
  bc.ca

Region 11
Michigan, Ohio
John W. Peck, ASA
Porter and Peck, Inc.
1001 Eastwind Drive, Suite 103
Westerville, OH 43081
Phone: 614-890-8384
Fax: 614-890-7351
e-mail: jwpeck@
  mindspring.com

Region 12
Alaska, Idaho, Montana,
Oregon, Washington
Donna J. Walker, ASA
Columbia Financial Advisors
650 Morgan Building
720 S.W. Washington Street
Portland, OR 97205-3508
Phone: 503-222-0562
Fax: 503-222-1380
e-mail: djwalker@cfai.com

Region 13
Northern half California,
Northern half Nevada
Michael H. Evans, ASA
Evans Appraisal Service, Inc.
1014 Sheridan Avenue
Chico, CA 95926-3539
Phone: 916-895-1212
Fax: 916-342-4453

Region 14
Hawaii, Philippines, Australia,
Pacific Rim, Far East, Pacific
Ocean Islands
John L. Lakes, ASA
P.O. Box 240013
Honolulu, HI 96824-0013
Phone: 808-373-2994
Fax: 808-373-2994
e-mail: lynde@hgea.org

Region 15
New York, Northern New
Jersey
Bernard M. Sencer, ASA
Sencer Appraisal Associates
2 Wooster Street
New York, NY 10013
Phone: 516-944-9456
Fax: 516-767-2112
e-mail: bsencer@aol.com

Region 16
Alabama, Georgia, Louisiana,
Mississippi,
Tennessee
Harold S. Clark, ASA MGA
P.O. Box 8344
New Orleans, LA 70182-8344
Phone: 504-286-1199
Fax: 504-286-1199
e-mail: harold.clark@apo.com

For other information pertaining to the ASA, contact their headquarters at:

American Society of Appraisers
P.O. Box 17265
Washington, DC 20041
Phone: 703-733-2109
e-mail: info@appraisers.org   http://www.appraisers.org

Business Valuation Data and Information

The **Merger & Acquisition/Capital Formation Network** is an Internet-based service that provides a comprehensive, daily updated listing of companies for sale, equity and debt sources, and valuation statistics from the network's valuation database.

Merger & Acquisition/Capital Formation Network
Phone: 919-471-0431
Fax: 919-471-0534
e-mail: M&AOnline@vintage.pdial.interpath.net   http://www.webpress.net/maol

The **M&A Source** is primarily an Internet-based resource which provides an extensive amount of information regarding mid-market mergers and acquisitions. Various databases provide information regarding the valuation of businesses.

The M&A Source
Attention: Yolande Nanayakkara
International Business Brokers Association
11250 Roger Bacon Drive, Suite B
Reston, VA 22090-5202
Phone: 703-437-7464 Fax: 703-435-4390
e-mail: IBBAInc@aol.com   http://www.ibba.com

The book titled *Valuing Small Business and Professional Practices* by Shannon P. Pratt, 2nd edition, contains the latest business valuation standards, transaction databases, litigation issues, and buy-sell agreements.

The book titled *Handbook of Small Business Formulas and Rules of Thumb* by Glenn Desmond, 3rd edition, contains a collection of 139 market valuation formulas for 78 categories of small businesses including professional, service, retail, and publishing.

The reference book titled *Financial Studies of the Small Business* by Financial Research Associates, Inc., 18th edition, contains composite statistics on 99 different industries. It includes balance sheet percentage relationships, income/expense statement percentages, balance sheet and income/expense ratios with a breakdown by sales volume and asset size.

The monthly newsletter, *Shannon Pratt's Business Valuation Update,* provides timely business valuation and sale information for a great number of actual mid-market transactions. For subscription information, contact Business Valuation Resources, 4475 SW Scholls Ferry Road, Suite 101, Portland, OR 97225. The telephone number is 800-846-2291.

Initial Public Offering, SCOR, and DPO

If you are interested in obtaining assistance for an Initial Public Offering (IPO), Small Corporate Offering Registration (SCOR) or Direct Public Offering (DPO) of your corporate stock, many of the investment banking firms listed earlier provide services in this field. For additional information you may contact the following organizations:

Securities Industry Association
120 Broadway, 35th Floor
New York, NY 10271
Phone: 212-608-1500 Fax: 212-608-1604
e-mail: info@sia.com

U.S. Securities and Exchange Commission
450 Fifth Street, NW
Washington, DC 20549
Phone: 202-942-7040
e-mail: help@sec.gov   http://www.sec.gov/smbus1.htm

North American Securities Administrators Association, Inc.
10 G Street, NE, Suite 710
Washington, DC 20002
Phone: 202-737-0900 Fax: 202-783-3571
e-mail: info@NASAA.ORG
http://www.nasaa.org

U.S. Small Business Administration
Office of Marketing and Customer Service
409 Third Street, SW, Suite 7600
Washington, DC 20416
Phone: 202-205-6744 Fax: 202-205-7064
e-mail: info@www.sbaonline.sba.gov   http://www.sba.gov

Glossary of General Terms
Common to the Purchase and Sale
of an Operating Business

The following is a glossary of common terms that you'll probably run across in buying, selling, or preparing a business for sale.

Accounting: The process of recording financial activities of a business, summarizing these activities, and analyzing the results.

Accounts payable: An obligation by a business to pay an amount to a vendor or other creditor for goods and services purchased on credit.

Accounts receivable: A financial claim by a business against a customer arising from a sale of goods or services on credit. One measure of the health of a business is how fast customers pay off their accounts. Less than 30 days is good, 30 to 60 days may be okay, and over 60 days could be a problem.

Accounting, cost: The process of collecting material, labor, and overhead costs and allocating them to products.

Accounting period: The period of time over which a business's income and expense statement summarizes changes (usually based on a fiscal year).

Accrued interest: Unpaid interest to date on a note or mortgage.

Accrued liabilities and expenses: Accumulated charges, such as interest or taxes, owed but not yet billed to the business, and therefore, not yet paid.

Accumulated depreciation: The total depreciation of an asset that has been charged as an expense to date.

Acid-test ratio: Also known as the "quick" ratio, it is the amount of current assets less the inventory, and divided by current liabilities; the standard is 1:1 and is a good snapshot indication of the health of the business. A business certainly needs enough current income to at least balance current expenses or it will be in trouble fast.

Agreement in principle: A preliminary agreement reached between the buyer and seller of a business that outlines the general terms under which more detailed negotiations will be undertaken.

Administrator: The person appointed by the court to manage your estate when you die without leaving a will.

Amortization: A spreading out of costs over a period of time similar to depreciation. For example, it can be a reduction in a debt or fund by periodic payments covering interest and part of the principal over a period of time. It is different from depreciation in that depreciation usually refers to physical things where amortization applies to things that expire (mortgages, patents, etc.).

Amortization schedule: A tabular presentation of the reduction in value of something being amortized.

Angel: A financial backer for a business enterprise.

Arms-length buyer: Any person, corporation, or other entity with whom you deal regarding the sale of your business and who has no prior financial or family involvement with you.

Assessed valuation: The taxable value of an asset as determined by a governmental source.

Assets: Everything a company owns or is due to it: current assets, such as cash, investments, money due, materials, and inventories; fixed assets, such as land, buildings (real estate), and machinery; and intangible assets, such as patents, and other goodwill.

Asset, current:	An asset which is either currently in the form of cash or is expected to be converted into cash within a short period, usually less than one year.
Asset, fixed:	Tangible physical property of relatively long life that generally is used in the production of goods and services.
Asset, intangible:	Assets which normally have no physical form such as: skilled employees, patents, trade names, good standing in the community, etc.
Asset, net book value of:	Original cost of the asset less the accumulated depreciation.
Asset purchase:	The process of buying a business's specified assets rather than purchasing its common stock.
Auction:	The process of offering your company for sale to a selected group of bidders. This is usually managed through an investment banker or mergers and acquisitions firm.
Audited financial statements:	A business's financial statements that have been prepared by a certified public accountant (CPA) independent of the business owner in accordance with generally accepted accounting principles. These statements show the business's financial position and its results of operations.
Balance sheet:	A statement showing the nature and amount of a business's assets, liabilities, and equity on a given date. In dollar amounts, the balance sheet shows what the business owned, what it owed, and the ownership interest in the company of its owners.
Base year:	A year chosen for comparison of numbers as the 100%, or "normal," year from which index numbers are computed.
Beneficiary:	Someone who receives benefits or funds under a will or other contract, such as an insurance policy.

**Book value
(of an asset):**

The accounting value of an asset shown on the balance sheet that is the original cost of the asset less its accumulated depreciation. Keep in mind that this value may have little or no relationship to the real market value of the asset. Frequently, depreciation expenses are charged much faster than the actual decline in the asset's value.

**Book value
(of a business):**

The book value of a business is determined from the financial records, by adding the current value of all assets (generally excluding such intangibles as goodwill), then deducting all debts and other liabilities. Book value of the business may have little or no significant relationship to actual market value due to depreciation and a lack of consideration for goodwill (intangible assets).

Bottom-line:

The net income enjoyed by a business.

Break-even point:

This is the point at which a business's net sales revenue equals its total costs. A quick look calculation for the business's break-even point is: Sales revenue = total fixed costs ÷ gross margin of profit.

Bridge loan:

Usually a very short term loan of funds to cover an unusual expense or fall-off in revenues. Sometimes bridge loans are used by buyers of businesses to get them over the initial 30- to 90-day transition period of the changeover in ownership of a business.

Business plan:

A written plan detailing a business's sales projections, expenses, marketing strategy, and objectives. A business plan is of great importance to anyone in business, but of paramount importance to anyone buying or starting a business. You will never get there if you don't know where you're going.

Bulk transfer:

Article 6 of the Uniform Commercial Code regulates the bulk transfer through the sale or ownership change of a large portion (usually greater than 50%) of a business's inventory, material, supplies, merchandise, and equipment. Requirements include the advance notification of creditors of the impending sale of a business and its assets listed above to prevent fraud. Provisions in each state are somewhat different so check your local statutes.

Capital:

The amount that an individual, partner, or stockholder has invested in a business; net worth of a business.

Capitalization:

The conversion of future income into a present value by use of a capitalization factor usually expressed as a percentage such as return on investment (ROI).

Capitalization (of an asset):

The accounting listing of an expenditure as a balance sheet asset rather than as an asset.

Capitalization (of a business):

The capital structure of a business consisting of the sum of the long-term debt and the owner's equity.

Capitalization of net profit:

A process recommended in this manual to determine the present value of a business by applying a capitalization rate (ROI) to the projected net profit of a business.

Capitalization rate:

A percentage number used to determine the present value (today) of a stream of future earnings.

Cash flow:

The difference between a business's cash receipts and its cash payments over a specific period of time.

Chattel mortgage:

A financial claim on specifically identified personal property (non-real estate) to secure money owed on the property.

Closely-held corporation: An incorporated business whose corporate shares are held primarily by the principals in the business and are not publicly traded.

Closing: The process of legally completing the purchase and sale of a business by exchanging asset titles, stock certificates, cash, and promissory notes.

Collateral: Asset(s) pledged by a borrower to secure repayment of a loan.

Commission: The negotiated fee, usually a percentage of the purchase and sale price of the total business cost, earned by a business broker for facilitating the sale of a business. Usually the value of the inventory and other noncapitalized assets are excluded from the calculation of the commission.

Common stock: Shares of ownership in a corporation.

Copyright: A legal form of protection granted to authors of original works both through common law and through registration with the U.S. Copyright Office.

C corporation: Entity or organization created by operation of law with rights of doing business essentially the same as those of an individual. The entity has continuous existence regardless of that of its owners and generally limits liability of owners to the amount invested in the organization. The entity ceases to exist only if dissolved according to proper legal process. It is easily transferred and has an unlimited life.

Cost-benefit analysis: Any financial analysis undertaken to relate the costs of taking a certain action to the benefits expected to be derived from that action.

Cost of goods sold: The price paid for the merchandise which has been sold by a business; beginning inventory plus net purchases minus ending inventory equals cost of goods sold.

Covenant not to compete: An agreement given by the seller of a business to the business buyer to not compete in that or a similar business for a specified period of time, and within a specified geographic area.

Current assets: Those assets of a business that are reasonably expected to be realized in cash, sold, or consumed during the normal operating cycle of the business. These include cash, U.S. Government bonds, accounts receivable, inventories, and short-term money due (usually within one year).

Current liabilities: Money owed and payable by a business, usually within one year.

Current ratio: The comparison of current assets to current liabilities which is the total current assets divided by total current liabilities. This ratio indicates a business's ability to pay its current debts with its current assets. A good target ratio is 2:1.

Debt service: This is the payment of principal and interest required on a debt (usually a loan or mortgage) over a specified period of time and interest rate.

Depreciation: Charges against earnings to write off the cost, less salvage value, of an asset over its estimated useful life. It is a bookkeeping entry for accounting and tax purposes and does not represent cash outlay.

Discount rate: A percentage representing future interest and used to calculate present value of future cash flow.

Draw, owners: Sometimes the owner of a small business (sole proprietorship or closely-held corporation) will take income as a draw as opposed to a salary. The terms are essentially the same except that generally a salary means that all withholding taxes, FICA, etc., are accounted for on the books of the business, whereas draw is straight cash to the owner who pays all tax obligations separately on a personal income tax return.

Due diligence: The process of investigation by a potential buyer into the business's claimed financial and operational performance. This means reviewing actual IRS returns and/or audited financial statements, verifying inventory, verifying customers and sales, etc., in general, as a verification of any and all claims made by the business owner concerning the operation of the business to satisfy the buyer that all representations made are accurate.

Earnest money: The deposit provided by a buyer to a seller as part of an offer to purchase a business under certain conditions. The money represents a serious intention to negotiate on the part of the potential buyer.

Earnings: This is the same as income and profit.

Earnings, normalized: Same as reconstructed earnings.

Earnings, recast: Same as reconstructed earnings.

Earnings, reconstructed: The new earnings calculated as a result of modifying the income and expect statement to eliminate the effects of variable accounting practices. Sometimes includes the add-backs of owner perks or potential reduction of other expenses.

Earn-out: Additional or deferred payment for your business usually tied to a company performance factor such as revenues over and above a set figure.

Employment agreement: This is an agreement whereby key employees agree to remain with the business for a specified period of time under certain conditions.

Equity: This is the net value of a business after all of the debts, claims, and assets are fully liquidated.

Estate: The property or assets you own or have rights to. Also commonly referred to as your possessions.

Estate tax:
A tax imposed at one's death on the transfer of most types of property to another.

Executor, executrix:
The person named in your will to manage your estate. This person will collect the property, pay any debt and distribute your property or assets according to your will.

Expense allocation:
The process of distributing an expense to a number of items or areas.

Factoring:
A process used by some businesses to improve their cash flow. A factoring company (usually a finance company or a bank) pays to a business a certain portion of the business's trade debt and then is repaid as the trade debtors pay their account. This may be one more reason not to buy the accounts receivable; you don't have to find and clear any factoring liens.

Fair-market value:
The highest price available in an open and unrestricted market between informed parties acting at arms-length and under no requirement to act.

Fictitious name:
A name frequently used by sole proprietors or partnerships to provide business name, other than those of the owners or partners, under which the business will operate. Also known as the trades name and the "doing business as" (d/b/a) name.

Fiduciary:
A position, person, or institution in a position of trust upon which certain reliance of facts may be placed.

FIFO:
The first-in/first-out method of inventory accounting that assumes that goods that enter the inventory first are the first to be sold.

Fiscal year:
The annual accounting period selected by a business to best correspond to its operations. A fiscal year can correspond to a normal calendar year or begin/end anywhere in between, e.g.; the federal government's fiscal year begins October 1 and ends September 30.

Floor price: The least amount of money you expect to be able to sell your business for. Usually the liquidation value.

Franchise: A form of business organization in which the franchisor (the primary company) provides to a franchisee (the local business) a market tested business package involving a product or service. The franchisee operates under the franchiser's trade name and markets goods and/or services in accordance with a contractual agreement.

Going concern: Any business that is operated in an active, for-profit way that creates value beyond the company's assets.

Golden parachute: An employment contract or agreement which financially protects a key employee in the event of an adverse action during the business sale process.

Goodwill: The collection of intangible assets represented in dollars by the difference between the total purchase price for the business and the net value of the tangible assets being purchased.

Grantor: The person who creates and transfers assets into a trust for the benefit of another.

Gross margin: The gross profit of the business stated as a percentage of net sales revenue.

Gross profit (also gross income): The net sales revenue of the business minus the direct cost of the products sold or services provided.

Income, before taxes: Net sales minus cost of goods sold minus all expenses.

Income, net: Excess of total revenues over total expenses in a given period.

Income and expense statement: A summary of a business's revenues, expenses, and profits for a specific period of time, usually for a full fiscal year.

Installment sale: The process of selling a business with the payments made over a period of time usually accompanied by a promissory note.

Intangible asset: A long-lived, nonphysical asset, such as a patent, a copyright, or a trademark.

Inventory: Finished goods being held for sale, and raw material and partly finished products that upon completion will be sold by the business.

Inventory turnover: Total cost of goods sold divided by the average value of inventory. Some businesses have very high inventory turnover and generally work on very small product markups. Other businesses have low turnover (such as furniture stores, jewelry stores, major equipment manufacturers, etc.) and consequently, usually have significantly higher markups.

Irrevocable: Indicating something that cannot be changed or terminated. As in an irrevocable trust.

Key person insurance: This has forever been called "key man" insurance, but to be politically correct (we do have a Democrat in the White House at this writing), I'll call it "key person." All this means is that the business is paying for the life insurance for key persons (usually the owner) with the business backers (partners, spouse, investors, etc.) as the beneficiaries. This protects the investors from a catastrophic loss. This is fully deductible and is sometimes used by small-business owners as a way to get Uncle Sam to underwrite part of their personal life insurance premiums. It is frequently an add-back in a reconstruction of business expenses.

Lease: The agreement between parties for the rent of a particular asset (real estate, automobile, equipment, etc.).

Leasehold improvements: Usually refers to the improvements made by a lessee to a lessor's property. Generally, leasehold improvements may be capitalized by a business and depreciated against income, but ownership reverts to the lessor upon completion of the lease.

Lehman formula: One method for calculating fees for investment bankers, business brokers and other intermediaries assisting in the sale of a business. A sliding scale percentage based on the selling price of the business.

Lessee: The person or entity to which a lease of real or personal property is given.

Lessor: The person or entity giving a lease for real or personal property.

Leverage: The use of borrowed funds to magnify the gain or loss on the principal amount involved. As in a leveraged buyout.

Leveraged buyout: The purchase of a company through various forms of debt that are paid off from the company's cash flow or sale of assets.

Liabilities: All the claims against a business. Liabilities can include accounts and wages and salaries payable, accrued taxes payable, and fixed or long-term liabilities, such as mortgage bonds, debentures, and bank loans.

Liability, current: Obligations against a business that become due within a short time, usually one year.

Lien: A legal claim on certain assets that are used to secure a loan.

Liquid assets: Those assets easily convertible into cash; marketable securities, receivables, checking and savings accounts, and cash itself.

Liquidation value: The market value of a business's tangible assets minus its liabilities under a forced sale.

Liquidity:	A measure of the quality and adequacy of current assets to meet current obligations as they come due.
Living trust:	A revocable trust established by a grantor during his or her lifetime in which the grantor transfers some or all of his or her property into the trust.
Long-term liability:	A liability due at a time after the next business year.
Loss, net:	Excess of total expenses over total revenues in a given period.
LIFO:	The last-in/first-out method of inventory accounting that assumes goods that enter inventory last are the first to be sold.
Marital deduction:	A deduction allowing for the unlimited transfer of any or all property from one spouse to the other, generally free of estate and gift tax.
Markup:	The amount added to cost to arrive at the retail price for goods or services.
Merger:	The legal combination of two companies by the selling company transferring its assets to the buying company.
Net asset value:	The value of an asset which is its original cost, less accumulated depreciation and liens.
Net profit (net income or net earnings):	Money remaining after deducting all operating expenses including taxes; gross profit minus operating expenses.
Net worth:	See the book value of a business (it's the same thing).
Note, promissory:	A written promise to repay a loan. Usually a key part of a business sale. Normally written from the buyer to the seller for a period of 5–10 years.

Note receivable: A debt that is evidenced by a note or other written acknowledgment.

Obsolescence: Loss of value of a fixed asset arising because improved assets become available.

Operating cash flow: This is cash flow directly generated by a business's operations. It is calculated by taking net income plus depreciation minus the increase in accounts receivable minus any increase in inventory plus any increase in accruals (money owned to the business as a result of operations). This is a mouthful to say but important to understand if you are going to underwrite a business expansion effort or anything else that requires cash flow generated by the business.

Operating income: This is earnings (profit) before deduction of interest payments and income taxes. This is a very important number for a buyer and seller of a business to know because it is the basis for the ability of the business to repay debt. In almost every case involving the purchase of a small business, the buyer will in some way finance the purchase (bank, SBA, seller, family, etc.).

Overhead: Method of allocating all non-labor costs to the various products manufactured or services performed.

Partner: One of multiple owners of an unincorporated business.

Partnership: A legal business association of two or more persons co-owning a business and sharing in the profits and losses. Although there are several kinds of partnerships, the two most common are; general and limited partnerships.

Patent: A right to a process or a product granted to its inventor or the inventor's assignee for their exclusive use.

Perks/perquisites:
The fees, profits, compensation or benefits accruing to a business owner or other persons in the company in excess of fixed income, wages, and salaries.

Physical inventory, taking of:
Counting all merchandise on hand, usually at the end of an accounting period.

Present value:
The value in current dollars of a future sum.

Price/earnings ratio:
The market value of a company expressed as a multiple of its earnings for the most recent fiscal year.

Private placement:
The sale of corporate stock to raise capital through direct negotiations with the purchasers.

Probate:
The review or testing of a will before a court of law to ensure that a will is authentic.

Profit:
The same as earnings and income.

Profit, gross:
Sales minus cost of goods sold.

Profit and loss statement:
The same as the income and expense statement.

Pro forma:
A set of projected financial statements which usually includes: income and expense statements, cash flow projections, and balance sheets. Generally, in a purchase and sale of a business, a seller prepares an optimistic pro forma statement. The buyer should ensure that a realistic pro forma is used as part of the business plan for the newly acquired business.

Promissory note:
A written promise to pay a sum of money at a specified future date in accordance with a predetermined interest rate and payment schedule.

Proprietor:
The only owner of an unincorporated business who is responsible for its operation and liabilities.

Prorate:	Spread equally over a period of time; allocate.
Quick ratio:	The ratio of liquid assets to current liabilities. This is also known as the "acid test" ratio. If an operating business routinely has fewer liquid assets than its current liabilities, problems are sure to follow.
Receipts:	Sometimes used interchangeably with sales and revenue.
Residual value:	Estimated scrap or resale value of a tangible asset.
Return on investment:	The annual income that an investment earns. Usually expressed as a percentage relative to the purchase and sale of a business.
Revenue:	The gross income received as a result of business operations.
Sales:	Same as revenue.
Service business:	A firm dealing in non-merchandising activities.
SIC Code:	Standard Industrial Classification Code assigned to businesses within an industrial category as determined by the U.S. Department of Commerce.
Simple interest:	Interest on principal only, as compared to compound interest which is interest on both principal and accumulated interest.
Sole proprietorship:	A form of business owned by one person who is responsible for the entire business operations and liabilities.
Solvency:	Ability of a business to meet interest costs and repayment schedules associated with long-term obligations.
Sub-chapter S corporation:	The IRS designation for a small corporation that offers the same liability limitations as a C corporation, but does not pay corporate taxes. Taxes on

company profits and losses are paid by the individual shareholders in proportion to their ownership.

Subsidiary operations: The operations of a business that are separately accounted for in the financial statements. Usually used for ease of business operations through separate profit centers.

Sweat equity: A slang term generally used to mean the value of a business over and above its net asset value. Also known as goodwill.

Stockholder: An owner of an incorporated business, the ownership being evidenced by stock certificates.

Tangible asset: A physical asset; a plant asset.

Taxable income: Income on which income tax is computed; gross income minus both exemptions and personal deductions.

The Book: A term used by some business brokers and investment bankers that refers to the collection of information prepared to fully describe a company for sale. Also referred to as a sales prospectus.

Tombstones: The details of a business sale transaction brokered by investment bankers and other intermediaries.

Trademark: A legal right given by the U.S. Patent and Trademark Office for a name or symbol, granting its creator exclusive use.

Trade name: The business name under which a business operates. Sometimes known as the d/b/a (doing business as...). Also referred to as the "fictitious name."

Trust: A written legal instrument created by a grantor during his or her lifetime or at death for the benefit of another.

Trustee: The person named in a trust document who will manage the property owned by the trust and distribute any income according to the document. A trustee can be an individual or a corporate fiduciary.

Turnover: The rate at which an asset is replaced within a given time period; usually refers to annual rate of replacement of stock (inventory turnover) or payment of accounts (accounts receivable turnover).

Unified credit: An estate tax credit equal to $192,800, which ultimately allows an exemption from tax on property transfers of up to $600,000. This amount will be increasing annually begining in 1998.

Valuation: The formal process of estimating the worth of a business.

Venture capitalist: A person or entity with the purpose of investing funds in business startups, expansions, acquisitions, new products, etc., generally for the purpose of realizing financial returns through ownership of equity positions in the business.

Will: A legal document directing the disposal of your property after your death.

Working capital: The readily convertible capital required in a business to permit the regular carrying forward of operations free from financial embarrassment. In accounting, the excess of current assets over current liabilities as of any date.

Write down: To reduce the book value of an asset to its current market value where the asset has actually decreased in value faster than it has been depreciated.

Yield: The return on one's investment, expressed as an annual rate of earnings as a percentage based on cost.

INDEX

Order Form

To order additional copies of this book

"Preparing Your Business For Sale"

- **Fax Orders:** (860) 691-1145
- **Telephone Orders:** 1-800-363-8867
- **E-mail Orders:** rds@businessbookpress.com
- **Mail Orders:** RDS Associates, Inc.
  291 Main Street
  Niantic, Connecticut 06357

❑ Please send____copies of *Preparing Your Business for Sale* at $29.95 each for softcover and $49.95 each for hardcover.

❑ Please send me a FREE catalog of your other great business book titles.

Company Name _____

Name _____

Address _____

City _____ State _____ Zip _____

Sales Tax: Connecticut residents please add 6% sales tax for each book.

Shipping: $4.95 for first book (for priority mail), plus $2.95 each additional book.

Method of Payment:

❑ Check ❑ Visa ❑ MasterCard ❑ Discover ❑ American Express

Card Number_____ Exp. Date _____

Name _____

Signature _____ Date _____

THANK YOU!
Be sure to visit our Web site at:
www.BusinessBookPress.com

Another Book
by Russell L. Brown

"Strategies for Successfully Buying or Selling a Business"

- **176 pages, softcover 8.5" x 11"**
- **Copyright 1998 ISBN: 0-9657400-0-5**

This book complements *Preparing Your Business For Sale* by providing the reader with this additional valuable information:

- **Where to find financially qualified and motivated buyers to buy your business.**
- **The ins and outs of negotiating and structuring a business sale deal which is to your best advantage.**
- **How to finance a business sale to maximize the number of potential buyers.**
- **Sample purchase and sale agreements and other vital forms which could save you money.**
- **And much more!**

To order this book:
- **Fax Orders: (860) 691-1145**
- **Telephone Orders: 1-800-363-8867**
- **E-mail Orders: rds@businessbookpress.com**
- **Mail Orders: RDS Associates, Inc.**
  291 Main Street
  Niantic, Connecticut 06357

• Please send____copies of *Strategies for Successfully Buying or Selling a Business* at $29.95 each.

Company Name _____

Name _____

Address _____

City _____ State _____ Zip_____

Sales Tax: Connecticut residents please add 6% ($1.80) sales tax for each book.

Shipping: $3.00 for the first book (or $4.00 for priority mail), plus $2.00 for each additional book.

Method of Payment:

❏ Check ❏ Visa ❏ MasterCard ❏ Discover ❏ American Express

Card Number _____ Exp Date _____

Name _____

Signature _____ Date_____

THANK YOU!
Be sure to visit our Web site at:
www.BusinessBookPress.com